PARADOXES IN POLITICS

PARADOXES IN POLITICS

**An Introduction to the Nonobvious
in Political Science**

Steven J. Brams

THE FREE PRESS
A Division of Macmillan Publishing Co., Inc.,
NEW YORK

Collier Macmillan Publishers
LONDON

The Free Press
A Division of Macmillan Publishing Co., Inc.
866 Third Avenue, New York, N.Y. 10022

Collier Macmillan Canada, Ltd.

Library of Congress Catalog Card Number: 75–28568

Printed in the United States of America

printing number

1 2 3 4 5 6 7 8 9 10

Library of Congress Cataloging in Publication Data

Brams, Steven J
    Paradoxes in politics.

    Includes bibliographical references and index.
        1.   Political science.   2.   Paradoxes.   I.   Title.
JA74.B7   320   75-28568
ISBN 0-02-904590-8

To Eva, my favorite paradox

CONTENTS

6.   THE ALABAMA PARADOX   137

7.   THREE PARADOXES OF POWER   167

LIST OF FIGURES

LIST OF TABLES

PREFACE

Political scientists often encounter difficulty in justifying the study of political science as anything more than the study of the obvious, that requires no special competence or expertise. Partially in reaction to the charge that their discipline involves only the accumulation of descriptive details, some political scientists have resorted to the use of esoteric mathematical and statistical methods that give their observations and analysis the stamp of scientific propriety.

Other political scientists have responded by developing more elaborate verbal models that attempt to impart greater theoretical structure to their subject matter. Still others have tried to make their discipline more "relevant" by freely offering prescriptions for the maladies of contemporary institutions, or by attempting to show that the wisdom of the great political philosophers can somehow be applied to today's problems.

All these responses, in my opinion, divert the attention of the student of politics from genuine problems in the discipline that can, by and large, be stated in nonesoteric language. Yet their solution, or resolution, is not susceptible to common sense alone but requires certain tools of analysis.

The particular problems I have focused on in this book are "paradoxes" for not only the reason that common sense is an unreliable guide in their analysis but also because commonsensical answers to such problems often contradict what a deeper analysis reveals. Because more careful analysis leads to conclusions that are in some way nonintuitive—that is, depart from common sense—these conclusions at first blush appear paradoxical.

The use of the word "paradox" in this book should be distinguished from its use in logic and mathematics. In these disciplines, paradoxes, which are sometimes called "antimonies," describe contradictions between two apparently equally valid principles, or inferences drawn from these principles. Only two of the paradoxes discussed in this book—one relating to inducement, the other to prediction—can properly be described as

Some ideas expressed in this Preface were first presented in somewhat different form in Steven J. Brams, "Paradoxes in Politics: A Perspective on the Methods of Political Inquiry," *DEA [Division of Educational Affairs] News*, 5 (Spring 1975), pp. 8–9, a publication of the American Political Science Association on the teaching of political science; the permission of the American Political Science Association to adapt material from this essay is gratefully acknowledged.

paradoxes in this sense, though formal contradictions could be extracted from some of the other paradoxes.

Rather than stress the derivation of formal contradictions, however, I have preferred to highlight the "surprise" aspects of these paradoxes. Of course, what I find surprising others may not; surprise, like beauty, is in the eye of the beholder. Indeed, some of the problems I call paradoxes were never conceived as such by those who previously analyzed them. Nevertheless, all these problems have provoked considerable controversy at one time or another, which seems one indicator of their nonobvious character; at least a few have produced major intellectual shocks. These shocks have usually stimulated new intellectual developments that have led to the removal, reconciliation, or better understanding of their most startling features.

In my search for paradoxes, I have undoubtedly developed a tendency to manufacture contradictions, and conjure up surprises, that are not always there. One test of authenticity that I tried to apply to all candidates for inclusion in this book is that they have important empirical or normative implications—that they be more than just clever theoretical contrivances devoid of any substance. In fact, I have devoted considerable space in each chapter to developing the substantive implications of the paradoxes and illustrating their relevance to dilemmas of contemporary politics.

In the exposition of each paradox, I present some historical background, indicate how the paradox in some way confounded or undermined common sense, and show how its unsettling aspects were finally exorcised—or at least dealt with. Since the resolution of paradoxes often requires the introduction of new concepts, or a new framework that generalizes the context in which the paradox first arose, it is necessary to spend some amount of time defining terms and elaborating conditions.

This approach is common in the natural sciences, wherein the student is encouraged to develop theoretical models, ponder and work out their logical implications, and test the truth of these in natural settings or in the laboratory. In the social sciences, by contrast, scientific analysis is not the main ingredient of most textbooks. Rather, there is an unfortunate tendency for the textbook writer to dish out a lot of information, often sprinkled liberally with his opinions and speculative pronouncements about what is best for society. Bits and pieces of information, and speculation as to their meaning, however, are no substitutes for logical and empirical analysis, the main activities encouraged in this book.

Since paradoxes, by their very nature, involve some rather subtle features, it is natural to ask whether these can be communicated in an essentially nontechnical work that assumes only a background in high school mathematics on the part of the reader. My answer is an unequivocal "yes"; *but,* the reader should be forewarned, the development of a sustained logical argument, and the determination of its empirical validity, require serious study and thoughtful reflection. This effort must be made if the nonobvious is to be made obvious. For most readers, I hope, this effort will be repaid by the insights and understanding they gain from the analysis.

ACKNOWLEDGMENTS

I would like to thank John A. Ferejohn and William H. Riker for carefully reading a first draft of this book and making many helpful suggestions. Comments by Nigel Howard and Kenneth A. Shepsle on specific parts of this book also proved helpful, though none of these people should be held responsible for deficiencies that remain. I also want to thank Donna S. Welensky for quickly and skillfully typing the manuscript, and Robert N. Harrington and Ellen Simon of The Free Press for their care in seeing the manuscript through to publication.

I am indebted to The Free Press for permission to use material from *Game Theory and Politics*.[1] This material constitutes about one-third of this book, but it is developed here in a rather different context, with technical details omitted that are not germane to the paradoxes.

Approximately another third of the book is also based on game-theoretic models, and the remaining third is based on other optimization and axiomatic models. The sources of these models are specifically acknowledged in the footnotes.[2]

Finally, I am grateful to my wife, Eva—to whom this book is dedicated —who, along with our children, has helped me immeasurably to understand and appreciate some very interesting paradoxes of life.

---

1. Steven J. Brams, *Game Theory and Politics* (New York: Free Press, 1975).

2. Why such a heavy emphasis on game-theoretic and related kinds of logical and mathematical analysis? I think the justification for the selection of paradoxes that are of interest must ultimately rest on the analysis in the book itself. But, briefly, I would argue that the utility of game-theoretic and related models stems from their ability to illuminate situations of complex interaction and interdependence which—because of this complexity—are almost bound to have unanticipated and, therefore, surprising consequences. Thomas S. Kuhn has argued that when such consequences become sufficiently puzzling are anomalous, the stage is set for a previously accepted framework or paradigm, within which these consequences cannot be explained, to be overthrown. See Thomas S. Kuhn, *The Structure of Scientific Revolutions*, 2nd ed. (Chicago: University of Chicago Press, 1970).

PARADOXES IN POLITICS

1

THE PARADOX OF
SECOND BEST

1.1. INTRODUCTION

"Rational behavior" is sometimes defined as choosing the most preferred
of one's alternatives. The problem with this definition is that there are
situations in which the choice of a less-preferred alternative would appear
sensible. An illustration of such a situation is provided by Anthony
Downs in his description of the quandary faced by some voters in the
1948 United States presidential election:

> When the Progressive Party ran a candidate . . . , some voters who
> preferred the Progressive candidate to all others nevertheless voted
> for the Democratic candidate. They did so because they felt their
> favorite candidate had no chance at all, and the more people voted
> for him, the fewer would vote Democratic. If the Democratic vote fell
> low enough, then the Republicans—the least desirable group from
> the Progressive point of view—would win. Thus a vote for their

The chapter is based largely on Steven J. Brams, *Game Theory and Politics* (© 1975 by
The Free Press, A Division of Macmillan Publishing Co., Inc.), chap. 2, which includes
additional technical material omitted here. The discussion has been somewhat reoriented
to reflect the title of this chapter, which was chosen before an article by R. G. Lipsey and
Kelvin Lancaster, "The General Theory of Second Best," *Review of Economic Studies*, 24
(1956–1957), pp. 11–32, was called to my attention by Roman Frydman. In this article,
a generel theorem is proved to the effect that if *any* of the conditions that lead to a Pareto
optimum in a general equilibrium system are relaxed, a "second-best" optimum situation
can in general be attained only by departing from *all* the other Paretian conditions; since
little can be said about the direction or magnitude of such departures, however, partial or
piecemeal policy measures that eliminate some (but not all) of the departures from the
necessary conditions for the Pareto optimum may be hazardous and actually decrease social
welfare. The vote-trading example given in Chapter 3 illustrates one aspect of this problem
based on external-cost considerations. For a general discussion of this problem in economic
theory, see William J. Baumol, "Informed Judgment, Rigorous Theory, and Public Policy,"
Southern Economic Journal, 32 (October 1965), pp. 137–145. See also M. G. Allingham
and G. C. Archibald, "Second Best and Decentralization," *Journal of Economic Theory*, 10
(April 1975), pp. 174–186, and references cited therein.

favorite candidate ironically increased the probability that the one they favored least would win. To avoid the latter outcome, they voted for the candidate ranking in the middle of their preference ordering.[1]

The fact that the Progressive candidate, Henry Wallace, got only 2 percent of the popular vote indicates that this irony was not acceptable to many Democratic voters who may have favored Wallace—at least as compared with the 50 percent who favored the Democratic candidate, Harry Truman.

Did the Democratic voters who favored Wallace, but nevertheless voted for Truman, act irrationally? It would appear not, for the reasons given by Downs, but the definition of rational behavior given at the outset of this chapter does not admit the choice of a second-best candidate. Either we must label this choice irrational or modify our notion of rationality. It is the latter course that we shall follow in this chapter in order to explain why people may on occasion choose a "second-best" alternative. We call this conflict between preference and choice the *paradox of second best*.

To be sure, the behavior of Democratic voters who switched from Wallace to Truman in 1948 may not appear paradoxical at all. Other instances of rational choice, however, are a good deal less obvious—and more devious, by the lights of some—than that illustrated by the behavior of voters in the 1948 presidential election. To facilitate their analysis, we begin by illustrating the influence of voting procedures on outcomes.

1.2. THE PROCEDURE MAKES A DIFFERENCE

Assume that the *preferences* of political actors, which refer to the values they attach to *outcomes*—or alternative social states—are given. These values need not be expressed quantitatively, but we do assume that actors can rank outcomes from best to worst. Since our interest is in explaining the best *means* that actors can choose to satisfy their preferences—however their preferences came into being—we do not inquire into the origins of preferences (which have been characteristic concerns in both psychology and sociology, with their emphasis on the study of socialization processes, roles, values, beliefs, and so forth).

We should also make clear that an *actor* does not necessarily refer to a single individual. This term can be applied to any autonomous decision-making unit, such as an organization or even a nation-state, as long as it makes sense to talk of its choices *as if* they were made by a single decision maker. This judgment, of course, will depend on the context in which the behavior one is trying to explain takes place and the level of analysis one wishes to achieve.

---

1. Anthony Downs, *An Economic Theory of Democracy* (New York: Harper & Row, 1957), p. 47.

For the purposes of our analysis in this chapter, we shall focus our attention on *voters*, who may represent either single individuals or groups of individuals acting in concert. We assume that each voter (or group of voters) can be represented by a *preference scale*, which is a set of outcomes or alternatives ordered by the preference ranking of a voter. We further assume that the context in which a voter acts is as a member of a collectivity (e.g., a committee, an assembly, or the entire electorate), wherein decisions are made according to some *decision rule* that specifies the minimum number of votes required for decisions to be binding on all members of the collectivity.

To lend some concreteness to these abstract concepts, consider the following situation. A bill is introduced in a legislature, and three outcomes are possible: (1) the original bill passes (O); (2) an amended bill passes (A); or (3) no bill passes (N). We assume that these possibilities are exhaustive: action on the bill may take only one of these three forms, so the set of possible outcomes is {O, A, N}.

In our hypothetical legislature we assume that there are three groups of voters whose members act in concert. The legislature may thus be thought of as effectively consisting of three distinguishable voters. We further assume that each of these collective voters ranks the set of outcomes as follows:

1. The *passers* prefer the original bill (O) to either of the other alternatives, but forced to choose between the other alternatives would prefer the amended bill (A) to none (N). Thus, their preference scale is (O, A, N).

2. The *amenders* most prefer the amended bill (A), but this failing would prefer the original bill (O) to none (N). Thus, their preference scale is (A, O, N).

3. The *defeaters*, if they cannot prevent passage of a bill (N), would prefer the amended version (A) to the original bill (O). Thus, their preference scale is (N, A, O).

Having tied the voters to the outcomes through their preference scales, we shall now show how different voting procedures affect the choice of an outcome by the voters. We begin by defining a *voting procedure* to be a way of arranging the outcomes to be voted upon, examples of which are given subsequently.

The first class of procedures that we shall consider is *binary*, which divides the set of outcomes into two subsets, each subset in turn into two further subsets, and so on, until a single outcome is reached. This is a rather common method of voting in committees and legislatures, perhaps being a reflection of the fact that the voting options available to members often are just two (i.e., binary): approval ("yea") or disapproval ("nay").

In one type of binary procedure, which we call the *successive procedure*, the first vote (or division) is taken on the original bill. If the bill is de-

---

FIGURE 1.1   SUCCESSIVE PROCEDURE

---

feated, then a second vote takes place on an amended bill; this vote may result either in the amended bill's passing (A) or its being defeated, in which case no bill passes (N). The sequence of votes may be depicted as a tree, with each fork corresponding to a vote and the endpoints of each branch corresponding to an outcome, as shown in Figure 1.1.

Since the subsets of outcomes at the endpoints of the branches of each fork (O and {A, N} at the endpoints of the branches of the first fork, A and N at the endpoints of the branches of the second fork)[2] have no members in common, we refer to this binary procedure as *disjoint*. In this procedure, one outcome (O) is singled out for initial consideration while the remaining two outcomes (A and N) are given identical treatment. Clearly, either of the latter two outcomes could occupy the place that outcome O does in the outcome tree, a fact we shall later exploit to contrast the effects produced by different arrangements of the alternatives on the outcome tree.

First, however, consider how our three voters might vote. The simplest assumption we can make is that each voter votes directly in accordance with his preferences, which we call *sincere voting*. A voter votes sincerely if, when choosing among subsets at a fork of the outcome tree, he selects the subset containing his most-preferred outcome. If, for example, a voter's preference scale is (O, A, N), as it is for the passers in our example, under the successive procedure he would vote for O over {A, N} at the first division, since outcome O is preferred to either A or N.

If no subset contains a voter's most-preferred outcome, a voter votes sincerely if he selects the subset containing the second most-preferred outcome (or failing the second, the third most-preferred, and so forth). Refer once again to the successive procedure of Figure 1.1. A voter with preference scale (O, A, N) would vote for A over N at the second division, since outcome A is preferred to outcome N.

Having defined and illustrated the meaning of sincere voting for single voters, we shall now explicate the relationship between individual choices

---

2. We enclose subsets of outcomes in braces only if they contain two or more members.

and the collective choice of a voting body. We start by assuming that none of the three voters in our previous example constitutes more than half the membership of the voting body. Assuming simple majority rule, this means that no individual voter is decisive. For an outcome, therefore, to be the collective choice of the voting body, it must be the choice of at least two voters at a terminal branch of the voting procedure.

A branch is *terminal* if the subset of outcomes at its endpoint contains only one member. This obviously follows from the fact that a one-member subset cannot be further subdivided.

To what extent do the results of sincere voting depend on the voting procedure adopted? To answer this question, consider our previously postulated three voters voting under the successive procedure of Figure 1.1. The first vote is taken on the original bill:

For original bill (O): passers

For amended bill (A) or no bill (N): amenders and defeaters

The original bill thus fails, and the second vote is between the amended bill and no bill:

For amended bill (A): passers and amenders

For no bill (N): defeaters

The amended bill thus passes.

Now assume that the *order* in which the three outcomes {O, A, N} are voted upon changes, which results in a reordering of outcomes for the successive procedure. Specifically, if the first alternative considered were the amended bill (A)—that is, if what we have called the amended bill were moved first, and, it failing, what we have called the original bill were then moved—the voting procedure would be as depicted in Figure 1.2.[3] This new ordering of outcomes results in passage of the original bill:

First Vote
    For A: amenders
    For O or N: passers and defeaters
    Intermediate result: O or N

Second Vote
    For O: passers and amenders
    For N: defeaters
    Final result: O

---

3. It is immaterial whether or not we consider this new ordering of the outcomes to be a "new" voting procedure. The new ordering does change the collective choice of the voting body from that generated by the ordering in Figure 1.1, as we show in the text, but structurally the procedures are identical (i.e., the outcome tree is the same—only the labeling of the endpoints of the branches is different).

FIGURE 1.2 NEW ORDERING OF SUCCESSIVE PROCEDURE

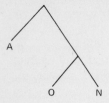

Thus, the reordering of outcomes changes the collective choice of the voters. For the sake of completeness, we mention that if N were considered first—for example, if the first vote were on the motion that O or A be tabled or postponed—then the resultant outcome would be A, duplicating the result for the original ordering given in Figure 1.1.

It should be evident from the foregoing examples and discussion that the voting procedure—or, in our example, simply the ordering of alternatives for a given outcome structure—may make a difference in the outcome selected by members of a voting body. Since a particular voting procedure or ordering of alternatives may affect choices on substantive issues, voters would have an incentive to try to anticipate the results of voting under each procedure or ordering of alternatives.

When voters are aware not only of the voting procedure or ordering to be followed but also know the preference scales of the other voters, we say that they have *complete information*. Given this information, it seems reasonable to assume that they will use it to predict the choices that other voters will make, although these predictions need not be based only on sincere voting, as we shall show presently. On the other hand, if voters have no information on each other's preference scales, they would have no basis on which to predict each other's choices—and so can do no better than vote sincerely.

Assume that the outcomes posed in our three-voter example are the sole concern of members of the voting body—that is, voting on no other issues matters or can be anticipated—and the members possess complete information. Then, given a prior choice on how these outcomes are to be voted upon under the successive procedure, the amenders and defeaters would prefer the ordering of Figure 1.1, the passers, the ordering of Figure 1.2. This follows from the fact that the preference scale of the passers is (O, A, N), so they would prefer the ordering of Figure 1.2 to ensure the adoption of O; the preference scale of the amenders is (A, O, N), so they would prefer the ordering of Figure 1.1 to ensure the adoption of A; and the preference scale of the defeaters is (N, A, O), so in the absence of an ordering that ensures the adoption of N, they would prefer the ordering of Figure 1.1 to ensure the adoption of A. Thus, a majority of voters (the amenders and defeaters) would prefer the ordering of Figure 1.1 to that of Figure 1.2.[4] On a vote, therefore, to determine whether to follow the Figure 1.1 ordering or the Figure 1.2 ordering, the Figure 1.1 ordering would win, with the consequence that A would be the collective choice of the voting body.[5]

All well and good for the amenders and defeaters—if they are given the opportunity to vote on, or otherwise determine, the ordering of alternatives. If they are not always successful in controlling the agenda, however, it may be advantageous for them *not* to vote sincerely—and for their most-preferred alternative at every division—as we shall subsequently show.

1.3. STRAIGHTFORWARD STRATEGIES AND VOTING PROCEDURES

Before considering alternatives to sincere voting, we must first define the strategies of a voter. By *strategy* we mean a complete plan that specifies a voter's choice at each division of an outcome tree. Under the successive procedure of Figure 1.1, for example, there are two divisions, at which each voter has two choices. Each voter therefore has four strategies, which specify all possible courses of action at all the divisions:

(a) Vote for O, that failing, for A.

(b) Vote for O, that failing, for N.

(c) Vote against O (i.e., for $\{A, N\}$), then for A.

(d) Vote against O (i.e., for $\{A, N\}$), then for N.

We now consider the conditions under which a voter can choose a strategy that, no matter what the choices of the other voters are, leads to at least as desirable an outcome as any other strategy. Of course, this strategy will not necessarily guarantee a voter his most-preferred outcome but rather an outcome no worse than would result from his choice of another strategy. We call such a strategy *straightforward* if, independently of the choices of other voters, it cannot be improved upon; we also refer to a voting procedure as straightforward for a voter if it affords him a straightforward strategy at all divisions.

---

4. This is an example of how an overarching "procedural rationality"—the ordering of voting on alternatives—can be derived from, or be revealed by, a "substantive rationality" that is based on the posited preferences of voters. For a discussion of these concepts, see William H. Riker and Peter C. Ordeshook, *An Introduction to Positive Political Theory* (Englewood Cliffs, N.J.: Prentice-Hall, 1973), pp. 14–16.

5. Such procedural votes are in effect allowed in the Swedish parliament, or riksdag. See Dankwart Rustow, *The Politics of Compromise: A Study of Parties and Cabinet Government in Sweden* (Princeton, N.J.: Princeton University Press, 1955), p. 194.

Robin Farquharson has shown that for binary voting procedures like the successive procedure, the procedure is straightforward for a voter if and only if every division of it separates his preference scale.[6] A scale is *separated* by a division if the top outcome of at least one subset at the division is not ranked higher than the bottom outcome of the other. This is true for the passers—preference scale (O, A, N)—and defeaters—preference scale (N, A, O)—under the successive procedure of Figure 1.1. The first division divides the set of outcomes {O, A, N} into the subsets O and {A, N}: for the passers, their top outcome A in the subset {A, N} is not ranked higher than outcome O; similarly, for the defeaters, outcome O is not ranked higher than their bottom outcome A in the subset {A, N}. This separation, however, is not possible for the preference scale of the amenders, (A, O, N): outcome O does rank higher than their bottom outcome N in the subset {A, N}; and their top outcome A in the subset {A, N} does rank higher than outcome O.

Another way of stating the separability condition is that a preference scale is separated by a division if the subsets into which the set of outcomes is divided do not overlap on the scale. To illustrate, we can draw lines cutting the preference scales of the passers and defeaters, (O/A, N) and (N/A, O), such that the members of one subset at the first division in Figure 1.1 lie to the left, members of the other subset lie to the right (i.e., there is no overlap). On the other hand, no line can separate the preference scale of the amenders, (A, O, N), into O and {A, N}.

If a voter does not have a straightforward strategy, he must, to make the best use of his vote, attempt to predict how the other voters are likely to vote (i.e., what strategies they are likely to adopt, given that he has complete information about their preference scales). This is easy for the amenders in our previous example because, as we showed, both the passers and defeaters have straightforward strategies under the successive procedure of Figure 1.1:

The passers, with preference scale (O, A, N), will choose strategy (a)—vote for O, that failing, for A.

The defeaters, with preference scale (N, A, O), will choose strategy (d)—vote against O (i.e., for {A, N}), then for N.

The best course of action for the amenders, with preference scale (A, O, N), taking the other voters' strategies as fixed, is to choose {A, N} over O on the first division, A over N on the second division, which is strategy (c)—vote against O (i.e., for {A, N}), then for A. This follows from the

---

6. Robin Farquharson, *Theory of Voting* (New Haven, Conn.: Yale University Press, 1969), p. 31. Much of the analysis in this chapter is based on Farquharson's masterful theoretical treatment, which is unfortunately marred by numerous errors. For a listing of these, see Richard D. McKelvey and Richard G. Niemi, "Strategic Voting: Some New Results and Some Old Questions" (Unpublished paper, University of Rochester, 1974).

fact that the amenders are the tie-breaking voter at each division [compare the opposite sides taken by the passers and defeaters choosing strategies (a) and (d)]. Whatever strategy the amenders adopt will, therefore, be decisive, so it is natural to assume that they will vote in such a way as to ensure adoption of their most-preferred outcome, A. This they accomplish by selecting strategy (c).

Coincidentally, if all three voters voted sincerely, they would have adopted precisely the "best" strategies we have specified—and the outcome, of course, would be exactly the same (i.e., A) as the one we showed on page 5 for sincere voting under the successive procedure of Figure 1.1. But under certain conditions, the outcome of sincere voting can be upset by the kinds of strategic calculations sketched in this section, as we shall next show.

1.4. EQUILIBRIUM CHOICES AND VULNERABILITY

To extend the logic of the last section, we start by considering the conditions under which a voter would be motivated *not* to vote directly according to his preferences. It seems reasonable to suppose that such an incentive would exist if the voter could, by changing his vote, change the collective choice of the voting body to one that ranks higher on his preference scale.

To illustrate a sincere collective choice that is vulnerable to such strategic calculations, consider the successive procedure of Figure 1.2, in which only the order of voting on outcomes has been changed from that of Figure 1.1. Here, it will be recalled (see page 5), the outcome of sincere voting was O, whereas the sincere outcome based on the ordering of Figure 1.1 was A.

We showed in section 1.3 that the sincere outcome A under the successive procedure of Figure 1.1 was not vulnerable to strategic calculations of our three voters. But under the procedure of Figure 1.2, if the defeaters vote for A instead of {O, N} at the first division, they will change the collective choice of the voting body from O to A:

First Vote
    For A: amenders and defeaters
    For O or N: passers
    Intermediate result: A

This intermediate result is in fact the final result, and no second vote is required, since A is a single outcome and thereby terminates the voting process.

The choice on the part of the defeaters, whose preference scale is (N, A, O), for A rather than {O, N} may not seem justified, given that {O, N} contains their most-preferred outcome. But in view of the facts that

(1) their vote is decisive at the first division, since the passers and amenders split their votes if they vote sincerely; and

(2) by voting "insincerely" they can effect a collective choice A that ranks higher on their preference scale than the sincere collective choice O,

the logic of their selection would appear to be sound. Yet, can we expect the passers, whose preference scale is (O, A, N), to sit idly by and continue to vote sincerely if the defeaters are able to change the sincere outcome to their own advantage and to the disadvantage of the passers?

This kind of problem did not crop up in our earlier discussion of voting under the successive procedure of Figure 1.1 because two of our three voters (the passers and defeaters) had straightforward strategies that could not be improved upon whatever strategy was selected by the third member of the voting body (the amenders). With the strategies of the passers and defeaters fixed, the amenders' strategy involved simply voting in such a way as to effect their higher-ranking outcomes at each division; no account had to be taken of possible subsequent responses on the part of the two other voters to their choices.

Under the successive procedure of Figure 1.2, however, the preference scale of only one voter, the amenders, is separated by the first division: (A/O, N). This means that the passers and defeaters must somehow "adjust" their voting not only to the straightforward strategy of the amenders but also to the strategies likely to be adopted by each other. How can we determine what strategies are "best" for each of these voters, and therefore likely to be adopted, when neither strategy can be taken as fixed but instead must be thought of as a response to the other voter's choice of strategies?

This is fundamentally a game-theoretic question and requires that we make additional assumptions that establish the bounds within which interdependent calculations can be made. (For our purposes here, a *game* may be considered an interdependent decision situation wherein voters can and do take account of the possible strategy choices of other voters based on complete information about their preference scales.) Since the solution to this game is the set of strategies that it is reasonable to assume the voters will adopt, we begin by specifying all four strategies available to each of the voters under the successive procedure of Figure 1.2, which are analogous to the four strategies under the successive procedure of Figure 1.1 that were given in section 1.3 (to distinguish them from the previous strategies we add primes):

(a') Vote for A, that failing, for O.

(b') Vote for A, that failing, for N.

(c') Vote against A (i.e., for {O, N}), then for O.

(d') Vote against A (i.e., for {O, N}), then for N.

TABLE 1.1   SIXTEEN OUTCOMES ASSOCIATED WITH THE DIFFERENT STRATEGIES OF PASSERS AND DEFEATERS UNDER SUCCESSIVE PROCEDURE OF FIGURE 1.2, GIVEN AMENDERS ADOPT THEIR STRAIGHTFORWARD STRATEGY (a′)

PASSERS' STRATEGIES	DEFEATERS' STRATEGIES			
	a′	b′	c′	d′
a′	A (E)	A (E)	A	A
b′	A (E)	A (E)	A	A
c′	A (E)	A (E)	O	O (S)
d′	A	A	O	N

Since the preference scale of the amenders is separated by the successive procedure of Figure 1.2, they have a straightforward strategy that can be read off directly from their preference scale, (A, O, N): vote for A, that failing, for O, which is strategy (a′). On the other hand, since the preference scales of the passers and defeaters are not separated by the successive procedure of Figure 1.2, they do not have straightforward strategies. We can begin the search for their best strategies by examining the sixteen outcomes associated with the four strategies that independently can be chosen by each of these voters, given that the amenders adopt their straightforward strategy (a′) (see Table 1.1).[7]

The outcomes associated with the intersection of the passers' and defeaters' strategies are based on majority choices at each division. For example, if the passers select strategy (c′), and the defeaters strategy (d′), the results will be as follows, given that the amenders adopt their straightforward strategy (a′):

First Vote
    For A: amenders
    For O or N: passers and defeaters
    Intermediate result: O or N

Second Vote
    For O: passers and amenders
    For N: defeaters
    Final result: O

---

7. If the amenders did not possess a straightforward strategy, we would have to consider the sixty-four (4 × 4 × 4) combinations of strategies that could be chosen by all three voters.

This result is not unfamiliar: the strategies (a'), (c'), and (d') happen to be the sincere strategies of the amenders, passers, and defeaters, respectively. In section 1.2 we showed that the sincere outcome under the successive procedure of Figure 1.2 is O, which we denote in Table 1.1 with the parenthetic expression (S).

This outcome is vulnerable to strategic calculations, however, as we showed at the beginning of this section. Specifically, if the defeaters vote for A instead of {O, N} at the first division [i.e., choose either strategy (a') or (b')], they will change the collective choice from O to A, which ranks higher on their preference scale. The sincere outcome O is therefore not an *equilibrium choice*—there is at least one voter who can, by changing his strategy, ensure a better outcome for himself. Formally, a collective choice is *vulnerable* (i.e., not an equilibrium choice) if another choice

(1) can be obtained from the first by substituting a strategy of one voter;

(2) is preferred to it by that voter.

We have indicated equilibrium choices by the parenthetic expression (E) in Table 1.1.

Sincere outcomes may or may not be equilibrium choices.[8] The sincere outcome under the successive procedure of Figure 1.2 is not, as we have shown. Under the successive procedure of Figure 1.1, on the other hand, the sincere outcome is an equilibrium choice. For, as we showed in section 1.3, given that the passers and defeaters choose their straightforward strategies (a) and (d)—which are also their sincere strategies—the amenders can do no better than choose strategy (c), which is their sincere strategy as well. The sincere outcome under this procedure, therefore, is invulnerable to the substitution of strategies that can lead to preferable outcomes for any voter.

If all voters have straightforward strategies under a particular voting procedure, their adoption will always produce an equilibrium choice. For, even if one or more voters could change the outcome by substituting a different strategy, none would have an incentive to do so since each voter's straightforward strategy is unconditionally best. The converse obviously does not hold—an equilibrium choice is not necessarily the product of straightforward strategies—since outcomes generated by the adoption of other strategies (e.g., the unanimous selection of one strategy by all voters) will also be equilibrium choices.

Sincere strategies are not necessarily straightforward [e.g., strategy (c) for the amenders under the successive procedure of Figure 1.1], but straightforward strategies are always sincere [e.g., strategies (a) and (d) for

---

8. For necessary and sufficient conditions for sincere voting to produce an equilibrium choice, see Prasanta K. Pattanaik, "On the Stability of Sincere Voting Situations," *Journal of Economic Theory*, 6 (December 1973), pp. 558–574.

FIGURE 1.3   RELATIONSHIPS AMONG STRATEGIES AND EQUILIBRIUM CHOICES

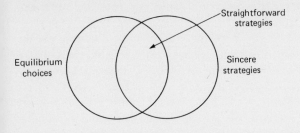

the passers and defeaters under the Figure 1.1 procedure]. The reason that the latter statement is true in general is that if a voter has a straightforward strategy, one subset of outcomes at each division will always provide him with an unconditionally best choice. Since this subset necessarily contains his single most-preferred outcome at every division, its selection is equivalent to voting sincerely.

The results we have just established are summarized in the Venn diagram of Figure 1.3. Straightforward strategies are a subset of sincere strategies, but only the selection of the former by all voters (if available under a particular voting procedure) will invariably result in an equilibrium choice.

1.5. DESIRABLE STRATEGIES AND EQUILIBRIA

In previous sections we suggested two criteria for narrowing down the set of strategies that voters would be likely to adopt. First, if a voter had a straightforward strategy, he would always adopt it since he could obtain no better outcome by choosing another strategy. For the class of binary voting procedures, we indicated that voters whose preference scales are separated by such a procedure possess a straightforward strategy, which is necessarily sincere.

Second, if a collective choice is not an equilibrium choice, there will be at least one voter who will have an incentive not to choose a strategy associated with that choice and, moreover, this voter can ensure that it will not be selected. Given that there is complete information about the preference scales of all voters, other voters could make the same strategic calculation. With every voter aware of the vulnerability of such an outcome, the strategies associated with a nonequilibrium choice would not be adopted by all voters.

But not all strategies associated with equilibrium choices will be appealing to voters. If we had not assumed that the amenders under the successive procedure of Figure 1.2 adopt their straightforward strategy (a'), but instead had assumed that they might select one of their other three strategies, then the sixty-four possible outcomes for the four strategies of each voter would reveal still more equilibrium choices than are shown in the reduced array of Table 1.1. Because the amenders have a straightforward strategy, however, the strategies associated with the additional equilibria have nothing to recommend them except their "stability," which is a necessary but hardly sufficient condition for adoption. On the other hand, the fact that a straightforward strategy is the best that a voter can do no matter what circumstances arise seems a compelling reason for its adoption.

If we assume that the amenders adopt their straightforward strategy in the preceding example, we are able to pare down the number of equilibrium choices to the six shown in Table 1.1. Associated with these choices, which all result in the collective choice of outcome A, are three strategies of the passers and two strategies of the defeaters, which still leaves multiple choices open to both voters. Are there any additional criteria that might enable the two voters to narrow still further their strategy choices?

To begin with, even if a voter has no information about the preference scales of the other voters, he can rule out those strategies which result in outcomes inferior to, or at least not superior to, those he can obtain by voting sincerely. To illustrate, if the passers under the successive procedure of Figure 1.2 adopt strategy (d'), the outcomes they obtain for every strategy choice of the defeaters are identical to those they would obtain if they adopted their sincere strategy (c')—except when the defeaters themselves select strategy (d') (see Table 1.1). Then their sincere strategy (c') gives them a better outcome, since O ranks higher on their preference scale than N. Thus, it would obviously be foolish for the passers ever to choose strategy (d'), which could result in outcome N. Likewise, strategies (a') and (b') of the passers can also be eliminated, because they lead to an outcome (A) inferior to that yielded by strategy (c') (O) when the defeaters choose strategy (c') or (d'). Hence, the passers' strategy (c') *dominates* their other three strategies, because it leads to outcomes no worse, and for at least one strategy choice of the defeaters a better outcome, than their other three strategies.

Similarly, we would expect the defeaters never to choose strategy (c'), because for every strategy of the passers it leads to identical outcomes as their sincere strategy (d')—except when the passers choose strategy (d'). Then the defeaters' sincere strategy (d') gives them a better outcome since they prefer outcome N to outcome O. Because strategies (a'), (b'), and (d') for the passers, and strategy (c') for the defeaters, are thus dominated by the sincere strategies of each voter, we can delete them from the rows and columns of Table 1.1, leaving the three outcomes shown in Table 1.2.

Because the removed strategies in some cases lead to outcomes less desirable, and in no cases more desirable, than some other strategies, we call them *undesirable*. On the other hand, assuming voters with straight-

TABLE 1.2   (PRIMARILY) DESIRABLE STRATEGIES AND OUTCOMES UNDER SUCCESSIVE PROCEDURE OF FIGURE 1.2

PASSERS' STRATEGY	DEFEATERS' STRATEGIES		
	a'	b'	d'
c'	A (E)	A (E)	O (S)

forward strategies always adopt them, a strategy is *desirable* (before deletion of the undesirable strategies) if there is no other strategy providing

(1) an outcome at least as good, whatever strategies are selected by the other voters without straightforward strategies;

(2) a better outcome for some selection of strategies of the other voters without straightforward strategies.

Obviously, straightforward strategies are desirable (there are no other strategies that can lead to better outcomes), and for a voter who possesses a straightforward strategy, it will be his only desirable strategy (not more than one strategy can be unconditionally best). Voters who do not possess straightforward strategies will have one or more desirable strategies, which can be found through a process of elimination of undesirable strategies, as we have shown in the case of the successive procedure of Figure 1.2.

1.6. SOPHISTICATED VOTING

The assumption that voters with straightforward strategies always adopt them initially facilitates the elimination of undesirable strategies by removing from the consideration of nonstraightforward voters all but one of the strategies of each of the straightforward voters. With the further removal of the undesirable strategies of nonstraightforward voters, only outcomes associated with desirable (and straightforward) strategies remain. Of these, it is reasonable to assume that those likely to be adopted will be limited to equilibrium choices.

In the case of the successive procedure of Figure 1.2, there are two desirable equilibria (see Table 1.2), these being the only ones of the original six equilibria listed in Table 1.1 to have survived the cut of the undesirable strategies (a'), (b'), and (d') of the passers and (c') of the defeaters.[9] Because this cut did not reduce the desirable outcomes to a single equilibrium, the defeaters are still left with more than one desirable strategy, associated with these equilibria, from which to choose. To reduce their desirable strategies still further, we now assume that each voter has not only knowledge of the preference scales of the other voters but also is able, on the basis of this information, to determine the desirable strategies of each of the other voters (as well as his own). In other words, we assume that he is able to convert the "raw information" he has on the preference scales of the other voters into new information about the strategies that they are likely to adopt. In this manner, all voters can become aware of the reduced set of desirable strategies shown in Table 1.2.

But the process need not stop here, for now some of these desirable strategies in the reduced table of outcomes (Table 1.2) become less appealing. This is so because, with the elimination of the undesirable strategies, the basis of comparison changes. For example, comparing the defeaters' strategy (d') with strategies (a') and (b') in Table 1.2, we see that the choice of (d') on the part of the defeaters is inferior to (a') and (b') since sincere outcome O ranks lowers on the defeaters' preference scale.

If we treat the reduced set of desirable strategies in Table 1.2 as if they were the original set of strategies, we may now delete the dominated strategy (d') of the defeaters. This leaves them with strategies (a') and (b'). The intersection of strategy (c') of the passers, and strategies (a') and (b') of the defeaters, admits one equilibrium choice: outcome A.

It may seem a bit strange that at the end of this elimination process two strategies can both be "best" for the defeaters, even though they result in the same outcome. Informally, we can show that this result is plausible by observing that both the passers and amenders prefer outcome O (the defeaters' worst outcome) to outcome N (their best). Outcome O would always win, therefore, if there should be a second vote between O and N under the successive procedure of Figure 1.2. With this outcome in effect foreordained if a second vote is required, it is of no import to the defeaters whether they choose strategy (a') or (b'), both of which involve an initial vote for outcome A that ensures its adoption—and that their worst outcome O will not be adopted—given that the amenders adopt their straightforward strategy, (a').

On the other hand, if a second vote is required, the passers, who also do not have a straightforward strategy, could make the difference between outcomes O and N since the amenders and defeaters would split their votes at the second division. On this vote, the passers would obviously choose

---

9. Recall from section 1.4 that we exclude from the category of "original equilibria" those associated with the three undesirable (i.e., nonstraightforward) strategies of the amenders. If we had counted these equilibria as "original," of course, many would not have survived the cut of undesirable strategies.

their most-preferred outcome O to ensure that their worst outcome N will not be adopted. Consistent with this choice would be a prior vote for {O, N}, which is strategy (c′), despite the fact that the passers can determine (for reasons given in the preceding paragraph) that their next to worst outcome A will be adopted.

It is precisely this informal "backwards" reasoning—designed to insure against (if possible) worst, then next to worst (and so forth) outcomes being adopted—which we systematized in the reduction process we have illustrated. To lay bare the structure of this process in somewhat more formal terms, it is helpful to define recursively a succession of desirable strategies for a voter:

A strategy is *primarily desirable* if it is either straightforward or if there is on other strategy which produces at least as good a result for every selection of strategies of the other voters with nonstraightforward strategies, and a better result for some selection.

A strategy is *secondarily desirable* if, on the assumption that all other voters use only primarily desirable strategies, it produces at least as good a result for every selection of strategies of the other voters with nonstraightforward strategies, and a better result for some selection.

In general, a strategy is *m-arily desirable* if it remains desirable on the assumption that all other voters use only (*m*-1)-arily desirable strategies.

For the successive procedure of Figure 1.1, the primarily desirable strategies are the straightforward strategies (*a*) and (*d*) of the passers and defeaters, respectively, and the sincere strategy (*c*) of the amenders. For the successive procedure of Figure 1.2, the primarily desirable strategies are those shown in Table 1.2, the secondarily desirable strategies are (*c*′) for the passers, (*a*′) and (*b*′) for the defeaters, with the straightforward strategy (*a*′) of the amenders primarily and secondarily desirable.[10]

At the highest level of desirability, all strategies are "ultimately" straightforward in the sense that they are unconditionally best, given the successive elimination of lower-level desirable strategies by all the voters. However, should one or more voters not adopt his "ultimately" straightforward strategy, only the straightforward strategy of the amenders remains *unconditionally* best and is therefore a *dominant* strategy. Whereas the desirable strategies of the passers and defeaters are *undominated* (best for some selections of strategies of the other voters but not for others), these voters have no straightforward strategies that are unconditionally best—except in the reduced game, but this is conditional on all voters' choosing successively more desirable strategies.

---

10. For rules for finding optimal strategies, see R. L. Kashyap and R. Mukundan, "Algorithms for Determining Equilibrium Points in N Stage Voting," Harvard University Technical Report no. 650 (Cambridge, Mass., 1975.)

The succession of desirable strategies corresponds to, but is not identical with, the succession of admissible strategies defined by Farquharson.[11] In game-theoretic terms, the successive elimination of strategies by voters—and outcomes associated with the eliminated strategies—produces a different and smaller game in which some formerly desirable strategies in the larger game cease to be desirable. The removal of undesirable strategies at successively higher levels of desirability in effect enables the voters to determine what outcome eventually *will* be adopted by eliminating those outcomes that definitely *will not* be chosen by the voters.

Driving this process is the assumption that all voters will rule out undesirable strategies at each stage, which seems quite reasonable in view of the fact that such strategies by definition can never lead to a better outcome than that which results from the choice of a desirable strategy, and for at least one selection of strategies of the other voters must lead to an unequivocally worse outcome. Or, as we showed by our informal "backwards" reasoning earlier, voters eliminate strategies that could result in their worst, next to worst (and so on) outcomes' adoption, even if the strategy or strategies left remaining offer no guarantee that their best outcome will be chosen. The assumption that other voters will do likewise renders the choices of all voters interdependent.

We call voting *sophisticated* if it forecloses the possibility that a voter's worst outcomes will be chosen—insofar as this is possible—through the adoption of successively more desirable strategies, given that other voters do likewise. In section 1.7, we shall show that the effects of a voting procedure disadvantageous to a majority when voting is sincere can be nullified through sophisticated voting.

1.7. VOTING ON VOTING PROCEDURES

At the end of section 1.2 we showed that if voting were sincere, the order in which alternatives are voted upon under the successive procedure would result in different outcomes.[12] Specifically, under the successive procedure of Figure 1.1, the outcome selected was A, but under the successive procedure of Figure 1.2, the outcome selected was O. Given that each voter has complete information about the preference scales of all other voters, we suggested that each voter could anticipate the results of sincere voting under both procedures. Should a voter be given the oppor-

---

11. The differences are spelled out in Brams, *Game Theory and Politics*, chap. 2. Difficulties in Farquharson's reduction procedure, and a different method for determining ultimately admissible strategies, are discussed in McKelvey and Niemi, "Strategic Voting: Some New Results and Some Old Questions."

12. For another example in which the procedure makes a difference, see T. C. Schelling, "What Is Game Theory?" in *Contemporary Political Analysis*, ed. James C. Charlesworth (New York: Free Press, 1967), pp. 224–232. The way in which alternatives are combined may also be significant, as we shall show in Chapter 2 in the case of platform voting (see section 2.1).

tunity to select which procedure to follow, he would choose the procedure that produced the better outcome, assuming that outcomes on other issues either did not matter or could not be anticipated.[13] We call voting *sincere-anticipatory* when voting on the substantive outcomes under each procedure is sincere, and voting on the procedures is based on an anticipation of the sincere outcomes produced by each procedure.

Because outcome A is preferred to outcome O by two of the three voters in our example (amenders and defeaters), we indicated that a majority would choose the procedure of Figure 1.1 over the procedure of Figure 1.2. The question we raised, but did not answer, in section 1.2 was the following: if there were *not* the opportunity to vote on procedures (i.e., the order in which alternatives would be voted upon), and the operative procedure were that of Figure 1.2, would the majority (amenders and defeaters) who do not favor the outcome selected by this procedure under sincere voting (O) have any recourse?

With a knowledge of sophisticated voting, we can now answer "yes" to this question. As we showed in section 1.6, the outcome under the successive procedure of Figure 1.2 would be A instead of O if voting were sophisticated rather than sincere. This is the same outcome that would have been produced if there were a prior procedural vote and voting were sincere-anticipatory, given the majority's preference for the Figure 1.1 procedure (i.e., outcome A) over the Figure 1.2 procedure (i.e., outcome O).

In general, for binary voting procedures like the successive procedure, if two different orderings in which outcomes are voted upon (Figures 1.1 and 1.2 in our example) produce two different outcomes under sincere voting, and these outcomes are anticipated on a procedural vote, then the outcome preferred on the procedural vote (outcome A in our example) can be obtained under the "losing" ordering (Figure 1.2 in our example) if voting is sophisticated.[14] In other words, if the would-be losers on a procedural vote (amenders and defeaters under Figure 1.2 procedure) recognize their disadvantageous position should they vote sincerely, they do not need the procedural vote to rectify it; the same outcome that would occur under sincere voting, preceded by a procedural vote, can be obtained immediately through sophisticated voting. Thus, a majority disadvantaged by a binary voting procedure when voting is sincere has a recourse: it can vote sophisticatedly and achieve the result favored by the majority, which is the same result it would obtain by voting sincerely under a procedure that leads to the majority outcome.

---

13. When voting is sophisticated, Gerald H. Kramer has generalized Farquharson's results to cover sequential voting processes on more than one issue, given that each voter's utility function across the various issues is additive. Gerald H. Kramer, "Sophisticated Voting over Multidimensional Choice Spaces," *Journal of Mathematical Sociology*, 2 (July 1972), pp. 165–180.

14. For a proof, see Brams, *Game Theory and Politics*, chap. 2.

The fact that sophisticated voting prevents the will of the majority from being thwarted is not inconsequential. (If there is no single majority, however, as in the case of the "cyclical majorities" discussed in Chapter 2, the will of the majority will depend on the alternatives compared.) By providing a safeguard against arbitrary orderings of binary procedures that produce outcomes inimical to a majority when voting is sincere, sophisticated voting ensures the selection of a socially preferred outcome. Thus, the strategic calculations of sophisticated voting would seem to be defensible as not only optimal for individual voters but socially desirable as well, and so would voting systems that encourage the exchange of information about voters' preferences that makes sophisticated voting possible.

Our main purpose, however, is not to defend sophisticated voting but to demonstrate that voting for one's most-preferred alternative at every division (i.e., sincere voting) may lead to the selection of a worse outcome than voting for a less-preferred alternative. Although we assume in our analysis that outcomes are the only things of value to voters, the best means (i.e., strategies) for achieving them clearly depend on both the preferences and strategy choices of the other voters. Since optimal strategies cannot be chosen solely on the basis of one's most-preferred outcome at every division, but instead must take account of the likely strategy choices of the other voters, "second-best" choices at some divisions that prevent the adoption of even worse choices would therefore seem to be rational.

1.8. PLURALITY VOTING

We introduced the analysis of this chapter with an example of a three-way contest for the presidency. Normally in races involving more than two candidates, the person with the most votes wins, or there is a runoff between the top two vote getters. In United States presidential elections, of course, there is the complicating factor of the Electoral College, whose anomalous effects we shall not analyze here.[15] Even without this complicating factor, however, voting under plurality procedures may lead to some thoroughly paradoxical results, as we shall illustrate here and later in Chapter 7.

The plurality procedure for our hypothetical example is depicted in Figure 1.4, in which the three possible outcomes are partitioned into three

---

15. For a discussion of these, see Steven J. Brams and Morton D. Davis, "The 3/2's Rule in Presidential Campaigning," *American Political Science Review*, 68 (March 1974), pp. 113–134; Claude S. Colantoni, Terence J. Levesque, and Peter C. Ordeshook, "Campaign Resource Allocations under the Electoral College," *American Political Science Review*, 69 (March 1975), pp. 141–154; followed by a "Comment" from Brams and Davis, pp. 155–156; and a "Rejoinder" by Colantoni, Levesque, and Ordeshook, pp. 157–161; and Guillermo Owen, "Evaluation of a Presidential Election Game," *American Political Science Review*, 69 (September 1975), pp. 947–953.

FIGURE 1.4   PLURALITY PROCEDURE

O   A   N

one-member subsets. Voting is not sequential, but involves immediately selecting one of the three outcomes. Since there is only division, at which each voter has three choices—to vote for O, A, or N—these choices completely specify a voter's strategies for every contingency that may arise.

If each of the three voters in our example votes sincerely, each would support his own first preference, and the result would be a three-way tie among the three alternatives. To prevent such an indeterminate result from occurring, we assume that one voter (say, the passers) either possesses more votes than the other two voters—but still less than a majority—or, if all the voters are equally weighted, can break a tie. Given that the alternative with the most votes wins, this assumption is sufficient to ensure that the sincere strategy of the passers—vote for O—is straightforward: no other choice would be better if the other voters split their votes, worse if the other voters chose a single outcome. If we assume that the passers adopt their straightforward strategy, then the outcomes available to the amenders and defeaters are as shown in Table 1.3.

The amenders have one primarily desirable strategy (vote for A), which is straightforward, whereas the defeaters have two primarily desirable strategies (vote for A, vote for N), both of which result in the solid boxed outcomes in Table 1.3. For the defeaters, however, only one strategy (vote for A) is secondarily desirable, which leaves outcome A (E) as the equilibrium choice of the voting body. Thus, for the preference scales of the three voters in our example, the plurality procedure results in the selection of a single outcome if voting is sophisticated. We call such a procedure *determinate*.

Suppose now that the preference scale of the amenders is (A, N, O) instead of (A, O, N), with the scales of the other two voters remaining the same as before [(O, A, N) for the passers, (N, A, O) for the defeaters]. The passers would still have a straightforward strategy, and the defeaters two primarily desirable strategies, but the amenders would now have two primarily desirable strategies (vote for A, vote for N)—instead of one (vote for A), as before. In this instance, the primarily desirable strategies of the amenders and defeaters cannot be further reduced, and the outcomes associated with these strategies include the three possible outcomes (O, A, and N) in the game (dashed boxed outcomes in Table 1.3). Although

TABLE 1.3 NINE OUTCOMES ASSOCIATED WITH THE DIFFERENT STRATEGIES OF AMENDERS AND DEFEATERS UNDER PLURALITY PROCEDURE OF FIGURE 1.4, GIVEN PASSERS ADOPT THEIR STRAIGHT-FORWARD STRATEGY (VOTE FOR O)

AMENDERS' STRATEGIES	DEFEATERS' STRATEGIES		
	Vote for O	Vote for A	Vote for N
Vote for O	O (E)	O	O
Vote for A	O	A (E)	O
Vote for N	O	O	N (E)[a]

[a] Equilibrium choice if preference scale of amenders is (A, N, O); see text for explanation.

two of these outcomes are now equilibrium choices, this confers no special status on them as far as the selection of strategies by the voters is concerned. The amenders would most prefer A, the defeaters N, but neither can avoid the possibility that their worst outcome (O) will be selected if they are not able to communicate and must choose strategies independently. Indeed, there is a fatal symmetry in this set of choices: if both voters try for their most-preferred outcome, both will end up with their worst outcome, O. Because this is only one of the three possible outcomes at the intersection of the three voters' primarily desirable strategies, the plurality procedure of Figure 1.3 is obviously not determinate for the preference scales postulated above.

The "fatal symmetry" alluded to is a paradox that can in principle be resolved if the voters are able to communicate with each other and coordinate their choices of strategies. Specifically, if the amenders and defeaters are able to agree on the selection of either outcome A or outcome N, then they can ensure its adoption by the choice of their appropriate primarily desirable strategies (see Table 1.3 for the strategies that intersect these outcomes). Whichever of these outcomes they settle on (given that they can agree on one)—outcome A favors the amenders, outcome N, the defeaters—it is better for both voters than outcome O, which is the rueful collective choice when both voters choose the strategy that offers them the possibility of their best (as well as worst) outcomes.

1.9. COALITIONS AND COOPERATION

The example just discussed illustrates how a willingness to cooperate on the part of some voters can lead to a better outcome for them—but for the voters left out of the bargain, it can spell disaster. If the amenders and defeaters settle on outcome N, for example, the passers will have to acquiesce in the adoption of their worst outcome, despite the fact that they have a straightforward strategy. Moreover, because this outcome is an equilibrium choice, no voter—even the passers—can do anything to alter the situation, at least as an individual actor.

If the passers do not act alone, however, but instead propose to the amenders that they form a coalition and both vote for A, presumably the amenders would accept this offer because they (like the passers) would prefer outcome A to outcome N. This agreement would appear to resolve the paradox of fatal symmetry, which the reduction of desirable strategies was not able to do: the equilibrium choice A will be preferred to N by a majority of voters (passers and amenders). Should members of the other two possible majority coalitions (passers and defeaters, amenders and defeaters) agree on an outcome other than A (O or N), at least one member of each coalition can be tempted to defect to the coalition of passers and amenders that proposes joint strategies that result in the adoption of A. Since there is no coalition that can block outcome A (i.e., whose members both would prefer some other outcome), it would appear to be the collective choice favored by a majority.[16]

Yet, this "resolution" of the paradox through the formation of coalitions assumes cooperation among voters. In contradistinction, sophisticated voting assumes no cooperation: communication among voters that could lead to binding and enforceable agreements is not permitted. As we shall show in Chapter 2, however, even if communication is allowed and voters can coordinate their choices of strategy, this may not be sufficient to ensure an enforceable agreement. In general, equilibrium choices may be vulnerable to subsets of members who form coalitions, which may in turn be vulnerable to other coalitions, and so forth.

It is possible to extend the concept of an equilibrium choice for individual members to an equilibrium choice for coalitions. Coalition equilibria would be invulnerable to subsets of voters of a specified size whose members can obtain a preferable outcome by agreeing to the joint selection of strategies. In the preceding example, outcome A is a coalition equilibrium of order two (i.e., not vulnerable to any subset of two voters)— as well as of order one—for, whatever strategies are selected by the three voters that lead to outcome A, the members of no subset of two voters can both obtain a preferable outcome by jointly altering their strategies.

In contrast, outcome N is an equilibrium of order one but not of order two. It is an equilibrium of order one since unilateral deviation by either the amenders or defeaters from the "vote for N" strategy always leads to outcome O, the worst outcome for each voter given the preference scales postulated earlier. It is not an equilibrium of order two, since when

---

16. For a formalization of the reasoning in this example in terms of the game-theoretic notion of "core," see Riker and Ordeshook, *Introduction to Positive Political Theory*, pp. 137–138.

both the passers and amenders select the strategy "vote for A," outcome A is the collective choice, which both voters prefer to outcome N.

1.10. EMPIRICAL EXAMPLES OF THE PARADOX OF SECOND BEST

Although the strategic calculations outlined in section 1.9 may seem farfetched, they help to elucidate some of the dilemmas political actors have faced in historical situations. Consider, for example, the United States presidential election of 1912, in which there were three major parties/candidates. These alternatives, and the likely preference scales of most of the electorate favoring each, are:

1. Democratic Party/Woodrow Wilson—(Wilson, Taft, Roosevelt)

2. Republican Party/William Howard Taft—(Taft, Roosevelt, Wilson)

3. Progressive Party/Theodore Roosevelt—(Roosevelt, Taft, Wilson)

In this election, Wilson was conceded to be the leading candidate (he eventually got 42 percent of the popular vote) since Roosevelt, who had bolted the Republican Party to form the Progressive ("Bull Moose") Party after failing to get the Republican presidential nomination, was expected to divide the Republican vote (he eventually got 27 percent of the popular vote and Taft got 24 percent, with minor candidates splitting the remainder).

Because Democratic voters were most numerous, they had a straight-forward strategy (vote for Wilson) under the plurality procedure of Figure 1.3. Republican and Progressive voters each had two primarily desirable strategies (vote for Roosevelt, vote for Taft), which admits all three possible outcomes as sophisticated. (This example provides a concrete interpretation of the game discussed on pages 21–22, wherein outcome O corresponds to Wilson, outcome A to Taft, and outcome N to Roosevelt.) If the Republican and Progressive voters could have combined on either Roosevelt or Taft, however, then they could have ensured the election of a candidate who, if not their favorite, would have been prefer-able to Wilson. (Carrying this reasoning one step further, if Wilson supporters had suspected such a coalition might form that would back Roosevelt, then it would have been wise for them to have supported Taft over Roosevelt and, with the support of Taft voters, to have made Taft the coalition equilibrium choice—which provides an interpretation of the cooperative game discussed on pages 22–23.) But it was precisely because Taft and Roosevelt refused to cooperate, and their supporters apparently voted sincerely, that the election went to Wilson.

It is reasonable to suppose that sophisticated voting has become more prevalent in recent presidential elections because, with the advent of public opinion polls and the wide dissemination of poll results, more complete information is available to the electorate. The case of the 1948 presidential election has already been mentioned. More recently, George Wallace's candidacy in the 1968 presidential election appears to have suffered from the fact that he was given little chance to win. In the final two months of the campaign, from the beginning of September up to Election Day, polls indicate that he lost (to both major candidates) more than one-third of his early supporters, which would seem to indicate sophisticated voting on their part.[17]

In elections that involve more than two candidates, it is extremely dismaying for some people to see a strong "extremist" candidate triumph over two or more "moderate" candidates only because the moderates split the centrist vote. Although we may be quick to attribute this result to sincere voting, it is important to point out that such an outcome can arise from sophisticated voting as well. As we saw in the case of the 1912 presidential election, sophisticated voting alone could have produced any of the three outcomes, but cooperation was needed to ensure one in particular. If the moderates do not cooperate, even the sophisticated voter may be quite helpless to do anything.[18]

In many elections today based on plurality voting, cooperation has been institutionalized in the form of a runoff election between the two top vote getters if no candidate in the plurality election receives a majority. This procedure forces supporters of the defeated candidates into agreement on either one of two alternatives, which prevents sophisticated voting in

---

17. Richard M. Scammon and Ben J. Wattenberg, *The Real Majority* (New York: Berkley Medallion Books, 1971), p. 193. This case is a bit ambiguous because it appears that the early Wallace supporters who switched split into two groups on their second-choice preferences: some favored Humphrey, others Nixon. With the two major candidates neck and neck in the final days of the campaign, neither group therefore had a surefire (sophisticated) strategy for blocking the selection of his last-place choice. For another example of sophisticated voting under the plurality procedure, see Farquharson, *Theory of Voting*, pp. 40–42, on the Roman Senate; for a general theoretical treatment of plurality voting under risk, see Ralph Joyce, "Sophisticated Voting in Three-Candidate Contests: Simple-Plurality Voting Systems" (Paper delivered at the 1973 Annual Meeting of the Midwest Political Science Association, Chicago, May 3–5). For data on sophisticated voting in West German elections, see Stephen L. Fisher, "A Test of Anthony Downs' Wasted Vote Thesis: West German Evidence" (Paper delivered at the 1974 Annual Meeting of the Public Choice Society, New Haven, Conn., March 21–23); for data and theoretical results on sophisticated voting in French labor elections, see Howard Rosenthal, "Game-Theoretic Models of Bloc-Voting under Proportional Representation: Really Sophisticated Voting in French Labor Elections," *Public Choice*, 18 (Summer 1974), pp. 1–23; and for evidence of manipulative voting practices generally in ancient Greece and Rome, see E. S. Stavely, *Greek and Roman Voting and Elections* (Ithaca, N.Y.: Cornell University Press, 1972).

18. Outside the world of professional politics, it is interesting to observe that the world of letters is not immune from such strategic kinds of activities. In several formal and informal votes, the five-member committee that awarded the 1973 National Book Award for fiction could not, after apparently extensive sophisticated voting, decide upon a winner. (There is not sufficient information to reconstruct complete preference scales for the committee members). Divided in the end on two books, the two factions agreed to cooperate by splitting the award between the two authors. See Eric Pace, "The National Book Award in Fiction: A Curious Case," *New York Times Book Review*, May 6, 1973, pp. 16–17.

the runoff election. It is not eliminated entirely, however, but simply pushed back to the plurality election, complicating the strategic calculation somewhat since more than one choice is made in the two elections.

To sum up, it appears that members of both small committees and large electorates may engage in game-theoretic kinds of strategic voting. On some occasions there seems to be cooperation among voters (if only implicit), on others, none. Our examples together suggest that one cannot always treat the choices of voters as a direct consequence of their preferences but must view them, instead, in the context of the preferences of other voters and relevant environmental constraints.

1.11. SUMMARY AND CONCLUSION

In this chapter we have looked at voting as a means for selecting alternatives that are in some sense socially preferred. We have shown that the social or collective choice arrived at depends on the following environmental constraints: (1) the voting *procedure* used, including the order in which alternatives are voted upon; (2) the *information* available to individual voters about the preference scales of other voters; and (3) *communication* among voters that allows them to coordinate their choices of strategies and to form coalitions. An awareness only of the procedure is consistent with sincere voting, whereby individuals vote directly according to their preferences. Additional information about the preference scales of other voters is consistent with sophisticated voting (as well as sincere-anticipatory voting) in a noncooperative game, whereby individuals may not choose their most-preferred outcome at a particular division in order to prevent less-preferred outcomes from ultimately being selected. Finally, an ability to communicate with other voters is consistent with the selection of joint strategies in a cooperative game, which may yield still better outcomes than can be achieved if there is no cooperation.

The idea that these environmental constraints are consistent with different kinds of voting is fundamentally rooted in the concept of *rationality*. Having previously offered commonsensical reasons why voters would make certain choices, we shall indicate how these reasons constitute, in effect, different definitions of rational behavior.[19]

---

19. For other conceptions of rational behavior relevant to the question of not only for whom to vote, but also whether or not to vote, based on the analysis of decision making under uncertainty, see John A. Ferejohn and Morris P. Fiorina, "The Paradox of Not Voting: A Decision Theoretic Analysis," *American Political Science Review*, 68 (June 1974), pp. 525–536; I. J. Good and Lawrence S. Mayer, "Estimating the Efficacy of a Vote," *Behavioral Science*, 20 (January 1975), pp. 25–33; and the several comments by Gerald S. Strom, Stephen V. Stephens, Lawrence S. Mayer and I. J. Good, Nathaniel Beck, Gordon Tullock, R. E. Goodwin and K. W. S. Roberts, and the reply by Ferejohn and Fiorina, in *American Political Science Review*, 69 (September 1975), pp. 908–928. One of the two election paradoxes discussed in Chapter 3 will be analyzed in terms of a model of decision making under uncertainty (or risk).

At the level of environmental constraint (1), a voter is rational if he *chooses his most-preferred outcome.* In this case we assume that a voter's knowledge of the social-choice process extends only to the voting procedure, so he can do no better than select his most-preferred outcome at each division (i.e., vote sincerely).

At the level of environmental constraint (2), a voter is rational if he selects strategies, insofar as possible, that *block the adoption of his least-preferred outcomes, assuming that other voters will do likewise.* If a voter has knowledge of the preference scales of other voters, then he can anticipate what strategies they will *not* select and thereby narrow down his own strategies to those which are most desirable. Since the choices of other voters may block the selection of a "most-preferred" outcome at any division, a voter's most sensible course therefore is to reduce the set of outcomes to those that are "not least preferred" by voting sophisticatedly.

At the level of environmental constraint (3), a voter is rational if he joins a coalition that can enforce an agreement, binding on its members, that *provides an outcome better than that which any other coalition can provide.* Clearly, if any member of a coalition can be tempted to defect to another coalition that can guarantee a better outcome, other voters will recognize this possibility, and the first coalition will not form. In this case, as in the previous case, a voter chooses from among outcomes that cannot be blocked, but now blockage can occur due to the selection of coordinated strategies by coalitions of voters.

In sum, the concept of rationality can be defined at various levels, depending on the environmental constraints assumed to be operative. At all levels the focus is exclusively on outcomes, which we have assumed are the only things valued by voters. Under environmental constraints (2) and (3), rationality is the force that fuels strategic calculations on the part of voters, who are linked to each other through a mutual perception of each other's rationality. Only when voters cannot perceive the effect of their individual choices on other voters' choices, and ultimately on the collective choice of the voting body—as when they are familiar only with the voting procedure—is a voting situation not a game.

Games may be cooperative or noncooperative, depending on whether voters are able to communicate and coordinate joint strategies that lead to enforceable outcomes. In noncooperative games, in which information is complete but there is no communication among voters, the sophisticated outcome will depend on the voting procedure. Whereas binary procedures are always determinate, leading to single outcomes if voting is sophisticated,[20] under other procedures sophisticated voting may not reduce the strategies of voters to those associated with only a single outcome.

In cooperative games, in which information is complete and there is communication among voters, the formation of coalitions does not

---

20. Farquharson, *Theory of Voting*, pp. 42–43.

depend on the voting procedure but only on the structure of voters' preference scales. This may render certain (equilibrium) outcomes incapable of being blocked, even by a coalition of voters.

But coalitions may not always form to block outcomes, as we saw in the case of the presidential election of 1912. In this election, voting was apparently sincere and Wilson, the leading vote getter, won under the plurality procedure (and, coincidentally, was also the electoral-vote winner). Yet, given the postulated preference scales of voters in this example, if voting had been sophisticated, the outcome would have been indeterminate (i.e., any of the three candidates might have won). In a series of pairwise contests, however, Taft would have defeated the other two candidates, making him the so-called *Condorcet winner;* indeed, if coalitions could have formed, Wilson supporters would have voted for Taft. On the other hand, if voters were sincere and there had been a runoff election between the two top vote getters (Wilson and Roosevelt), Roosevelt would have been elected.[21] What then, if anything, makes Wilson—the historical winner—the rightful winner?

From this example it is apparent that different combinations of voting procedures and types of voting can produce a rather rich menu of outcomes, none of which seems to have an incontrovertible a priori claim to being considered *the* rightful outcome. For those who have a low tolerance for ambiguity, this richness may be quite unpalatable. It may, however, be an accurate reflection of the general incoherence of social-choice processes, about which we shall have more to say in subsequent chapters.

We set out in this chapter to show that sincere voting may not always be advantageous. Specifically, it may be advisable on occasion not to vote for one's most-preferred alternative, which we referred to as the paradox of second best. To show that second best may really be best from a strategic viewpoint required first that we show how different environmental constraints mediate the selection of outcomes for voters with given preference scales. Untangling the effects of these different constraints enabled us then to explicate different concepts of rationality, some of which clearly revealed the advantages of insincere voting—and the possible conflict between preference and choice. Empirical evidence, particularly from three-way presidential elections, indicated that sophisticated and coalition strategies on the part of candidates and voters are considered— if not always followed—in real-life voting situations.

---

21. For a similar analysis of this election, see Riker and Ordeshook, *Introduction to Positive Political Theory*, p. 98, n. 13, who incorrectly identify Roosevelt as the Condorcet winner.

2

THE PARADOX OF VOTING

2.1. INTRODUCTION

Of all the paradoxes discussed in this book, the paradox of voting has probably been the source of more intellectual controversy and confusion than any other, at least as judged by the amount that has been written about it. First discovered in the eighteenth century, it was largely forgotten until the pioneering work of Duncan Black and Kenneth J. Arrow in the late 1940s and early 1950s resurrected interest in it and its ramifications. Since then, an enormous literature has developed concerning the paradox of voting, much of which is highly abstruse and mathematical.

There seem to be three reasons for the consuming interest in this paradox. First, in its most elementary form it can be simply stated (a characteristic of some of the most famous unsolved problems in mathematics, e.g., the four-color problem). Second, this paradox is not only puzzling, it is also pathological—it says that there are fundamental problems connected with the idea of social or collective choice. Third, the implications of the paradox seem pervasive, though there remains a good deal of controversy on this last point.

The standard example of the paradox of voting involves three voters who rank a set of three alternatives $\{x, y, z\}$ as shown in Table 2.1. The paradox arises from the fact that if every voter is assumed to have a *transitive* preference scale (i.e., if he prefers x to y and y to z, then he prefers x to z), the social ordering nevertheless is intransitive: a majority (voters 1 and 3) prefers x to y, a majority (voters 1 and 2) prefers y to z, but a majority (voters 2 and 3) prefers z to x, rather than x to z. This means that given at least three alternatives, there may be no social choice that is decisive in a series of pairwise comparisons—that is, is a Condorcet winner—since every alternative that receives majority support in one comparison can be defeated by another majority in another comparison. For this reason, the majorities that prefer each alternative over some other in a series of pairwise comparisons are referred to as *cyclical majorities*, though the paradox is not dependent on a specific decision rule like majority rule, as we shall show in subsequent sections.

TABLE 2.1   PARADOX OF VOTING

VOTER	PREFERENCE SCALE FOR ALTERNATIVES
1	(x, y, z)
2	(y, z, x)
3	(z, x, y)

Cyclical majorities may manifest themselves in other forms, including voting on party platforms.[1] Consider a voting procedure in which the voters do not have the opportunity to vote on single issues, but instead must choose among candidates who take positions on two or more issues. For example, if there are two issues, assume that the alternatives (i.e., positions a candidate might take) on the first issue are x and x', and on the second, y and y'. If the preferences of three voters for the four possible platforms, comprising positions on the two issues, are as shown in Table 2.2, then there is no platform that can defeat all others in a series of pairwise comparisons. As shown by the arrows in Figure 2.1, which indicate majority preferences between pairs of platforms, the majorities are cyclical and the social preferences are therefore intransitive.

What is particularly striking about this example is that if separate votes were taken on the two issues, x would be preferred to x' by voters 1 and 2 and y would be preferred to y' by voters 1 and 3 (compare the first preferences of the voters in Table 2.2). But despite the fact that a majority would prefer alternatives x and y were the issues voted on separately, platform $x'y'$ defeats platform xy since it is preferred by a majority (voters 2 and 3). Thus, a platform whose alternatives, when considered separately, are both favored by a majority may be defeated by a platform containing alternatives that only minorities favor. A recognition that a majority platform may be constituted from minority positions is what Anthony Downs argued may make it rational for politicians to construct platforms that appeal to coalitions of minorities.[2]

The divergence between less-preferred individual alternatives and a more-preferred platform that combines them depends on the existence of

1. Claude Hillinger, "Voting on Issues and on Platforms," *Behavioral Science*, 16 (November 1971), pp. 564–566. See elso Joseph B. Kadane, "On Division of the Question," *Public Choice*, 13 (Fall 1972), pp. 47–54, for an analysis of the effects of combining different alternatives. For other examples of intransitive relations in tournaments, card games, bingo, and coin-tossing experiments, see Martin Gardner, "Mathematical Games," *Scientific American*, October 1974, pp. 120–124.

2. Anthony Downs, *An Economic Theory of Democracy* (New York: Harper & Row, 1957), chap. 4.

TABLE 2.2   PLATFORM VOTING

VOTER	PREFERENCE SCALE FOR PLATFORMS
1	$(xy, xy', x'y, x'y')$
2	$(xy', x'y', xy, x'y)$
3	$(x'y, x'y', xy, xy')$

FIGURE 2.1.   CYCLICAL MAJORITIES FOR PLATFORM VOTING

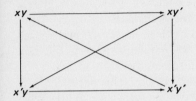

the paradox.[3] In the preceding example, the paradox of voting makes no platform invulnerable, which helps to explain the importance that politicians attach to anticipating an opponent's positions so that they can respond with a set that is more attractive to the voters. Of course, many politicians try to avoid this problem by being intentionally vague about their positions in the first place, as Downs pointed out.[4] Some consequences of uncertainty and ambiguous strategies that involve the fuzzing of positions on issues will be analyzed in Chapter 3.

2.2. ARROW'S GENERAL POSSIBILITY THEOREM

Before attempting to generalize the preceding analysis, let us be clear about what the paradox of voting says. Clearly it demonstrates, at least in the previous examples, that a concept of rationality based on transitivity cannot be transferred directly from individuals to a collectivity via some decision rule like that of simple majority. Something queer happens on the way, something comes apart, which complicates the idea of a "social choice" based on this kind of internal consistency. Indeed, this lack of

---

3. Hillinger, "Voting on Issues and on Platforms," p. 565, claims this is not the case, but this is refuted in Nicholas R. Miller, "Logrolling and the Arrow Paradox: A Note," *Public Choice*, 21 (Spring 1975), p. 110.

4. Downs, *Economic Theory of Democracy*, chaps. 8 and 9.

consistency in social choice reflects, as Riker and Ordeshook point out, a qualitative difference between individual and social decisions:

> Social decisions are not the same kind of think as individual decisions, even though the former are constructed from the latter. As a consequence of that difference, social decisions are sometimes arbitrary in a way personal decisions are not; personal decisions follow from persons' tastes, but social decisions do not follow from the taste of society simply because it is never clear what the taste of society is.[5]

In a way, this difference might be viewed as a second major crack in the concept of rationality—at least commonsensical notions of it that we may harbor. In Chapter 1 we showed that it was not sufficient to view *individual rationality* simply in terms of the choice of one's most-preferred alternative. One had to take account of the preferences of other actors, and the resultant social preference implied by these individual preferences, to ascertain what choices were rational for individual voters. But now there is a new wrinkle: there seems to be something awry with the very idea of a coherent social preference or social choice. This naturally leads us to inquire into the means by which society constructs a social preference order from the preference scales of its individual members.

Kenneth J. Arrow's approach to this question was not to analyze a specific method for summing individual preferences but rather to postulate a set of abstract conditions that *any* summation method should meet.[6] He then asked what implications summation methods satisfying these conditions have for the *collective rationality* of social outcomes—specifically, whether they lead to transitive social choices—given that the preferences of individuals are transitive. To ensure the latter, Arrow made two assumptions about the relation—which may indicate either preference or indifference—by which *individuals* order pairs of alternatives. Letting R symbolize this relation (read "is preferred to" or "is indifferent to"), the assumptions are:

(a) *Connectivity.* For any two alternatives x and y, either xRy or yRx. That is, the alternatives (e.g., political candidates) possess some common property (e.g., positions on an issue) that allows individuals to compare them with respect to their values.

(b) *Transitivity.* For any three alternatives x, y, and z, if xRy and yRz, then xRz. That is, individuals are consistent (i.e., transitive) in their ranking of alternatives.

---

5. William H. Riker and Peter C. Ordeshook, *An Introduction to Positive Political Theory* (Englewood Cliffs, N.J.: Prentice-Hall, 1973), pp. 114–115.

6. Kenneth J. Arrow, *Social Choice and Individual Values*, 2d ed. (New Haven, Conn.: Yale University Press, 1963); the first edition of this classic work was published in 1951.

Given that there exist connected alternatives that individuals can transitively order, Arrow postulated five conditions that he believed would render social choices democratic. These conditions may be thought of as "reasonable" requirements that any method of aggregating or summing individual preferences into a social outcome should satisfy, where the social outcome is simply society's ranking of the alternatives. Very roughly, given at least three alternatives, Arrow's conditions are:

1. *Universal Admissibility of Individual Preference Scales.* All possible orderings of alternatives by individuals are admissible; there are no institutions (e.g., political parties) that can restrict the orderings so that certain preference scales cannot be expressed.

2. *Positive Association of Individual and Social Values.* Given that xRy is the social ordering, if individuals either raise or do not change the ranking of x in their preference scales, and the ranking of y remains unchanged, it is still the case that xRy. This restriction ensures that the method of summing individuals' preference scales reflects, in a nonperverse way, these preferences: the social ranking of x does not respond negatively to changes in rankings by individuals.

3. *Independence from Irrelevant Alternatives.* If S is a subset of the set of available alternatives, and the preference scales of individuals change with respect to alternatives not in S, then the social ordering for alternatives in S does not change. This has been by far the most controversial of Arrow's conditions; we shall discuss its implications in detail in section 2.3.

4. *Citizens' Sovereignty.* For any two alternatives x and y, there exist individual preference scales such that x is preferred to y in the social ordering. In other words, the social outcome is not imposed; at the extreme, if all individuals should prefer x to y, x cannot be prohibited as the social outcome. This condition, in effect, outlaws the possibility that a social outcome is unrelated to the preference scales of society's members.

5. *Nondictatorship.* For any two alternatives x and y, there is no individual such that whenever he prefers x to y, x is always preferred to y in the social ordering. In other words, there is no individual who can dictate the social ordering of alternatives. Thus, by this condition an alternative cannot be prescribed from the *inside* (e.g., by a dictator), just as by condition 4 an alternative cannot be imposed from the *outside* (e.g., according to some societal ethic).[7]

The intent of these conditions is to link the ordering of alternatives by society to individuals' preference scales in a nonarbitrary way—that is, in a way that would make the social outcome responsive to the preference

---

7. Riker and Ordeshook, *Introduction to Positive Political Theory*, p. 91.

scales of individuals (as spelled out in conditions 2–5), whatever they may be (as guaranteed by condition 1). Remarkably, there is *no* method of summing individual preferences that satisfies all these conditions and yields a *social ordering* satisfying assumptions (a) and (b), previously postulated for individuals. Every method of summation that satisfies conditions 1–3 either does not produce a connected and transitive social ordering or, if it does, violates either condition 4 (Citizens' Sovereignty) or condition 5 (Nondictatorship). Hence, it is impossible to construct a method of summing individual preferences, satisfying the notions of fairness and justice embodied in the five conditions, that does not result in an intransitive social order. [Note that social intransitivities cannot arise from individual intransitivities since the latter are ruled out by assumption (b).] If cyclical majorities are to be avoided, therefore, the social outcome must be either imposed or dictated.

This is the essence of Arrow's General Possibility—sometimes called Impossibility—Theorem. Although the proof of this famous theorem is beyond the scope of this book, there is no difficulty in explaining its import. In effect, it condemns to an ineradicable arbitrariness all methods of summing individual preferences that satisfy the five conditions. At least for some preference scales of individuals (by condition 1, none can be precluded), the method of summation will lead necessarily to cyclical majorities, thus making the social outcome dependent on which pair of alternatives is compared.

This means that the paradox of voting cannot be dismissed as an aberration of majority rule or any other method of summing individual preferences. Either the method does not satisfy all of Arrow's five conditions or, if it does, it necessarily leads to an intransitive social ordering for at least some preferences of individuals. The strength of Arrow's abstract formulation of the five conditions is that he did not have to examine every summation method that has ever been proposed or is ever likely to be proposed. By abstractly defining a *class* of methods, rather than concretely defining a particular summation procedure, he was able to administer the coup de grâce to all procedures that possess the properties of this class. Given the defining properties of this class (Arrow's five conditio.·s), the paradox of voting cannot be avoided, which renders the notion of "social consensus" achieved by procedures having these properties somewhat of a contradiction in terms.

2.3. INDEPENDENCE FROM IRRELEVANT ALTERNATIVES

Perplexed and dismayed by the negativeness of this result, many theorists, not surprisingly, have attacked the reasonableness of certain of Arrow's conditions. This attack has led to various refinements in Arrow's statement of the original conditions, new axiomatizations of social choice, and many new theorems.[8] But except for one minor flaw found in Arrow's original proof (discussed in the second edition of *Social Choice and Individual Values*), Arrow's basic impossibility result has remained intact for a generation.

If the correctness of Arrow's theorem has proved logically unassailable, there nevertheless remains a good deal of controversy over its interpretation and its significance for the study of social and political processes. Because this controversy is based in part on a fundamental confusion over the meaning of one of Arrow's conditions, however, it seems useful to try to clarify the meaning of this condition in order to understand better the significance of the General Possibility Theorem.

Since the conditions in Arrow's proof of the General Possibility Theorem are all necessary, and together sufficient, to ensure the occurrence of the voting paradox, one way to avoid the paradox is to drop one of the conditions. The most controversial, and some have argued the most unrealistic, of the conditions is condition 3, Independence from Irrelevant Alternatives. Unfortunately, practically all the *examples* that have been used to illustrate the meaning of this condition, including one given by Arrow himself, misinterpret it, as Charles R. Plott has recently demonstrated.[9] Here is Arrow's example:

The reasonableness of this condition can be seen by consideration of the possible results in a method of choice which does not satisfy condition 3 [Independence from Irrelevant Alternatives], the rank-order method of voting frequently used in clubs. With a finite number of candidates, let each individual rank all the candidates, i.e., designate his first-choice candidate, second-choice candidate, etc. Let pre-assigned weights be given to the first, second, etc., choices, the higher weight to the higher choice, and then let the candidate with the highest weighted sum of votes be elected. In particular, suppose that there are three voters and four candidates, x, y, z, and w. Let the weights for the first, second, third, and fourth choices be 4, 3, 2, and 1, respectively. Suppose that individuals 1 and 2 rank the candidates in order x, y, z, and w, while individual 3 ranks them in order z, w,

---

8. For recent reviews and syntheses of the social-choice literature related to the General Possibility Theorem, see Peter C. Fishburn, *The Theory of Social Choice* (Princeton, N.J.: Princeton University Press, 1972); Prasanta K. Pattanaik, *Voting and Collective Choice: Some Aspects of the Theory of Collective Decision Making* (New York: Cambridge University Press, 1971); Amartya K. Sen, *Collective Choice and Social Welfare* (San Francisco: Holden-Day, 1970); and David J. Mayston, *The Idea of Social Choice* (New York: St. Martin's Press, 1974).

9. Charles R. Plott, "Recent Results in the Theory of Voting," in *Frontiers of Quantitative Economics*, ed. M. D. Intriligator (Amsterdam: North-Holland Publishing Co., 1971), pp. 109–129; Plott, "Ethics, Social Choice Theory and the Theory of Economic Policy," *Journal of Mathematical Sociology*, 2 (July 1972), pp. 181–208; and Plott, "Rationality and Relevance in Social Choice Theory," California Institute of Technology Social Science Working Paper no. 5 (Pasadena Calif., August 1971).

x, and *y*. Under the given electoral system, *x* is chosen. Then, certainly if *y* is deleted from the ranks of the candidates, the system applied to the remaining candidates should yield the same result, especially since, in this case, *y* is inferior to *x* according to the tastes of every individual; but, if *y* is in fact deleted, the indicated electoral system would yield a tie between *x* and *z*.[10]

If one refers to the statement of condition 3, it is clear that what it does *not* assume is that the set of alternatives changes; rather, only individual preferences are allowed to vary. In Arrow's example, however, the set of alternatives changes from $\{w, x, y, z\}$ to $\{w, x, z\}$, whereas individual preferences are held fixed.[11] In fact, rather than violating the Independence condition, this example satisfies it.[12] Given the initial preferences and the set of alternatives $S = \{w, x, z\}$, the social choice is $\{x, z\}$. Now if individuals 1 and 2 continue to rank the three alternatives in the order *x*, *z*, *w*, and individual 3 ranks them in the order *z*, *w*, *x*, the choice under the rank-order method remains $\{x, z\}$ since *z* and *x* both get 7 votes, *w* gets 4 votes. This is true regardless of how the individuals feel about alternative *y* because the condition assumes that the postulated set of alternatives $S = \{w, x, z\}$ from which a choice is made does not change. Unavailable

---

10. Arrow, *Social Choice and Individual Values*, p. 27.

11. The literature is filled with other examples in which this mistake is committed, even by perceptive scholars. See, for example, Riker and Ordeshook, *Introduction to Positive Political Theory*, pp. 88–90 and 109–114, a generally outstanding work which we have cited frequently throughout this book.

12. Other examples based on the rank-order method could be given, however, in which a change in individual *preferences* produces a change in the social choice, which would appear to violate condition 3. For instance, if the preference scales of five voters change from (1) (*x*, *y*, *z*) to (*x*, *z*, *y*), (2) (*x*, *y*, *z*) to (*x z*, *y*), (3) (*y*, *z*, *x*) to (*z*, *y*, *x*), (4) (*y*, *z*, *x*) to (*y*, *x*, *z*), and (5) (*z*, *x*, *y*) to (*x*, *z*, *y*), no change occurs in each voter's ranking of alternative *x* vis-à-vis alternative *y*. Nevertheless, the first set of preference scales yields 10 votes for *x* versus 11 votes for *y*, whereas the second set of preference scales yields 12 votes for *x* versus 8 votes for *y*. However, since condition 3 is usually interpreted to mean that the social choices be taken only over the subset $S = \{x, y\}$, not the set $\{x, y, z\}$ containing the "irrelevant" alternative *z* (see text), even after the change in preference scales over the three-member set $\{x, y, z\}$, *x* is still preferred to *y* over $S = \{x, y\}$ by 10 votes to 5 votes. This example, therefore, satisfies *this interpretation* of condition 3—that the social choice over "relevant" alternatives (in *S*) not change, despite the change in the ranking of alternative *z*. Since the rank-order method satisfies the four other conditions of the General Possibility Theorem as well, we know that it can lead to cyclical majorities, which is verified by the fact that for the original set of preference scales of the five voters in our example, a majority prefers alternative *x* to alternative *y*, alternative *y* to alternative *z*, and alternative *z* to alternative *x*. A precise mathematical statement of condition 3, interpreted as above, can be found in Fishburn, *Theory of Social Choice*, p. 204, where condition 3 is referred to as C6. Alternatively, if we interpret condition 3 to specify that social choices be taken over the entire set $\{x, y, z\}$, our example demonstrates that the rank-order method does *not* satisfy this condition: the voters' ranking of alternative *z* is not irrelevant to the social choice—*y* in the case of the first set of preferences, *x* in the case of the second—for the subset *S* containing alternatives *x* and *y*. According to *this interpretation*, therefore, the rank-order method does not satisfy all five conditions, *given* that the social ordering is transitive, which is another way of stating the General Possibility Theorem. For a set of conditions that uniquely characterizes the rank-order method (also called Borda's rule), see H. P. Young, "An Axiomatization of Borda's Rule," *Journal of Economic Theory*, 9 (September 1974), pp. 43–52.

alternatives not included in this "feasible" set are assumed to have no effect on the social-choice process, which Plott argues is a rather innocuous assumption to make, even on ethical grounds: "As a question of 'ethics' the axiom simply says 'best' depends upon preferences over candidates for 'best' and not on unavailable alternatives."[13]

Arrow's example does violate what Plott calls a (collective) "rationality" condition, which in essence refers to assumptions (a) and (b), but applied to the social ordering. It says that over one set of alternatives x is preferred to z, but over another set of alternatives (the set of alternatives, but not individuals' preferences, is allowed to vary under this condition) neither candidate is preferred to the other (i.e., the social choice is one of indifference between the two candidates). Since there is no single relation R that can "rationalize" these variable social choices over different sets of alternatives, the rationality condition is not satisfied.

Should we be unduly upset by this fact? Plott thinks not, arguing that the idea of "better" inherent in a (binary) preference relation is excessively narrow and "uninteresting." He offers examples of social-choice processes that violate various rationality conditions but yet do not depend on the sequence in which alternatives are voted upon (i.e., are independent of the "path" of choice over two-element sets), which Arrow and others have argued justifies the rationality conditions. Thus, to devise social-choice processes that are path independent—unlike several voting procedures discussed in Chapter 1, wherein the outcome is sensitive to the order in which alternatives are voted upon—does not require that we impose the rationality conditions. Although rationality implies path independence, path independence does not imply rationality.[14]

Since the rationality and independence-of-path conditions are not equivalent, there exist social-choice processes that satisfy all Arrow's conditions except rationality and still possess the independence-of-path property. Hence, they are not subject to the General Possibility Theorem and would appear to yield "reasonable" outcomes that are not simply artifacts of the voting procedure or social-choice process used.

2.4. SINGLE-PEAKED PREFERENCES

The relaxation of Arrow's rationality conditions are not the only conditions that provide an escape from the paradox of voting. It is possible to

---

13. Plott, "Recent Results in the Theory of Voting," p. 116. Even dropping the Independence condition, however, does not eliminate related paradoxes. See Dennis J. Packard, "Social Choice Theory and Citizens' Intransitive Weak Preference—A Paradox," *Public Choice*, 22 (Summer 1975), pp. 107–111.

14. Plott, "Rationality and Relevance in Social Choice Theory" pp. 27–29; and Plott "Path Independence, Rationality, and Social Choice," *Econometrica*, 41 (November 1973), pp. 1075–1091. See also Douglas H. Blair, "Path-Independent Social Choice Functions: A Further Result," *Econometrica*, 43 (January 1975), pp. 173–174; and John A. Ferejohn and David M. Grether, "On Normative Problems of Social Choice," California Institute of Technology Social Science Working Paper no. 80 (Pasadena, Calif., April 1975).

FIGURE 2.2. GEOMETRIC REPRESENTATION OF SINGLE-PEAKED PREFERENCE SCALES OF THREE INDIVIDUALS

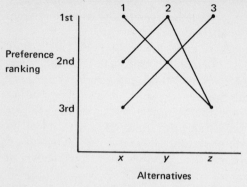

weaken other conditions and thereby avoid the consequence of social incoherence endemic to all summation methods that fulfill the conditions of the General Possibility Theorem.

Even before Arrow proved this famous theorem, Duncan Black showed in a series of articles in the late 1940s that by imposing certain restrictions on individuals' preference scales (which, of course, violates condition 1, Universal Admissibility of Individual Preference Scales), an outcome favored by a majority could be ensured.[15] Given a decision rule of simple majority and sincere voting, one obvious condition sufficient to guarantee that a majority favors a particular outcome is that more than half of all individuals rank that outcome highest on their preference scales.

This condition is highly restrictive, and, except when individual preferences are very homogeneous, is probably rarely satisfied in practice. In fact, however, to ensure that one outcome is preferred by a majority to all others, one need insist only that the preference scales of individuals be "single peaked." Black defined this condition in terms of a coordinate system in which the outcomes or alternatives are arranged along the horizontal axis and the preference rankings by individuals of these alternatives along the vertical axis. The preference scale of each individual can then be represented geometrically by a set of connected lines, or curves, as illustrated in Figure 2.2. In this example, individual 1 ranks alternative x first, alternative y second, and alternative z third, so his preference scale is (x, y, z). Similarly, the preference scales of individuals 2 and 3 are (y, x, z) and (z, y, x), respectively.

Note that each individual's preference curve in Figure 2.2 (1) has a single "peak" and (2) always slopes downward from this peak in one or

15. Black's results are included in Duncan Black, *Theory of Committees and Elections* (Cambridge: Cambridge University Press, 1958).

FIGURE 2.3. NONSINGLE-PEAKED PREFERENCE SCALES

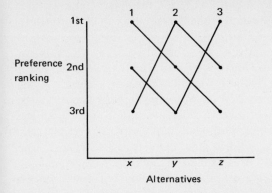

both directions. By contrast, the preference scales of not all individuals in Figure 2.3 are single peaked: individual 3's preference curve first slopes downward from his most-preferred alternative (z), then changes direction and slopes upward (reading from right to left). Only when an individual's preference curve increases up to a peak—or is at a peak immediately—and then decreases after the peak is his preference scale said to be single peaked.

The preference scales of a *set* of individuals are said to be *single peaked* if there is *some* arrangement of alternatives along the horizontal axis such that the preference curves of *all* individuals are single peaked. The reader can check that no matter how the alternatives in Figure 2.3 are ordered along the horizontal axis (there are six possible arrangements), there is *no* ordering that renders the preference curves of all individuals single peaked.

Black demonstrated that if the preference scales of all individuals can be represented by a set of single-peaked preference curves, then there is one alternative that is preferred by a majority to all others (i.e., is a Condorcet winner). This ensures that there are no cyclical majorities and the social ordering is transitive. In the case of the preference scales represented in Figure 2.2, for example, alternative y is preferred by individuals 2 and 3 to alternative x, and by individuals 1 and 2 to alternative z. Thus, alternative y is the social choice; it is also easy to show that a majority (individuals 1 and 2) prefers alternative x to alternative z, so the social preference order is (y, x, z).

In general, for a set of single-peaked preference curves, the social choice will be the alternative at the peak of the *median curve*, or the curve to the left of whose peak there lie exactly as many preference curve peaks as to the right. Obviously, if the number of persons is even, there is no single median curve and the possibility of ties exists. In this case, therefore, there may be no single alternative preferred by a majority to all others, though there will be one that is undefeatable if all preference curves are single peaked.

Single peakedness provides a useful criterion for determining whether the preference scales of individuals are sufficiently similar, or homogeneous, for there to be an alternative that defeats or—in the even case—is undefeatable by all other alternatives in a series of pairwise comparisons. Moreover, if there is an odd number of individuals, it tells us which alternative—that coincident with the median preference curve—is the majority, or Condorcet, winner. Roughly, single peakedness can be interpreted to mean that there exists a single dimension underlying the preferences of all individuals (e.g., a liberalism-conservatism scale) along which the alternatives (e.g., political candidates) can be ordered. The existence of such a dimension *is* consistent with individuals' having diametrically opposed preference scales; it implies only that they exercise a uniform—if opposed—standard in ordering the alternatives.

Methods for determining the "degree" of single peakedness of a set of preference scales have been developed and applied to empirical data. In section 2.6 we shall discuss some empirical instances of the paradox of voting wherein the single-peakedness condition was apparently not met. At this point, however, it is helpful to consider an alternative characterization of single peakedness that sheds considerable light on the nature of individual preference scales that give rise to the voting paradox. This characterization will also facilitate our analysis of the probability of occurrence of the paradox in section 2.5.

From the preceding discussion and examples, it is apparent that there may be a majority winner even when the preference scales of individuals differ markedly. For example, for the preference scales depicted in Figure 2.2, every person most prefers a different alternative (i.e., the peak of each preference curve is located at a different point on the horizontal axis). Nevertheless, a majority still prefers alternative y to either other alternative. This raises a question: how heterogeneous must individual preference scales be for the paradox of voting to occur?

Looking at the preference scales of individuals in Figure 2.3, where there is a paradox, one finds that only not do the first preferences of each individual differ but so do the second preferences: the second choice of individual 1 is alternative y; of individual 2, alternative z; and of individual 3, alternative x. Given that the first and the second choices of all three persons differ, it necessarily follows that the least-preferred alternatives of everyone also differ, which a glance at Figure 2.3 confirms. Situations wherein each alternative is ranked differently by every individual—first on one person's preference scale, second on another's, and last on the third's—always result in the paradox.

To characterize situations—not necessarily involving just three individuals or three alternatives—in which the paradox cannot occur, Amartya K. Sen defined a set of preference scales to be *value restricted* if all individuals agree that there is some alternative that is never best, medium, or worst for every set of three alternatives, or "triple." Thus, the triple in Figure 2.2 is value restricted since alternative y is not worst on anyone's preference scale. Given that a set of alternatives is value restricted, Sen proved that majority rule satisfies all of Arrow's conditions [and assumptions (a) and (b)], except, of course, condition 1,[16] Universal Admissibility of Individual Preference Scales.

It is evident from our preceding discussion that the paradox of voting can be circumvented if individuals' preference scales reflect a certain modicum of similarity. Since the preferences of citizens in democracies and other social collectivities to which conditions 2–5 of Arrow's theorem might apply undoubtedly exhibit some similarities, an evaluation of the real-world implications of the paradox must take account of its expected frequency of occurrence. If it is very small, the paradox can quickly be dismissed as a curious but unimportant aberration. If it has a high probability of occurring, on the other hand, it may have serious ramifications for the social coherence of democratic societies. In sections 2.5 and 2.6 we shall evaluate the significance of the paradox in light of both some theoretical calculations and empirical case studies.

2.5. PROBABILITY OF THE PARADOX OF VOTING

If we make the simplifying assumption that all orderings of alternatives are equally likely for every individual, it is not difficult to calculate the probability of the paradox for three individuals who choose among three alternatives. There are six ways in which each individual may order the set of three alternatives $\{x, y, z\}$:

1. (x, y, z)
2. (x, z, y)
3. (y, x, z)
4. (y, z, x)
5. (z, x, y)
6. (z, y, x)

Hence, there are $6^3 = 216$ ways in which three individuals can express their preferences. For a social intransitivity to occur, as we know from our earlier discussion of value restriction, neither the first, second, nor third preferences of the three individuals can agree. Thus, once one individual has chosen a preference scale [e.g., (x, y, z)], which he can do in six ways, a second individual has a choice between only two preference

---

16. Sen, "A Possibility Theorem on Majority Decisions," *Econometrica*, 34 (April 1966), pp. 491–499. For other characterizations of partial agreement that ensures a transitive social preference, see Sen, *Collective Choice and Social Welfare*, pp. 169–171.

TABLE 2.3   PROBABILITIES OF NO MAJORITY WINNER

NUMBER OF ALTERNATIVES	NUMBER OF INDIVIDUALS						
	3	5	7	9	11	...	Limit
3	0.056	0.069	0.075	0.078	0.080	...	0.080
4	0.111	0.139	0.150	0.156	0.160	...	0.176
5	0.160	0.200	0.215	0.230	0.251	...	0.251
6	0.202	0.255	0.258	0.284	0.294	...	0.315
7	0.239	0.299	0.305	0.342	0.343	...	0.369
⋮	⋮	⋮	⋮	⋮	⋮	⋮	⋮
Limit	1.000	1.000	1.000	1.000	1.000	...	1.000

scales [i.e., (y, z, x) or (z, x, y)], on which none of the alternatives is ranked in the same position as on the first individual's preference scale. Given the choices of the first two individuals, the third individual is limited to just one preference scale. Hence, given three alternatives, there are $6 \times 2 \times 1 = 12$ ways in which three individuals can choose preference scales that will yield an intransitive social preference. The probability, therefore, of a social intransitivity is $\frac{12}{216} = 0.056$, assuming all preference scales are equiprobable.

The probabilities that no alternative will be preferred to all others for three or more individuals choosing among three or more alternatives are shown for several cases in Table 2.3, based on several recent studies in which both exact and approximate calculations of the probabilities were made (all figures are accurate to the number of decimal places shown).[17] The probability values reveal an interesting pattern as the number of individuals and alternatives increases. For a fixed number of alternatives, the values increase—most rapidly in the beginning—as the size of a voting body approaches infinity, but not generally by a great amount. In the case of three alternatives, for example, the probability of the paradox increases from 0.056 to 0.088, or to less than one chance in eleven. For a fixed number of individuals, on the other hand, the prob-

17. Richard G. Niemi and Herbert F. Weisberg, "A Mathematical Solution for the Probability of the Paradox of Voting," *Behavioral Science*, 13 (July 1968), pp. 317–323; Mark B. Garman and Morton I. Kamien, "The Paradox of Voting: Probability Calculations," *Behavioral Science*, 13 (July 1968), pp. 306–316; Richard G. Niemi, "Majority Decision-Making with Partial Unidimensionality," *American Political Science Review*, 63 (June 1969), pp. 488–497; Frank Demeyer and Charles Plott, "The Probability of a Cyclical Majority," *Econometrica*, 38 (March 1970), pp. 345–354; Robert M. May, "Some Mathematical Remarks on the Paradox of Voting," *Behavioral Science*, 16 (March 1971), pp. 143–151; Jerry S. Kelly, "Voting Anomalies, the Number of Voters, and the Number of Alternatives," *Econometrica*, 42 (March 1974), pp. 239–251. For a discussion of related "paradoxes" of voting, see Peter C. Fishburn "Paradoxes of Voting," *American Political Science Review*. 68 (June 1974), pp. 537–546.

ability of the paradox always approaches 1.00 as the number of alternatives increases. Clearly, the occurrence of the paradox is much more sensitive to the number of alternatives than the number of individuals.[18]

2.6. EMPIRICAL EXAMPLES OF THE PARADOX OF VOTING

It is hard to evaluate the empirical significance of the paradox from the probalistic calculations outlined in section 2.5 since they are based on an equiprobability assumption about individuals' preference scales which in practice is probably violated. The question is: in what direction do deviations from this assumption occur?

Since political actors may have an incentive to contrive a paradox that exploits an apparent lack of consensus among voters, Riker and Ordeshook argue that the theoretical calculations probably understate the significance of the paradox.[19] Moreover, because the manipulation of outcomes requires a not inconsiderable amount of planning and effort, one would expect that the more important and controversial an issue is, the more likely political actors will be motivated to contrive a paradox that is not inherent in the distribution of preferences.

As evidence for this proposition, Riker gives two empirical examples.[20] The first concerns federal aid for school construction, which was considered by the U.S. House of Representatives in 1956 in terms of the following

---

18. The effects of other parameters have also been tested. On the effects of single peakedness and voter agreement, see Bernard Grofman, "A Note on Some Generalizations of the Paradox of Cyclical Majorities," *Public Choice*, 12 (Spring 1972), pp. 113–114; Peter C. Fishburn, "Vote Concordance, Simple Majorities, and Group Decision Methods," *Behavioral Science*, 18 (September 1973), pp. 364–376; Fishburn, "Single-Peaked Preferences and Probabilities of Cyclical Majorities," *Behavioral Science*, 19 (January 1974), pp. 21–27; and Kiyoshi Kugn and Hiroaki Nagatani, "Voter Antagonism and the Paradox of Voting," *Econometrica*, 42 (November 1974), pp. 1045–1067. On the effects of unequally weighted voters and conflict, see Bo H. Bjurulf. "A Probabilistic Analysis of Voting Blocs and the Occurrence of the Paradox of Voting," in *Probability Models of Collective Decision Making*, ed. Richard G. Niemi and Herbert F. Weisberg (Columbus, Ohio: Charles E. Merrill Co., 1972), pp. 232–249. On the effects of uncertainty, see Kenneth A. Shepsle, "The Paradox of Voting and Uncertainty," in *Probability Models of Collective Decision Making*, pp. 352–370. For an elegant argument, based on an elementary geometric construction, that the paradox of voting is ubiquitous, see Howard Margolis, "What It Takes To Avoid Arrow's Paradox" (Paper delivered at the 1974 Annual Meeting of the American Political Science Association, Chicago, August 30–September 2); see also Charles R. Plott, "A Notion of Equilibrium and Its Possibility under Majority Rule," *American Economic Review*, 57 (September 1967), pp. 787–806. Of related interest is Gerald H. Kramer's proof that in essentially quantitative kinds of social-choice situations—not the kind of "all-or-nothing" qualitative kinds of choice situations discussed in this chapter—cyclical majorities are ineradicable unless the (quantitative) preferences of voters are nearly coincidental. See Kramer, "On a Class of Equilibrium Conditions for Majority Rule," *Econometrica*, 41 (March 1973), pp. 285–297.

19. Riker and Ordeshook, *Introduction to Positive Political Theory*, p. 97.

20. William H. Riker, "Arrow's Theorem and Some Examples of the Paradox of Voting," in *Mathematical Applications in Political Science*, ed. John M. Claunch (Dallas: Arnold Foundation of Southern Methodist University, 1965), pp. 41–60.

FIGURE 2.4   AMENDMENT PROCEDURE

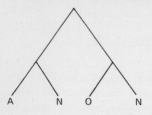

---

three alternatives: (1) an original bill (O) for grants-in-aid for school construction; (2) the bill with the so-called Powell amendment (A), which provided that no federal money be spent in states that had segregated public schools (i.e., the southern states); and (3) no bill (N) (i.e., the status quo). As Riker reconstructed the situation, there were basically three groups of voters with the following preference scales:

1. The passers (mostly southern Democrats) favored school aid, but they were so repelled by the Powell amendment that they preferred no bill to the amended bill. Thus, their preference scale was (O, N, A).

2. The amenders (mostly northern Democrats) were pro-integration, but if the Powell amendment were not successful, would still prefer school aid to no action. Thus, their preference scale was (A, O, N).

3. The defeaters (mostly Republicans) preferred the status quo over either version of the bill, with the pro-integration bill apparently more palatable than the original bill. Thus, their preference scale was (N, A, O).

The voting procedure used in Congress (and in many other voting bodies) is a type of binary procedure called the *amendment procedure*. Unlike the successive procedure discussed in Chapter 1 (see section 1.2), wherein the subsets at each division have no members in common, the usual procedure for voting on amendments includes a division into *nondisjoint* subsets. For this reason, we refer to this binary procedure as "overlapping."

In the example before us, the procedure would pit the subset of outcomes {A, N} against the subset {O, N}. If the amendment is adopted, the second vote is on the amended bill (A) versus no bill (N). If the amendment is defeated, the second vote is on the original bill (O) versus no bill (N). Defeat can thus occur in two different ways under this procedure, as shown diagramatically in Figure 2.4. Since each successive vote involves only two subsets of outcomes, this procedure, like the successive procedure, is binary; it is distinguished from the successive procedure only by the fact that both subsets of outcomes at the first division have more than one member.

Using the amendment procedure, the roll-call votes on the Powell amendment, which passed, and on the amended bill, which failed, reveal that the northern Democrats needed (and got) the support of Republicans—whose first preference was defeat of any school-aid bill—on the Powell amendment. Riker's interpretation is that the Republicans, realizing that a majority probably favored the original bill, may have voted for the amendment so as to disattach southern Democratic support on the vote for final passage (of the amended bill).

Since the Republicans did not introduce the Powell amendment, however, it seems unfair to blame them for using it to defeat the school-aid bill. If there had been contrivance on their part, it would have arisen from not voting sincerely to effect a better outcome.[21] Yet in fact most Republicans preferred outcome A to O, which is consistent with their postulated preference scale.[22] Indeed, the sincere outcome under the amendment procedure of Figure 2.4 is N, which did in fact occur.

Since the sophisticated outcome under this procedure is O, it would seem that it was the northern Democrats, and not the Republicans, who had the opportunity to contrive an outcome that would have been preferred by them over N—but they failed to exploit this opportunity. Specifically, if they had voted for {O, N} instead of their sincere choice {A, N} on the amendment vote, {O, N} would have been selected. Then outcome O would necessarily have been the choice of the voting body on the final vote, since two of the three voters (southern Democrats and northern Democrats) would have preferred it to outcome N.

Given the preference scales of the different groups of voters postulated in this example, therefore, it was not contrivance on the part of the Republicans which sank the federal school-aid bill, but rather a failure to contrive (by voting sophisticatedly) on the part of the northern Democrats.

---

21. Riker, it should be pointed out, does not use the word "contrivance" to refer to insincere voting but only to the device of introducing a third alternative that creates a paradox-of-voting situation whereby a previous Condorcet winner (O in our example) is rendered vulnerable to the new alternative (A in our example) [which is in turn vulnerable to the third alternative (N), which is itself vulnerable (to O), thereby completing the cycle]. In Riker's terms, then, the introduction of the amendment is prima facie evidence of contrivance. But, as we argue in this and the later examples, contrivance that creates a paradox of voting says nothing about contrivance *in voting* by which the sincere outcome in a two-alternative situation can be sustained—rather than defeated—in a three-alternative paradox-of-voting situation if the voters are sophisticated.

22. The proposition that the Republicans contrived the paradox by not voting directly according to their preferences could be supported only if their preference scale were (N, O, A) instead of (N, A, O)—that is, if they actually preferred the original bill to the amended bill but nonetheless voted for the amended bill. Yet, if their preference scale were (N, O, A), then the outcome of both sincere and sophisticated voting would be O, which means that contrivance on their part would have been fruitless. Furthermore, not only is this outcome inconsistent with what actually happened, but given the preference scale (N, O, A) of the Republicans, the paradox of voting does not occur since O defeats N, N defeats A, but O defeats A. On the other hand, if the preference scale of the Republicans were (N, A, O), as postulated in the text, there is a paradox since O defeats N, N defeats A, and A defeats O, which is consistent with the facts in this case (see text).

Apparently, this possibility for contrivance was recognized by Representative Dawson (an Illinois Democrat), who was alone among black congressmen in voting against the Powell amendment.

The fact that in 1957, a year after the Powell amendment succeeded (in effect, A defeated O) but final passage failed (N defeated A), the bill in its original form got majority support in the House (O defeated N) is convincing evidence that a paradox of voting actually existed: O defeats N, N defeats A, and A defeats O. But our analysis strongly suggests that the failure of either version of the school-aid bill to pass in 1956 was not a contrivance of the Republicans, at least in terms of the way in which they voted on the three alternatives. Furthermore, since they did not propose the amendment, it is hard to accuse them of splitting the Democratic opposition; the fault seems, rather, to lie with the Democrats themselves.

In his second example of the paradox, Riker presents more convincing evidence that an amendment was specifically proposed to divide the support of the voters favoring the original bill. In this case, which occurred in the U.S. Senate in 1911, the original bill (O) was a proposal to amend the Constitution to provide for direct popular election of senators (which eventually became the Seventeenth Amendment in 1913). The amendment (A) provided that the guarantee against federal regulation of these elections in the original bill be deleted; by jeopardizing the ability of southern states to exclude blacks from the election process, it was specifically designed to antagonize senators from the South. The final alternative was the status quo, or no bill (N).

The preference scales of the southern Democrats, northern Democrats, and Republicans for {O, A, N} duplicate those in the previous case, with the sincere outcome N once again triumphant due to the failure of the northern Democrats to vote sophisticatedly. If there were contrivance on the part of the Republicans in introducing an amendment to drive a wedge through Democratic support, there was certainly no contrivance on the part of the northern Democrats to thwart this strategy. Although the idealist might characterize the voting behavior of the northern Democrats in the two cases we have described as "sincere," the realist might consider the epithet "naive" more fitting.[23] In cases like these, it is hard to believe that a knowledge of party positions, past voting, and so forth did not

---

23. When the possibility of sophisticated voting was pointed out to Jean-Charles de Borda (1733–1799) under his method of vote counting, he replied, "My scheme is only intended for honest men." Black, *Theory of Committees and Elections*, pp. 183, 238. Recent results, closely related to the General Possibility Theorem, indicate that any scheme that is "strategy proof" is necessarily dictatorial. See Mark Allen Satterthwaite, "Strategy Proofness and Arrow's Conditions: Existence and Correspondence Theorems for Voting Procedures and Social Welfare Functions," *Journal of Economic Theory*, 10 (April 1975), pp. 197–218. See also Alan Gibbard, "Manipulation of Voting Schemes: A General Result," *Econometrica*, 41 (July 1973) pp. 587–601; and Richard Zeckhauser "Voting Systems, Honest Preferences, and Pareto Optimality," *American Political Science Review*, 67 (September 1973), pp. 934–946.

provide members with sufficient information on which to base predictions about outcomes—and, accordingly, vote sophisticatedly.

Certainly in contemporary times, extensive debate and media coverage of controversial issues exposes the preferences of many members. Perversely, however, this may inhibit sophisticated voting, for reasons we shall now give.

When preferences are more fully exposed, members will vote sincerely if the sanctions from their party, constituency, and other groups for taking the "wrong" (i.e., insincere) public positions on roll-call votes override strategic considerations. Although the means used to achieve particular ends are irrelevant to our analysis, in principle the costs associated with the diabolical aspects of sophisticated voting could be incorporated in the valuation of the ends themselves (e.g., by distinguishing outcomes achieved by "devious" means from those achieved by "nondevious" means).

Another possible explanation for sincere voting might stem from the inability of members who do have something to gain from sophisticated voting to agree to coordinate their strategies. In situations wherein a party or coalition leader is skilled in parliamentary maneuver and persuasion, however, he may be able to convince a sufficiently large number of voters to take concerted action whose immediate effect is disadvantageous but whose expected ultimate effect is, on balance, beneficial. Such a person seems to have been Lyndon B. Johnson, who as majority leader of the U.S. Senate was instrumental in the following case.

In 1955 members of the Senate faced the following three alternatives:[24] (1) an original bill (O) for an $18 billion highway program, which included the so-called Davis-Bacon clause that set up fair-pay standards for workers on federal construction projects; (2) the bill as amended (A), with the Davis-Bacon clause deleted; and (3) no bill (N) (the status quo). Since the Davis-Bacon clause was anathema to southern Democrats, the voters, as before, divided into three groups:

1. Northern Democrats, with preference scale (O, A, N)
2. Southern Democrats, with preference scale (A, N, O)
3. Republicans, with preference scale (N, O, A)

Under the amendment procedure of Figure 2.4, the sincere outcome is N and the sophisticated outcome is A. The latter outcome eventually resulted, for southern Democrats, led by Johnson, were able through parliamentary maneuvering to get the Davis-Bacon clause removed without a roll-call vote,[25] which was tantamount to getting northern Demo-

---

24. Robin Farquharson, *Theory of Voting* (New Haven, Conn.: Yale University Press, 1969), pp. 52–53.

25. *Congressional Quarterly Almanac*, vol. 11, 84th Cong., 1st sess. (Washington, D.C.: Congressional Quarterly News Feature, 1955), p. 438.

crats to support them on {A, N} by voting sophisticatedly under the amendment procedure of Figure 2.4.[26] Then, on the vote pitting A against N, the northern Democrats joined the southern Democrats and supported A.

Farquharson quotes *Time* as reporting that the "Republicans flubbed their chance,"[27] presumably because their least-preferred outcome was adopted. Certainly this possibility exists since they did not have a straightforward strategy (see section 1.3): the top outcome for them of each subset at the first division (N) is ranked higher than the bottom outcome (A or O) of the other subset.

The situation is more complicated, however, if one assumes that the voters can communicate with each other for the purpose of coordinating joint strategies. Then A, the outcome adopted, is vulnerable to a coalition of northern Democrats and Republicans who support outcome O. Similarly, O is vulnerable to a coalition of southern Democrats and Republicans who support outcome N; and N is in turn vulnerable to a coalition of northern and southern Democrats who support outcome A. In other words, we have once again the paradox of voting since no coalition is an equilibrium choice of order two, and there is thus no outcome that cannot be defeated—including that which the Republicans most favored, N. Thus, if the Republicans flubbed their chance, it was not because they had any surefire strategy for winning.

In the three instances of the paradox we have described, the sincere outcome was chosen twice and the sophisticated outcome, once.[28] To a certain extent, these outcomes are an artifact of the voting procedure used.

---

26. Whereas contrivance of the paradox normally involves introduction by amendment of a third alternative, here an amendment was used in effect to suppress an alternative.

27. Farquharson, *Theory of Voting*, p. 53.

28. For accounts of paradoxes, some apparently contrived, that involved more than three alternatives and/or voters, see Michael J. Taylor, "Graph-Theoretical Approaches to the Theory of Social Choice," *Public Choice*, 4 (Spring 1968), pp. 45–46, n. 1, who analyzes voting in a committee of a university department; Richard G. Niemi, "The Occurrence of the Paradox of Voting in University Elections," *Public Choice*, 8 (Spring 1970), pp. 91–100, who analyzes voting in several elections held by a university faculty; John C. Blydenburgh, "The Closed Rule and the Paradox of Voting," *Journal of Politics*, 33 (February 1971), pp. 57–71, who analyzes voting in the U.S. House of Representatives on amendments to the Revenue Acts of 1932 and 1938; and William H. Riker, "The Paradox of Voting and Congressional Rules for Voting on Amendments," *American Political Science Review*, 52 (June 1958), pp. 349–366, who analyzes voting on amendments to an appropriations bill for the Soil Conservation Service in the U.S. House of Representatives in 1952. In the last article, Riker suggests a procedural rule that would enable the House and Senate to discover the paradox and, at the prerogative of the presiding officer, prevent the arbitrary passage of a bill or resolution that happened to be successful only because of the order in which amendments were voted upon (up to four amending motions to a bill or resolution can be considered simultaneously in both houses of Congress); but see my comment on this rule in note 30 below. The most systematic investigations of the paradox in the Senate and House are Bruce D. Bowen, "Toward an Estimate of the Frequency of the Paradox of Voting in U.S. Senate Roll Call Votes," and Herbert F. Weisberg and Richard G. Niemi, "Probability Calculations for Cyclical Majorities in Congressional Voting," both in *Probability Models of Collective Decision Making*, pp. 181–203 and pp. 104–131.

If the voting procedure had been that of the successive procedure of Figure 1.1, for example, both the sincere and sophisticated outcomes would have been different in the first two instances, though the same in the last instance.

What these examples share, however, whatever the sincere or sophisticated outcomes are, is the absence of a decisive coalition. Given that groups of voters cooperate with each other, which seems a fairly reasonable assumption to make about members of both houses of Congress, some group of members in any coalition that forms can be tempted to defect and join another coalition. This means that the outcome that is supported by a particular coalition and eventually prevails is very much an artifact of the stage in the voting process at which it forms. Assuming that it takes some time to mount a challenge to a coalition after it has formed, it is evident that the later a coalition forms when there exists a paradox of voting, the more successful it will be in warding off such challenges.[29]

2.7. SUMMARY AND CONCLUSION

Our subject in this chapter has been probably the most famous paradox in the social sciences. Called the paradox of voting, it occurs when the preference scales of voters are such that there is no alternative that is socially preferred—that is, that will defeat all other alternatives in a series of pairwise comparisions. As manifested in the phenomenon of cyclical majorities, it may crop up either in direct voting on alternatives, or indirect (platform) voting on parties and candidates, as we illustrated by examples.

More generally, we showed that the existence of the paradox of voting does not depend on any particular voting procedure or decision rule. *Any* method of summing connected and transitive individual preferences that satisfies the five conditions of Arrow's General Possibility Theorem is vulnerable to the paradox. We discussed the most controversial of these conditions—Independence from Irrelevant Alternatives—in some detail and showed that its proper interpretation does not, as had been thought by some, involve comparing social choices when certain (irrelevant) alternatives are precluded. Rather, it involves comparing social choices when the preferences of individuals change with respect to these irrelevant alternatives.

---

29. Duncan Black advances a similar argument that the later an alternative is introduced into the voting, the more likely it will be adopted (by a majority, but not necessarily a coalition whose members have agreed to cooperate). Black, *Theory of Committees and Elections*, pp. 39–45. But Farquharson shows that although this is true when voting is sincere, if voting is sophisticated an alternative fares better the earlier it is introduced. Farquharson, *Theory of Voting*, Appendix I, p. 62. See also Bernard Grofman, "Some Notes on Voting Schemes and the Will of the Majority," *Public Choice*, 7 (Fall 1969), pp. 65–80.

The restriction of individual preference scales to those that are single peaked violates condition 1, Universal Admissibility of Individual Preference Scales, and—in so doing—provides an escape from the paradox of voting. This restriction also provides a means for identifying the majority, or Condorcet, winner, from the median curve in a geometric representation of single-peaked curves. The concept of value restriction offers another way of characterizing individuals' preference scales reflecting a uniformity of judgment inconsistent with Arrow's condition 1 and the occurrence of the paradox.

We next summarized several theoretical studies that conclude that the greater the number of voters or alternatives—especially the latter—the greater the probability that the paradox will occur, which is a relationship reinforced if voters do not exercise a common standard of judgment in deciding among alternatives. Besides its statistical frequency, we gave examples of important and controversial issues in Congress for which there was some evidence that certain members tried to contrive a paradox that was not inherent in the distribution of preferences.

Does the existence of the paradox doom any social-choice process to an inescapable arbitrariness? In one sense it does, because there is no procedure or type of voting so far considered that can surmount the arbitrariness of the paradox—except, perhaps, one that demonstrates its existence, but this does not lead to a recommended course of action.[30]

Certainly the outcomes in our legislative examples of the paradox had nothing to justify them as the most-preferred alternatives; they were simply the products of sincere and sophisticated voting under a particular voting procedure. Whereas in two of the three legislative examples of the paradox sincere voting resulted in the maintenance of the status quo, in the third case a parliamentary maneuver that had the effect of sophisticated voting led to a result different from the status quo.

It seems that a judgment on whether the strategies that produced these outcomes are clever contrivances or brilliant maneuvers must ultimately rest on a value judgment about the desirability of the outcomes themselves. In the absence of an unambiguous first choice of voters in these cases, it is hard to think of any other ground for labeling one outcome as socially preferred.

The arbitrary social choices that may be foisted on members of a society because of the paradox have alarmed some analysts, though others have argued that this consequence is of little moment.[31] Although the

---

30. Riker has recommended that further action in such cases be at the discretion (with restrictions) of the presiding officer, but this simply substitutes one person's arbitrariness for the arbitrariness of a fixed procedure for voting on alternatives. Riker, "The Paradox of Voting and Congressional Rules for Voting on Amendments," pp. 364–366. The value of exposing the paradox is questioned in Roger H. Marz, Thomas W. Casstevens, and Harold T. Casstevens II, "The Hunting of the Paradox," *Public Choice*, 15 (Summer 1973), pp. 97–102, wherein details on the number of votes required to reveal its existence are also given.

31. For a penetrating assessment of different views, see Riker and Ordeshook, *Introduction to Positive Political Theory*, chap. 4.

latter judgment is difficult to accept in light of both the probabilistic calculations and—more important—the empirical instances of the paradox that we have discussed, various of Arrow's conditions, especially Universal Admissibility of Individual Preference Scales, are probably violated sufficiently often in practice that the General Possibility Theorem cannot be considered an impenetrable barrier to coherent social processes. In any event, it is probably foolish to expect that the standards by which we judge individual choices are appropriate to judgments about social choices. As Riker and Ordeshook put it:

> We are not deeply disturbed by the paradox, for it serves mainly to remind us that society is not the same as the people who compose it. People are not invariably disturbed by the inconsistencies and incoherencies of market outcomes—such as the oft-discovered fact that society spends more on liquor than education though surely a majority would wish otherwise. Markets have been churning out such inconsistencies for centuries without leading us to reject them as useful tools. Similarly there is no reason to reject other institutions of summation simply because they also are incoherent by human (i.e., individual) standards.[32]

Thus, probably the most important lesson of the paradox of voting is that not only is there a qualitative difference between individual and social choice, but—on reflection—one should not expect otherwise.

---

32. Riker and Ordeshook, *Introduction to Positive Political Theory*, p. 114.

3

TWO ELECTION PARADOXES

3.1. INTRODUCTION

We continue in this chapter our exploration of complications that arise in the choice of alternatives in voting situations. The first paradox we shall discuss relates to the choice of alternatives in an uncertain, or risky, environment; the second, to the prediction of choices that take account of the likely reactions of voters to knowledge about the prediction. We shall refer to the first paradox as the *ambiguity paradox* and the second paradox as the *reaction paradox*.

The ambiguity paradox arises from the fact that, under certain circumstances (to be described), it may be rational for candidates in an election to take equivocal positions on issues in order to maximize their appeal to voters. Yet, this equivocation would appear not to be rational for voters trying to evaluate the candidates according to the positions they take.

This apparent inconsistency between candidate rationality and voter rationality has greatly disturbed some democratic political theorists. Thus, the literature of democratic political theory is strewn with exhortations that political parties and candidates should be more "responsible"—clearer about what they regard as the central issues in an election and more forthright about the positions they take on them—in political campaigns. Unfortunately, this literature usually ignores the fact that such "responsible" behavior may be disastrous to the political fortunes of a candidate or party.

This is so because equivocation, under certain circumstances, may be a candidate's best political strategy for winning an election. Moreover, this strategy, far from being contrary to the interests of voters, will in general coincide with these interests. To demonstrate this result and thereby resolve the ambiguity paradox, we shall introduce new parameters—in particular, the notions of risk and intensity of preference—into the decision-making calculus of voters and candidates.

The reaction paradox has less worried democratic political theorists than political practitioners, especially political pollsters and those for whom they take polls. The problem arises when their private predictions, upon being published, upset these predictions because the public, treating the prediction as new information, uses it to make new calculations about the likely outcome, whom to vote for, and so forth. Thereby a private prediction, when made public, may falsify the outcome it originally predicted.

This problem cannot be resolved by simply taking the public reaction into account (if possible) in making the prediction, because this new prediction may itself generate still another reaction that could in turn falsify it. And so it goes ad infinitum, with apparently no resolution to the prediction–reaction–new prediction cycle that can stabilize a correct prediction once and for all.

The reaction paradox may be simply stated: subject to some rather innocuous conditions, one *can* make a public prediction that is confirmed, rather than falsified, by a public reaction to it. Although this paradox is of a more constructive nature than other paradoxes treated in this book—most of which relate to the destruction of a plausible inference rather than construction of an implausible generalization—it seems still to deserve the name "paradox" for its nonobvious and surprising qualities. As we shall show, the reaction paradox, by providing an escape from the prediction–reaction–new prediction cycle, bears directly on the question of how bandwagon and underdog effects may be incorporated into predictions of election outcomes.

3.2. DECISION MAKING UNDER RISK

From Chapter 2 (see section 2.2) we know that the violation of any one of Arrow's five conditions is sufficient to remove the ironclad guarantee, provided by the General Possibility Theorem, that the paradox of voting will occur. In fact, we know that the paradox definitely will not occur if the preferences of voters can be represented by single-peaked curves (see section 2.4), which violates the condition of Universal Admissibility of Individual Preference Scales.

In most real-life situations, however, it is probably not the case that the preferences of voters can be ordered along a single dimension or scale, which single peakedness implies. The empirical examples of the paradox of voting discussed in section 2.6 certainly attest to the fact that voter preferences are not in general unidimensional.

An institutional feature of real-world voting situations much more pervasive than unidimensionality of preferences is the uncertainty associated with preferences. To Anthony Downs "it is a basic force affecting all human activity. . . . Coping with uncertainty is a major function of nearly every significant institution in society; therefore it shapes the nature of each."[1] Little wonder, then, why Downs devotes one-third of *An*

---

1. Anthony Downs, *An Economic Theory of Democracy* (New York: Harper & Row, 1957), p. 13.

Economic Theory of Democracy to "the general effects of uncertainty."[2]

Obviously, introducing uncertainty into the analysis of election strategies complicates the analysis a good deal. If the relationship between outcomes and strategies is not only a function of what strategies other players choose (see Chapter 1) but some random variable (based on chance) as well, then one is indeed plunged into murky waters.

We shall not take the plunge all the way in this chapter, but instead restrict our analysis to situations involving *decision making under risk*, which does not involve game-theoretic choices (see note 6 below). That is, we shall treat the ambiguous relationship between strategies and outcomes as a *lottery*, wherein one chooses not from a set of n outcomes $O = \{o_1, o_2, \ldots, o_n\}$ but from a set of m actions $A = \{a_1, a_2, \ldots, a_m\}$, where each action a_i is a lottery over the outcomes:

$$a_i = \{p_1^i o_1, p_2^i o_2, \ldots, p_n^i o_n\}.$$

By this calculation, each of the n outcomes is "weighted" by a probability p_j^i, where $\sum_{j=1}^{n} p_j^i = 1$ for the set of n probabilities corresponding to each action a_i. Thus, each a_i may be thought of as producing not a single outcome but a "weighted average" of outcomes, each with a designated probability of occurring.

Which outcome does occur when an action a_i is taken will depend entirely on these probabilities. One cannot, therefore, say for sure what the outcome will be—except in the degenerate case when some p_j^i is equal to one and all the other p_j^i's are equal to zero—so there is obviously risk associated with the choice of an action.

For the purposes of our analysis, risk and uncertainty may be taken to be synonymous: the action a_i which a person chooses is risky precisely because the outcomes it leads to are uncertain—their probabilities of occurrence are all that are known. (If these probabilities were completely unknown, one could surmise very little about the consequences of choosing different actions, which Kenneth A. Shepsle argues would be tantamount to assuming a world of total ignorance.)[3] A world in which persons are instead *partially ignorant*, and make lottery-like choices that involve risk, seems better to capture the exigencies that voters and candidates face in political life.

In this model of decision making under risk, a voter chooses from among candidates who take stands, sometimes ambiguous, on various issues, but he does not have the opportunity to select directly levels and kinds of governmental activity. The candidate who desires to win an

2. Downs, *Economic Theory of Democracy*, part 2.

3. Kenneth A. Shepsle, "Parties, Voters, and the Risk Environment: A Mathematical Treatment of Electoral Competition under Uncertainty," in *Probability Models of Collective Decision Making*, ed. Richard G. Niemi and Herbert F. Weisberg (Columbus, Ohio: Charles E. Merrill Publishing Co., 1972), pp. 273–297, esp. p. 278.

election formulates his positions to appeal to voters whose preferences he does not know completely, so the consequences of his actions (i.e., choices of positions, or probability distributions over positions) are necessarily risky, too.

In the subsequent analysis, we shall simplify the contingent calculations of voters and candidates by assuming that the preferences of voters are fixed and known to the candidates. Given that voters want to maximize their expected utility (defined in section 3.3), we shall explore the question of what positions a candidate should take on one or more issues to maximize his attractiveness to as many voters as possible. Some of the strange effects that uncertainty may produce in risky decision-making environments, wherein the preferences of the voters result in a paradox of voting, will be described in section 3.3.

3.3. AMBIGUITY AND THE PARADOX OF VOTING

Assume an electorate consisting of three voters $V = \{1, 2, 3\}$, whose preference scales for three alternatives $A = \{x, y, z\}$ are as follows: voter 1—(x, y, z); voter 2—(y, z, x); voter 3—(z, x, y). As we showed in Chapter 2 (see section 2.1), these preference scales define a paradox of voting: a majority (voters 1 and 3) prefers x to y, a majority (voters 1 and 2) prefers y to z, and a majority (voters 2 and 3) prefers z to x. Since x defeats y, y defeats z, but z defeats x, the social ordering is intransitive.

Assume that a candidate running for office in this three-voter electorate (which may be thought of as consisting of three factions) must take a position on an issue defined by the three alternatives just given; the alternatives represent different positions on the issue. If the position a candidate takes is likely to decide his electoral fate, then there is no single position that is clearly superior to the others. Any position (alternative) he chooses can be defeated by another position (alternative) chosen by another candidate.

To be sure, if one candidate were able to choose his position *after* his opponent already had made a choice, the candidate choosing second could always choose a position that would defeat his opponent's. The strategic advantage of choosing second in paradox-of-voting situations would appear most to help candidates running against incumbents since incumbents—by virtue of the actions they must take while in office— would more often be forced to commit themselves to positions before their opponents announced their own positions.[4]

A more interesting and perhaps more realistic case is one in which both an incumbent and his opponent must announce their positions simultaneously, or develop them in such a way that neither the in-

---

4. For an extended discussion of this problem, see Downs, *Economic Theory of Democracy*, pp. 55–62.

cumbent nor his opponent can react to an already chosen position of the other. Obviously, in this case, neither candidate has any surefire winning strategy—the outcome will depend on what *both* candidates choose as their positions. However, if we modify this problem slightly and assume that the incumbent is constrained to one of the three "pure" positions, but his opponent can "straddle" these pure positions, then it is always advantageous for the nonincumbent to pursue a strategy of ambiguity, *regardless of what (pure) position the incumbent adopts.*[5]

More precisely, assume that the incumbent is restricted to the set of certain positions (degenerate lotteries) x, y, and z, but his challenger is not so constrained: he can choose a set of probabilities (p_x, p_y, p_z) over the three positions (alternatives) that defines the likelihood that he will choose, respectively, position x, position y, and position z. Thus, he offers to the voters not a pure position but a lottery over these positions, which may be interpreted to mean an ambiguous position which nevertheless indicates varying propensities (i.e., probabilities of his adopting) one pure position or another.

This is the kind of position reflected in such statements as "I will give careful consideration to . . ." (all alternatives are open and presumably equally likely), "I am leaning toward . . ." (one alternative is favored over the others), and "I will do this if such and such . . ." (probabilities depend on such-and-such factors). Of course, incumbents may also adopt such fence-straddling positions, but since they are running at least in part on their previous records, it seems inherently more difficult for them to fuzz their positions by covering up actions they already have taken while in office. Moreover, even if an incumbent repudiates a previous position, he would most likely (and convincingly) do so in favor of championing another alternative, which is *not* an ambiguous strategy and therefore not necessarily helpful in a paradox-of-voting situation, as we have already shown.

Given that an incumbent is constrained to one of the three pure positions, when would it be to the challenger's advantage to pursue a strategy of ambiguity? To facilitate the calculation of optimal strategies, we assume that each of three voters attaches *cardinal utilities* (numbers that indicate their degree of preference), as shown in Table 3.1, to the three alternatives (positions). In this table, we assume that each voter assigns a utility of 1 to his most-preferred position, a utility of 0 to his least-preferred position, and some utility—represented by the letters k, m, and n in Table 3.1—greater than 0 but less than 1 to his middle-ranked position.

5. The calculations set forth in the following discussion are described in Kenneth A. Shepsle, "A Note on Zeckhauser's 'Majority Rule with Lotteries on Alternatives': The Case of the Paradox of Voting," *Quarterly Journal of Economics*, 84 (November 1970), pp. 705–709; for further details and a more mathematical treatment, see Kenneth A. Shepsle, "The Paradox of Voting and Uncertainty," in *Probability Models of Collective Decision Making*, pp. 252–270.

TABLE 3.1   PARADOX OF VOTING: UTILITIES OF VOTERS FOR POSITIONS[a]

VOTER	POSITION		
	x	y	z
1	1	k	0
2	0	1	m
3	n	0	1

[a] Utilities k, m, and n of voters 1, 2, and 3 for middle-ranked alternatives y, z, and x have the following range of values: $0 < k, m, n < 1$.

By this symbolic assignment, we do not specify with numbers *how much* more preferred each voter's first choice is to his middle choice, or less preferred his last choice is to his middle choice. This (unspecified) assignment simply says that the three positions can be ranked from best to worst; in our subsequent analysis, however, we shall indicate the constraints *any* such assignment must satisfy in order for (1) a (lottery) choice of the challenger to defeat any (nonlottery) choice of the incumbent and (2) this lottery to exist.

Consider first the question of what assigmnent of probabilities to each position by a challenger will defeat the (certain) choice of position x, y, or z by the incumbent. For each voter we define his *expected utility* for the challenger in our example to be the probability (p_x, p_y, or p_z) that the challenger chooses position x, y, or z times the voter's utility for that position, summed across all positions.

In order for the challenger to have a surefire winning strategy, a majority of voters must derive greater expected utility from his (lottery) position than from any (nonlottery) position of the incumbent. For the ambiguous challenger to offer a majority of voters greater expected utility than the nonambiguous incumbent, the three voters' expected utilities must be such that

$$p_x(1) + p_y(k) + p_z(0) > k,$$
$$p_x(0) + p_y(1) + p_z(m) > m,$$
$$p_x(n) + p_y(0) + p_z(1) > n,$$

where p_x, p_y, and p_z, which we assume sum to 1, are the probabilities that the challenger—as the voters perceive his ambiguous position—will choose each of the three positions, x, y, and z, respectively. (We assume that the voters agree on their perceptions of candidate positions but not on their preferences for these positions.) Thus, in order that a majority favor the challenger, the expected utility of the challenger's ambiguous position must be greater for each voter than the utility he attaches to the candidate position that ranks second in his preference scale.

To see why this is so, suppose that the incumbent chooses position x and the challenger chooses the lottery (p_x, p_y, p_z). Then, given the inequalities specified in the preceding paragraph, from Table 3.1 it is evident that whereas voter 1 will prefer the incumbent (from whom he derives a utility of 1 versus expected utility of $p_x + kp_y < 1$ [since $k < 1$] for the challenger), voters 2 and 3 will prefer the challenger (deriving expected utilities of $p_y + mp_z$ and $np_x + p_z$, respectively, which are greater than the utilities of 0 and n that each gets from the incumbent). Hence, the challenger will be preferred by two of the three voters (voters 2 and 3), so he will win if the voters vote sincerely. Similarly, one can show that if the incumbent chooses either position y or position z, a majority of voters will prefer the challenger. Thus, if the above inequalities are satisfied, the challenger will always win no matter what (pure) position the incumbent chooses, given that voting is sincere.[6]

Does such a lottery exist? To show that it does, one must demonstrate that the three inequalities given previously can be satisfied simultaneously and that the probabilities sum to 1. Shepsle has proved that there is a simultaneous solution to these inequalities that yields the following condition for the existence of a lottery: $kmn \leq (1 - k)(1 - m)(1 - n)$; if $kmn = (1 - k)(1 - m)(1 - n)$, the lottery is unique.[7]

This existence condition implies (but we shall not show) that at least one of the voters assigns utility k, m, or n to his middle-ranked position that does not exceed 0.5. Because this means that at least one voter attaches at least twice as much value to his first-ranked position as to his second-ranked position,[8] Shepsle concludes that at least one of the voters must—for the ambiguous strategy of the challenger to be socially preferred —intensely prefer his first-ranked alternative. He adds:

> The risky candidate, then, thrives in an environment of intense preference. The implication here is that on the so-called critical issues in an election (which are "critical" precisely because many people have intense feelings on them), we might expect politicians to be

---

6. Having fixed the preferences of the voters, and not defined a game they might play with the candidates—by misrepresenting their preferences—or among themselves (as discussed in Chapter 1), then it is clear that the concept of "insincere" voting on their part is not germane in this context. The game we have described is strictly between the candidates, with the voters, by their choices of candidates based on the expected-utility calculation, serving only to define the payoffs to these players.

7. Shepsle, "The Paradox of Voting and Uncertainty," pp. 261–262.

8. It also implies that the voter would never prefer the certainty of obtaining his second-ranked position to the lottery giving equal probabilities of obtaining his first-ranked and last-ranked positions. This implication is the interpretation given to the concept of "risk acceptance" in section 3.4.

vague and ambiguous. Considered in this light, Richard Nixon's vague rhetoric on the Viet Nam issue in the 1968 presidential campaign, e.g., "I have a plan," is explicable.[9]

Although Nixon's rhetoric is a nice illustration of an ambiguous strategy, it is not clear that it is related to Shepsle's formal result. This result, after all, pertains only to paradox-of-voting situations; that there were three different positions on the Vietnam issue that resulted in cyclical majorities, and rendered Nixon's ambiguous campaign strategy in 1968 efficacious against some pure strategy of Humphrey's, is not apparent.

Shepsle's analysis, nonetheless, is instructive in demonstrating that when there is no socially preferred alternative, and the existence condition that implies an intense preference on the part of at least one voter (in the three-voter case) obtains, the cyclical majority problem can be avoided: there *is* an ambiguous strategy, defined by a nondegenerate lottery, that defeats all nonambiguous strategies, defined by degenerate lotteries, in a series of pairwise comparisons. In the case in which voters with intense preferences form cyclical majorities, then, there is an incentive for non-incumbent candidates to fuzz their positions on an issue.

3.4. ATTITUDES OF VOTERS TOWARD RISK

In section 3.3 we dealt with the rather special case in which one candidate (the incumbent) was restricted to the set of pure positions, but his opponent (the challenger) was free to construct lotteries on these positions. Given the further constraint that at least one voter intensely prefers his first-ranked alternative, it was shown that in paradox-of-voting situations the challenger could offer the voters a lottery that would defeat any (pure) position of the incumbent's.

These constraints, like the single-peakedness restriction described in section 2.4, violate conditions of the General Possibility Theorem. The first constraint, limiting the incumbent to a certain (nonlottery) position, violates the connectivity assumption that permits all alternatives to be compared, both certain and risky; the second constraint on intense preferences violates the Universal Admissibility of Individual Preference Scales, which admits all individual preference scales, irrespective of preference intensities (see section 2.2). Thus, the fact that the paradox of voting is obviated in the case discussed in section 3.3 is entirely consistent with Arrow's theorem.

When these constraints are removed, it is not difficult to show that cyclical majorities are ineradicable, as guaranteed by the General Possibility Theorem. In particular, if *both* candidates in our earlier example are free to advocate *any* position, risky or certain, then there is no position

---

9. Shepsle, "The Paradox of Voting and Uncertainty," p. 263.

which a majority of voters prefers to all other positions. Generally, in the absence of individual and social constraints of the kind discussed in section 3.3 (i.e., that restrict preference intensities of voters or admissible positions of candidates), the pure positions of candidates, and an infinity of lotteries on these positions, may—but will not always (depending on the distribution of voter preferences)—cycle.[10]

Even when all voters have single-peaked preferences, which is sufficient to ensure that the median sure prospect will defeat all others (see section 2.4), cyclical majorities may reappear when lotteries are admitted on the two extreme alternatives. Indeed, whenever some lottery in single-peaked situations is able to defeat the median alternative, it is always the case that another alternative can in turn defeat the lottery.[11]

In real elections, of course, there is typically a variety of constraints that may make some positions more viable than others, though not necessarily for all candidates. One candidate, for example, may consider his election prospects to hinge on generating major financial support; toward this end, he may pitch his appeal to a minority of the electorate who feels intensely about an issue and, as a consequence, is more likely to contribute to his campaign. A better-heeled candidate, less dependent on financial contributions, may seek to appeal to a larger segment of the electorate, but he may be constrained by his own previous record or that of his party, which prevents him from deviating sharply from particular positions.

In general, the effects of peculiar constraints faced by candidates in a particular election can be analyzed on a case-by-case basis only. There is, however, one important parameter in all elections—the attitudes of voters toward risk—that may crucially affect the relative attractiveness to candidates of lottery versus nonlottery positions. Since this parameter enables one to characterize voter preferences more finely, it also enables one to look more closely at the question of whether candidates, reacting to voter preferences by the positions they take, do violence to voter rationality. If the positions that candidates take to attract maximum voter support are lotteries, and these lotteries prevent voters from maximizing their own expected utility, then there is an evident conflict between candidate rationality and voter rationality, which is the essence of the ambiguity paradox.

When we admit the possibility that political candidates may choose lotteries on a set of positions, the choices of voters will depend not only on their preferences for these positions but also on their attitudes toward the risk inherent in the choice of a candidate who takes a lottery position.

---

10. This is always the case if the distribution of voter preferences among the pure positions results in a paradox of voting. For a proof, see Shepsle, "The Paradox of Voting and Uncertainty," pp. 268–270.

11. See Richard Zeckhauser, "Majority Rule with Lotteries on Alternatives," *Quarterly Journal of Economics*, 83 (November 1969), pp. 696–703.

FIGURE 3.1. VOTER UTILITY FUNCTIONS

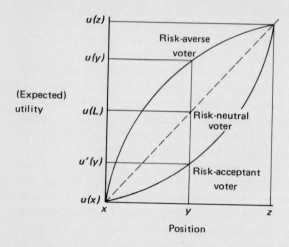

Position

For unlike a candidate who offers a sure prospect, a voter cannot know for sure what to expect of a candidate who refuses to commit himself with certainty to a single position.

Some voters may deplore the ambiguity of such a position, but others may find such a risk quite acceptable, depending on the alternatives. For analytic purposes, we may distinguish two types of voters—risk-averse and risk-acceptant (the use of these terms will be explained shortly)—who are defined by the *shape* of their utility functions. Although the two utility curves for the risk-averse and risk-acceptant voters in Figure 3.1 have different shapes, both types of voters attribute greater utility to position z than to position y, and to position y than to position x.

Now consider position y of both voters on the horizontal axis, which we assume lies midway between positions x and z. The height on the vertical axis at which this position intersects each utility curve is indicated by $u(y)$ for the risk-averse voter and $u'(y)$ for the risk-acceptant voter.

Suppose each voter must choose between two candidates:[12]

1. Candidate A says he will choose position y with certainty.

2. Candidate B wavers between position x and position z; that is, he takes an ambiguous position, assigning equal probability to x and z. Thus, his position may be represented by the lottery $L = (\frac{1}{2}x, \frac{1}{2}z)$.

---

12. If we admit the possibility either of abstention or of there being more than two candidates, the analysis is considerably complicated and raises another set of paradoxical questions related to the decision of whether or not to vote. See John A. Ferejohn and Morris P. Fiorina, "The Paradox of Not Voting: A Decision Theoretical Analysis," *American Political Science Review*, 68 (June 1974), pp. 525–536, and references cited therein.

Clearly, the utility of candidate A's position is $u(y)$ for the risk-averse voter, $u'(y)$ for the risk-acceptant voter. The utility of candidate B's position is the expected utility of L:

$$u(L) = \tfrac{1}{2}u(x) + \tfrac{1}{2}u(z) = \tfrac{1}{2}u(z),$$

since $u(x) = 0$. This is the midpoint on the vertical axis lying between $u(x) = 0$ and $u(z)$, which corresponds to the midpoint of the diagonal dashed line in Figure 3.1.

As can be seen from Figure 3.1, the risk-averse voter prefers candidate A to candidate B since $u(y) > u(L)$. By comparison, the risk-acceptant voter prefers candidate B to candidate A since $u(L) > u'(y)$. Thus, despite the fact that the risk-averse and risk-acceptant voters rank the pure positions of the candidates in the same way, their different attitudes toward risk—specifically, the ambiguous position represented by the lottery L—dictate different candidate choices.

In general, voters who possess concave utility functions (i.e., with an "upward" hump) will prefer a certain prospect to a lottery over the "extreme" alternatives; for this reason, they are said to be *risk-averse*, with decreasing marginal utility for positions x, y, and z. In contrast, voters who possess convex utility functions (i.e., with a "downward" hump) will prefer a lottery to a certain prospect; for this reason, they are said to be *risk-acceptant*, with increasing marginal utility. We may, in addition, distinguish a third type of voter, called *risk-neutral*, who is indifferent between (i.e., equally inclined toward) sure prospects and lotteries with the same expectation. His utility function would correspond to the diagonal dashed line shown in Figure 3.1.

3.5. RESOLUTION OF THE AMBIGUITY PARADOX

Whatever the attitudes of the voters toward risk, we assume that they always act to maximize their expected utility (or utility in the case of sure prospects). For risk-acceptant voters, this maximization process entails their selection of candidates who offer them risks with greater expected utility than the utility offered by candidates who offer them sure prospects. In the case of such voters, there is nothing irrational about their gambling against a sure prospect if the gamble means greater expected utility for them.

The more voters in the electorate who are risk-acceptant, the more attractive equivocal strategies will be to candidates who wish to maximize their chances of winning an election. By lowering the utility of the middle-ranked alternative relative to the most-preferred alternative [compare $u'(y)$ and $u(y)$ in Figure 3.1], a risk-acceptant attitude increases the preference *intensity* of voters for their most-preferred alternative (z in Figure 3.1). Thus, risk acceptance and preference intensity are simply two different ways to describe the same phenomenon, which explains why the appeal of an equivocal strategy is enhanced if some voters feel intensely about issues, as we showed for the special case of cyclical majorities in section 3.3.[13] Intuitively, the reason that a candidate, who wavers between extreme positions about which most of the electorate feel intensely, is potent in a risk-acceptant environment is that the moderate (pure) position of an opponent satisfies almost no one (i.e., is a position only marginally preferred to the worst positions of most voters).[14]

To the degree that incumbents are forced by their previous actions into pure positions on issues that polarize the electorate (i.e., intense, or "critical," issues), these positions are rendered tenuous, and their chances of reelection accordingly reduced, by equivocal challengers who can present themselves as acceptable risks. On the other hand, if there is a paucity of critical issues, voters will be less inclined to take risks and more inclined to settle on middle-ranked alternatives, which will tend to favor the pure position of a middle-of-the-road incumbent. For these reasons, we would expect incumbents to try to manipulate the risk environment in favor of low-key issues (on which their pure positions are more acceptable), and challengers to push hard on divisive issues (on which their ambiguous positions are more acceptable). This is why the ability of candidates to define the issues in a campaign is all-important, as E. E. Schattschneider has pointed out.[15]

If it is to the electoral advantage of a candidate to adopt an ambiguous strategy, it is equally to the advantage of voters to be able to choose a candidate who advocates such a strategy. For the candidate's optimal strategy is that which best reflects the interests of the electorate to whom he is appealing. If the candidate fails to offer the voters a lottery on positions that would defeat the pure position of an opponent, then he is impeding, not helping, the exercise of rational choice by the voters.

It is not the case, then, as Anthony Downs argues, that "rational behavior by political parties [i.e., the choice of ambiguous positions] tends to discourage rational behavior by voters."[16] Voters, as we have seen, may actually prefer a lottery choice to any sure prospect. Thus, the "rationality crisis"—to use Downs's terminology[17]—created by the inability of voters to evaluate the ambiguous positions of candidates is an illusion. There is, in fact, no necessary conflict between candidate equivocation and voter rationality; quite the contrary, it is the rationality of

---

13. For an example not involving cyclical majorities in which a risky strategy dominates the median position, see Zeckhauser, "Majority Rule with Lotteries on Alternatives," p. 697; and Kenneth A. Shepsle, "The Strategy of Ambiguity: Uncertainty and Electoral Competition," *American Political Science Review*, 66 (June 1972), pp. 555–568, esp. pp. 562–563.

14. For a more rigorous development of these ideas, see Shepsle, "The Strategy of Ambiguity: Uncertainty and Electoral Competition," pp. 561–565; and Shepsle, "Parties, Voters, and the Risk Environment: A Mathematical Treatment of Electoral Competition under Uncertainty," pp. 280–297.

15. E. E. Schattschneider, *The Semisovereign People: A Realist's View of Democracy in America* (New York: Holt, Rinehart and Winston, 1960).

16. Downs, *Economic Theory of Democracy*, p. 136.

17. Downs, *Economic Theory of Democracy*, p. 139.

voters which may force candidates to choose ambiguous positions if they (the candidates) are to act rationally themselves.

The conclusion that we draw from this analysis is that ambiguous positions that maximize the appeal of candidates are entirely consistent with the exercise of rational choice by voters. Indeed, it would seem that candidates act not only rationally but responsibly when, reacting to the preferences of the voters, they fuzz positions that on an individual basis would be unacceptable to a majority of the electorate. (This fuzziness, when read by voters as an indication of open-mindedness, is precisely what makes such candidates acceptable risks.)

It is also worth noting that the explanation for candidate ambiguity we have offered here does not require the introduction of new variables in Downs's basic model, which have been suggested by other theorists in proposed revisions. Riker, for example, suggests in his criticism of Downs's model that candidates are vague when they have imperfect information about the preferences of voters.[18] Although, empirically, this may be so in some instances, logically it is not necessary to introduce imperfect information about voter preferences—as opposed to candidate positions— to show why candidates are motivated to fuzz positions. In fact, the presumption that candidates' equivocate because they have imperfect information about voter preferences leads to obvious difficulties in explaining why there is so much blurring of issues in presidential elections, wherein, presumably, more information is developed about voter preferences than in lower-level elections.

In the foregoing analysis, we have assumed that political candidates respond to the fixed preferences of voters in trying to formulate positions on issues that maximize their appeal to voters. In our analysis of the second election paradox, we shall not treat the preferences of voters as fixed but instead assume that the preferences—and voting behavior—of at least some voters change when they are confronted with information about the probable outcome of an election.

3.6. CONDITIONS FOR CORRECT PREDICTION

Our analysis of the reaction paradox starts from the assumption that candidates have already chosen their campaign strategies and, on the basis of these choices, some prediction can be made about the outcome of the election. The question then is: how stable is this prediction in the light of voter reaction to it that may change the preferences—and voting behavior— of some voters? The surprising answer that *some* prediction can be made (1) that is "adjusted" for voter reaction, and (2) that a subsequent reaction to the adjusted prediction cannot disconfirm, is what constitutes the paradox.

---

18. William H. Riker, *The Theory of Political Coalitions* (New Haven, Conn.: Yale University Press, 1962), pp. 100–101. For an alternative theory of ambiguity that requires additional information on the salience of issues, see Benjamin I. Page, "The Theory of Political Ambiguity," *American Political Science Review*, forthcoming.

It is important to note at the outset what this kind of prediction does *not* assume, which makes it an even more surprising feat. It does not assume that once a prediction is made and the reaction to it is anticipated, the reaction to the adjusted prediction will be smaller, the reaction to a subsequently adjusted prediction still smaller, and so on. In such a case, presumably, smaller and smaller reactions could be adjusted for all at once, enabling one to converge on a correct prediciton that would already have taken account of all possible reactions and made all necessary adjustments.

Just as this assumption about the convergence of reactions is un-necessary, neither is it necessary to assume that public reactions to a prediction increase or decrease in a particular way or follow any other pattern. The one assumption of any practical import sufficient to ensure that a correct prediction can be made is that the "reaction function" (to be illustrated later) be *continuous*: given small changes in the "unadjusted" prediction, there is no abrupt, or discontinuous, change in the reaction of the public to it. A second, technical assumption that is also required is that the outcome to be predicted be bounded, which means roughly that there are upper and lower finite limits within which it falls.[19] We shall illustrate the meaning of these assumptions in section 3.9.

3.7. SELF-FULFILLING AND SELF-FALSIFYING PREDICTIONS

By an *unadjusted prediction*, we mean a prediction of an election outcome based on such information as the resources and strategies used by the candidates in a campaign, the attitudes and demographic characteristics of voters, public opinion polls on how people plan to vote, and so forth. Assuming that accurate *private* predictions of voting behavior and election outcomes based on this kind of information can be made, what will be their effect when they are made public?

When the results of a private prediction are published, or otherwise become known, it is useful to distinguish between two kinds of possible public reaction to it:

1. The prediction is *self-fulfilling*: people act in such a way as to confirm its correctness. If, for example, it is predicted that the economy will move into a recession, consumers may, consonant with the prediction, spend less and save more, thereby helping to bring the recession about.

2. The prediction is *self-falsifying*: people act in such a way as to disconfirm its correctness. If, for example, a war is predicted between two countries that would be disastrous to both sides—such as a nuclear war—efforts may be made to prevent it that bring about a peaceful settlement instead.

---

19. For further details and discussion of these assumptions, see Emile Grunberg and Franco Modigliani, "The Predictability of Social Events," *Journal of Political Economy*, 62 (December 1954), pp. 465–478; and Grunberg and Modigliani, "Discussion: Reflexive Prediction," *Philosophy of Science*, 32 (April 1965), pp. 173–174.

Clearly, only predictions of the second kind, which public reaction to invalidates, present any problems of adjustment.[20]

This is not to say that private (unadjusted) predictions, which are subsequently confirmed by events after they are published, do not evoke any public reaction. On the contrary, a prediction about an election may generate switches on both sides, but if the switches are equal and opposed and, consequently, cancel each other out, they will have no effect on the predicted outcome. In such a case, even though there is a public reaction, we consider the prediction to be a self-fulfilling prediction since it has no effect on the election outcome. If the private prediction concerned the number of party switchers, however, which its publication then changed, this prediction would be self-falsifying.

For the purposes of the analysis that follows, we shall be concerned exclusively with private predictions that public reaction to, upon publication, alters. Whatever the nature of the alteration, these are the only predictions that publication renders problematic, however the private prediction was made. Although we proceed from the assumption that accurate private predictions can be made, and investigate their public consequences only, this assumption may not well describe our predictive capabilities in many areas of political science—as well as the social sciences generally—which is a point to which we shall return later.

3.8. EFFECTS OF POLLS ON VOTING BEHAVIOR

Elections are the most significant recurring feature of democratic political systems and have probably been subjected to more systematic study than any other political events. By and large, however, studies of elections, especially in American politics, have focused on the peculiarities of a particular race or set of races, with comparatively little attention being devoted to the development of theoretical models of elections.[21] Although a prodigious search has been conducted to unearth empirical regularities in the voting behavior of the electorate—and to a lesser extent the cam-

---

20. Note that our economic example of a prediction of the first kind could be easily turned into a prediction of the second kind if the predicted recession altered consumer spending and saving habits to such an extent that a depression, rather than a recession, ensued. For further discussion of such predictions, see Ian Budge, "The Scientific Status of Political Science: A Comment on Self-Fulfilling and Self-Defeating Predictions," *British Journal of Political Science*, 3 (April 1973), pp. 249–250; and J. S. Sorzano, "The Scientific Status of Political Science: A Note on the Oedipus Effect," *British Journal of Political Science*, 4 (April 1974), pp. 254–256. In these essays, the authors seem not to be aware of the theoretical studies subsequently described in this chapter, which could have sharpened their own analyses considerably.

21. The work of Anthony Downs, alluded to earlier in this chapter, is the outstanding exception to this statement in the last twenty years. More recently, several theorists have followed in the tradition he set, but the models they have developed have generally not been tested empirically. For a summary and review of this more recent work, see William H. Riker and Peter C. Ordeshook, *An Introduction to Positive Political Theory* (Englewood Cliffs, N.J.: Prentice-Hall, 1973), chaps. 11 and 12.

paign behavior of politicians—these findings are perenially disconfirmed as new data are accumulated and analyzed. The conceptual foundations of this empirical-inductive approach, as one might imagine, are rather weak, with constant attempts being made to repair the problem areas.[22]

To be sure, one hardly requires a theory of elections to make accurate election forecasts, on the basis of voters' expressed candidate preferences, just before an election.[23] Ever since 1936, when George Gallup first applied rudimentary sampling techniques to predict correctly the outcome of that year's presidential election—and refute the predictions of an ill-conceived *Literary Digest* poll—election forecasts have been part of the American political landscape.[24]

Since election predictions based on scientific public opinion polls first achieved prominence in the 1930s, they have met with uneven success. The erroneous predictions by pollsters that Dewey would beat Truman in the 1948 presidential election led to the use of more refined procedures, which improved the subsequent success rate of election eve predictions considerably. In the eight national elections between 1954 and 1968, the average deviation between the predicted and actual outcomes was only 1.4 percent.[25]

Many analysts have been troubled by the fact that poll findings, divulged in the course of an election campaign, may themselves change voting attitudes and behavior and thereby interfere with the election outcome. These anxieties have not been allayed by the fact that election outcomes have, for the most part, confirmed the accuracy of the polls, at least in presidential elections. (This has not been true of presidential primaries, in which voter attitudes, especially in multicandidate races, tend to be much more unstable.)

Theories of voting behavior, which one might expect would provide some information about the effects of poll information on voting behavior, do not generally treat this question, much less describe the conditions under which knowledge of the relative standing of candidates in a poll may affect the attitudes of voters. In one experimental study, the appeal of the underdog was shown to be stronger than the appeal of the front-runner, but no reasons why this should be the case were offered except that "common folklore holds that Americans are inclined to come to the aid of the underdog in an unequal fray between two antagonists."[26]

---

22. For a critique of this literature, see Robert Abrams, *Some Conceptual Problems of Voting Theory*, Sage Professional Paper in American Politics, vol. 1, no. 04-005 (Beverly Hills, Calif. Sage Publications, 1973).

23. The predictions of pollsters, however, are not based simply on the raw data they collect, but are modified to take account of the likelihood that different categories of voters will actually vote in an election.

24. Charles W. Roll, Jr., and Albert H. Cantril, *Polls: Their Use and Misuse in Politics* (New York: Basic Books, 1972), p. 10.

25. Harold Mendelsohn and Irving Crespi, *Polls, Television, and the New Politics* (Scranton, Pa.: Chandler Publishing Co., 1970), p. 73.

26. Daniel W. Fleitas, "Bandwagon and Underdog Effects in Minimal Information Elections," *American Political Science Review*, 65 (June 1971), p. 438.

There is some evidence from presidential elections suggestive of voter predispositions toward the underdog. Gallup poll trend data since 1948, when polls were first taken sequentially over the course of presidential campaigns, show that

> . . . the pattern is for the margin between Presidential candidates to get smaller in the final weeks of the campaign. This trend was dramatically the case in 1968, when Humphrey all but wiped out an early 13 percentage point deficit by regaining strength among normally Democratic blue-collar workers. But, it also occurred in 1964, 1960, 1952, and 1948. This decreasing margin is in large part the result of the return to the fold of potentially defecting members of the trailing candidate's party.[27]

This trend was again present in the 1972 presidential election; its only apparent disconfirmation came in 1956, when Eisenhower maintained an almost constant 12–14 percent lead over Stevenson throughout the campaign.[28]

The three most significant last-minute surges in support for underdogs in recent presidential elections (1948, 1960, and 1968) have invariably helped Democratic candidates—in two cases (1948 and 1960) by enough to win. In view of the fact that there are many more registered Democrats than Republicans, this Democratic bias is not surprising. It has in fact been contended that the success of a Democratic candidate in rallying support among his partisans is the crucial determinant of election outcomes in close presidential races.[29]

If the inclination of voters toward underdogs in presidential elections has been primarily a Democratic phenomenon, can this inclination be said to be a manifestation of the *underdog effect*—the supposed force that predisposes voters to vote for the candidate they expect to lose? Similarly, can a *bandwagon effect*, which predisposes voters to vote for the candidate they expect to win—and which is often alleged to characterize the behavior of voters in presidential primaries and of delegates in national party conventions—be divorced from the particular selection factors at work in actual voting situations?

These are thorny empirical questions to answer; they are rendered even more obdurate by the rather ad hoc nature of election theory. Although some theoretical conditions associated with bandwagons in three-candidate contests[30] and coalition situations[31] have been identified,

---

27. Mendelsohn and Crespi, *Polls, Television, and the New Politics*, p. 20.

28. Mendelsohn and Crespi, *Polls, Television, and the New Politics*, p. 19.

29. See Vic Fingerhut, "A Limit on Campaign Spending—Who Will Benefit?" *Public Interest*, 25 (Fall 1971), pp. 3–13.

30. Richard D. McKelvey and Peter C. Ordeshook, "A General Theory of the Calculus of Voting," in *Mathematical Applications in Political Science, VI*, ed. James F. Herndon and Joseph L. Bernd (Charlottesville, Va.: University Press of Virginia, 1972), pp. 32–61, esp. pp. 58–59.

31. Steven J. Brams and José E. Garriga-Picó, "Bandwagons in Coalition Formation: The 2/3's Rule," *American Behavioral Scientist*, 18 (March–April 1975), pp. 472–496.

they have not been subjected to empirical tests. By the same token, an extensive review of the empirical literature on the effects of published polls on voting behavior, which found there to be "no absolutely conclusive [empirical] evidence that . . . the publication of poll results does or does not affect the subsequent votes,"[32] must be qualified by the fact that the studies reviewed were not informed by any theory that indicated conditions under which reaction effects might be expected to occur in the first place.

Given the lack of conclusive evidence on reaction effects one way or the other, we shall postulate in section 3.9 *hypothetical* bandwagon and underdog effects of published election predictions. Our main argument will be that these effects provide no barrier, *in principle*, to correct predictions.

3.9. CORRECT PREDICTIONS WITH BANDWAGON AND UNDERDOG EFFECTS[33]

Assume that a *private* poll taken before an election indicates that p_i percent of the voters intend (i) to vote for candidate A. Assume that the pollster taking this poll desires to make a *public* prediction P that will be subsequently confirmed by the percentage p_a of voters who actually (a) vote for candidate A on election day. If he knows that the actual percentage p_a who vote for A will be a function of *both* the percentage p_i who intend to vote for A and his prediction P [$p_a = f(p_i, P)$], can he choose a P such that $P = p_a$, i.e., his prediction will agree with the election outcome?

Obviously, if P has no effect on p_a—that is, if p_a is a function only of p_i [$p_a = f(p_i)$]—then he should let $P = p_i$ (or whatever other functional relationship obtains). In the nontrivial case in which his prediction does alter the voting intentions of at least some voters, however, he would want to choose a P which not only has already "factored in" the public reaction to itself (say, ΔP) but has also "factored out" the subsequent reaction to the adjusted prediction (say, $\Delta P'$). But as we indicated in section 3.6, a prediction P adjusted for both ΔP and $\Delta P'$ effects would be a new prediction and would itself evoke a new public reaction, and so on ad infinitum.

How can we circumvent this infinite regress? Assume that p_i is fixed (by the results of the poll). Then p_a will be a function solely of $P[p_a = f(P)]$.

32. Joseph T. Klapper, *Bandwagon: A Review of the Literature* (Office of Social Research, Columbia Broadcasting System, June 17, 1964), quoted in Mendelsohn and Crespi, *Polls, Television, and the New Politics*, p. 18. Of course, the effects of polls on fund-raising efforts, the morale of party workers, the behavior of politicians, and so on may *indirectly* affect a candidate's vote-getting ability, but we restrict our analysis here to the *direct effects* of poll information on voting behavior.

33. The discussion that follows in this section parallels closely that in Herbert A. Simon, "Bandwagon and Underdog Effects in Election Predictions," *Public Opinion Quarterly,* 18 (Fall 1954), pp. 245–253.

FIGURE 3.2. BANDWAGON EFFECT

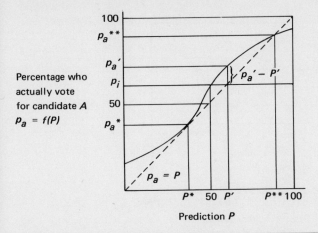

That is, with the number of voters intending to vote for candidate A given—a constant—the percentage who actually vote for A will vary only with the published prediction P.

This situation is illustrated in Figure 3.2 in the case of a possible bandwagon effect, which we compare with the situation in which there are no reaction effects. In the latter situation, the actual percentage p_a who vote for candidate A would coincide with the percentage p_i who indicated in the poll that they intended to vote for A. Thus, one could predict that $p_a = p_i$, represented by the horizontal straight line that intersects the vertical axis at p_i in Figure 3.2.

Now assume that p_a is also sensitive to the prediction P and, when $P > 50$ percent, there is an additional swing to candidate A because of a bandwagon effect. This phenomenon is represented by the solid curve in Figure 3.2, which lies above the line $p_a = p_i$ when the prediction is that candidate A will get more than 50 percent of the vote ($P > 50$ percent), below this line when $P < 50$ percent, and on this line when $P = 50$ percent.

A prediction P will be confirmed if it lies on the 45 degree diagonal $p_a = P$, represented by the dashed line in Figure 3.2, since for all points on this line the actual percentage p_a who vote for candidate A agrees with the prediction P. Since the curve $p_a = f(P)$ intersects this diagonal at two points, (P^*, p_a^*) and (P^{**}, p_a^{**}), in Figure 3.2, the pollster could make either of two predictions that, if published, would be confirmed. Moreover, whereas the prediction P^{**} will not change the outcome (candidate A would have won anyway if the prediction were not published since $p_i > 50$ percent), the prediction P^* would change the outcome. For as the predicted loser, candidate A would lose votes because of the bandwagon effect which otherwise would have made him the victor were there no published prediction.

FIGURE 3.3. UNDERDOG EFFECT

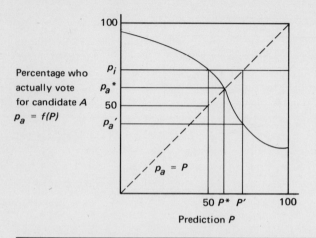

Prediction P

It is worth noting that if the pollster had predicted $P' = p_i$, as given by the poll, his prediction would have been too low by the margin $p'_a - P'$ (see Figure 3.2), but candidate A still would have won. In general, the percentage p_i who indicate that they intend to vote for a candidate will not coincide with a point where the curve $p_a = f(P)$, and the diagonal $p_a = P$, intersect.

A possible underdog effect is illustrated in Figure 3.3. When $P <$ 50 percent, the percentage p_a who actually vote for candidate A exceeds the percentage p_i, as given by the poll, who indicated that they intended to vote for A; when $P > 50$ percent, the reverse is true; and when $P =$ 50 percent, there is no effect. The point at which the curve $p_a = f(P)$ intersects the diagonal $p_a = P$ reveals that although the correct public prediction P^* hurts candidate A (since $p_a^* < p_i$), it does not change the election outcome (candidate A still wins since $p_a^* > 50$ percent). On the other hand, were the pollster to predict (incorrectly) $P' = p_i$, as given by the poll, his prediction would change the election outcome since $p'_a < 50$ percent. There is, as Simon puts it, no "simple relationship" between the election outcomes that are predicted and changes in these outcomes that are induced by the predictions.[34]

We call the curves illustrating bandwagon and underdog effects in Figure 3.2 and 3.3 *reaction curves*. They represent, in effect, predictions about how the public will react to the predictions of the pollster. The presumed effects of these predictions reverse the causal mechanism underlying the analysis in Chapters 1 and 2: instead of assuming that

34. Simon, "Bandwagon and Underdog Effects in Election Predictions," p. 85.

individual preferences (and choices) determine social choices, we assume in this analysis that expectations about social choices condition individual choices.[35]

The reaction curves are strictly bounded between the lower and upper limits of $p_a = 0$ and $p_a = 100$ percent. As drawn, they are also continuous—smooth, with no "breaks." Reaction curves that satisfy the conditions of boundedness and continuity *must* intersect the diagonal $p_a = P$ at one or more points between the lower and upper limits $p_a = 0$ and $p_a = 100$ percent in the domain $0 \leq P \leq 100$ percent. (If this fact is not intuitively obvious, without lifting your hand from the paper try drawing a smooth line from $P = 0$ to $P = 100$ percent which does not intersect the diagonal somewhere in the range between $p_a = 0$ and $p_a = 100$ percent.)

Mathematically, we say that there must exist some "fixed point" at which this intersection occurs. Its existence, given the conditions of boundedness and continuity, is guaranteed by Brouwer's Fixed-Point Theorem in topology.[36]

We have indicated the points of intersection of the reaction curves with the diagonal lines by the coordinates (P^*, p_a^*) and (P^{**}, p_a^{**}) in Figure 3.2, and (P^*, p_a^*) in Figure 3.3. Since at these fixed points on the reaction curves $P = p_a$, the pollster, by predicting $P = P^*$ or $P = P^{**}$ (Figure 3.2), or $P = P^*$ (Figure 3.3), would be assured that these predictions would be confirmed by the public reaction.

All other predictions P would be invalidated by a public reaction, including the prediction $P' = p_i$, which (as indicated in Figure 3.2) diverges from the actual percentage p_a' by the increment $p_a' - P'$; if this increment were "added on" to the prediction, it would give some new prediction P'', which in general would not coincide with some P^* (representing a fixed point) on the horizontal axis. Hence, P'' would also be invalidated, as would all other predictions P where $P \neq p_a$.

The fact that there exist two fixed points in the Figure 3.2 illustration of the bandwagon effect means that the pollster could make one of two public predictions, either of which would be confirmed. Specifically, he could correctly predict either that candidate A would lose with p_a^* percent of the vote, or win with p_a^{**} percent of the vote. By contrast, his only correct prediction in the case of the underdog effect, illustrated in Figure 3.3, would be that candidate A would win with p_a^* percent of the vote.

If there exist two or more fixed points from which a pollster might choose, this choice may give him an ability to manipulate election out-

---

35. This latter assumption, to be sure, was operative in our earlier analysis insofar as voters, taking account of the preferences of others, also anticipated the social choices implied by these preferences.

36. For a nontechnical exposition of this theorem, see Richard Courant and Herbert Robbins, *What Is Mathematics?* (London: Oxford University Press, 1941), pp. 251–255; for an informal proof, see Mark Kac and Stanislaw M. Ulam, *Mathematics and Logic: Retrospects and Prospects* (New York: New American Library, 1969), p. 36.

comes. Since at this time we have no theoretical or empirical basis for speculating about the existence—much less the shape—of possible reaction curves (those given in Figures 3.2 and 3.3 are purely hypothetical for particularly assumed p_i's), it does not seem particularly worthwhile to worry unduly about his manipulative ability. Given a better understanding of reaction effects, however, the potential for manipulation of election outcomes is present; it certainly cannot be ruled out altogether.

3.10. SOME PRACTICAL CONSIDERATIONS

The preceding analysis demonstrates that irrefutably correct public predictions can, in principle, be made. By simply locating the fixed point(s)—which we know must exist—at which the diagonal line $P = p_a$ intersects the reaction curve, normally self-falsifying predictions can be turned into self-fulfilling predictions.

The mathematical conditions that ensure that such predictions are possible do not seem to impose severe practical limitations on real-life applications. The boundedness condition says simply that there are well-defined upper and lower limits that circumscribe predictions of the event. The continuity condition does present a potentially more serious problem, however, if public reactions change abruptly at some threshold (say, $P = 50$ percent). For example, assume that a poll reveals that $p_i = 46$ percent prefer candidate A and $p_i = 44$ percent prefer candidate B, and the remaining 10 percent of the voters will vote for the candidate they expect to lose (i.e., there is an underdog effect). Then any prediction that candidate A will not obtain a majority ($P \leq 50$ percent) will result in his winning with $p_a = 56$ percent, and any prediction that he will obtain a majority ($P > 50$ percent) will result in his losing with $p_a = 46$ percent. Since the reaction curve that results does not intersect the diagonal line $p_a = P$ because of the discontinuity at $P = 50$ percent (where it "breaks" from $p_a = 56$ percent to $p_a = 46$ percent), there is no fixed point that will yield a stable prediction (see the solid lines in Figure 3.4).[37]

It is important to note that although the conditions of boundedness and continuity are sufficient to ensure a fixed point, neither is necessary: there may be fixed points even though one or both conditions are not satisfied. If there is a bandwagon, rather than an underdog, effect in the preceding example, for instance, $p_a = 46$ percent for $P \leq 50$ percent and $p_a = 56$ percent for $P > 50$ percent. In this case, even though there is a discontinuity at $P = 50$ percent, the reaction curve intersects the diagonal line $p_a = P$ at (56, 56) and (46, 46) (see the horizontal dashed lines in Figure 3.4), yielding two possible correct predictions, one a winning outcome and the other, losing.

---

37. This example is adapted from Grunberg and Modigliani, "The Predictability of Social Events," p. 473.

FIGURE 3.4.   REACTION CURVES WITH DISCONTINUITIES

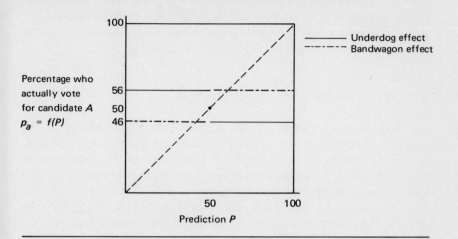

In addition to the mathematical conditions of boundedness and continuity, correct public conditions depend on two assumptions of a more substantive nature that may not be easy to satisfy in practice. The first is that the forecaster or predictor be possessed of sufficient information— and the ability to analyze and draw conclusions from this information— to enable him to make accurate private predictions. This assumption seems to be reasonably well met in the field of election predictions, but it very definitely is not met for the prediction of other social and political events. We still have, for example, only very scant knowledge of the causes of war, and, as a consequence, predictions about the outbreak of wars tend to be crude and inaccurate. Economic forecasting models, until recently thought to be in a rather advanced state, have of late led to some spectacular predictive failures.

If we generally lack the ability to make accurate private forecasts of important social-political events, we know even less about how predictions—when made public—feed back on the occurrence of these events. For example, though there is some evidence that arms races have a strong reactive component fueled in part by what each side predicts the other will spend on defense, no systematic studies have been conducted of how *public* reactions to these predictions influence defense spending. As another example, predictions about what the stock market will do evidently affect stock market performance, but exactly in what way remains somewhat of a mystery. Similarly with election predictions, there is as yet no conclusive evidence, as we indicated earlier, that the publication of poll results generates any public reaction at the polls.

It thus seems that the relevant information and knowledge required to develop accurate private predictions, and plot reaction functions, may be severely lacking in many cases of practical interest. Nonetheless, a demonstration that certain kinds of predictions can, in principle, be made and not invalidated by a public reaction seems an important and constructive result. Insofar as it belies the plausible claim that such predictions can never escape an infinite series of adjustments before they are rendered correct, this result would seem to qualify as a paradox.

3.11. SUMMARY AND CONCLUSION

We have analyzed two paradoxes in this chapter, one related to the selection of optimal candidate strategies and voter choices in an election, the other related to the prediction of election outcomes. The first paradox, which we called the ambiguity paradox, poses the question of whether ambiguous strategies that may be rational for candidates in an election are also rational for the voters who must choose from among the candidates. The second paradox, which we called the reaction paradox, asks whether the public reaction to a private prediction necessarily renders it incapable of being adjusted—with the public reaction taken account of— so that a correct public prediction can be made.

With respect to the first paradox, it has been argued by advocates of a "responsible" party system that a voter cannot make intelligent choices among candidates (or parties) when they fuzz their positions on issues. Plausible as this contention seems, however, we showed that under certain circumstances voters would actually prefer a candidate who offers them a lottery over alternative positions to any certain position. For the case in which there exist cyclical majorities on a set of positions, for example, a majority of voters (in three-voter–three-alternative situations) will prefer a lottery on the two extreme positions to the median position if the preferences of at least one voter are "intense."

Ambiguous positions may even be preferred to one or more pure positions when the preferences of voters are single peaked, but lottery positions are not dominant in such situations; they can in turn be defeated by at least one pure position. Thus, if candidates are permitted to construct lotteries on pure positions, single peakedness does not preclude the existence of a paradox of voting.

These results, it should be emphasized, are in accord with the General Possibility Theorem, which asserts that cyclical majorities are ineradicable (under certain conditions), whether or not lotteries are allowed. The introduction of lotteries simply permits candidates greater flexibility in their choices of positions on issues. In general, lottery positions are sensible choices for candidates when voters are risk-acceptant, which may be translated to mean that they feel intensely about certain positions on issues.

The presumed tension between ambiguous positions that are optimal for candidates, and clear-cut positions that are optimal for voters, is resolved by demonstrating that voters may prefer—subject to the risk-acceptance–intensity conditions we have outlined—ambiguity to clarity. When this is the case, the interests of voters and candidates coincide, and the ambiguity paradox is thereby resolved. Moreover, contrary to those who equate ambiguity with irresponsibility, we argued that candidates act most responsibly when they mirror the interests of voters who—as we showed—may under certain circumstances prefer risky choices to sure prospects.

The reaction paradox was developed in the context of a pollster's trying to make an election prediction that would not be invalidated by a public reaction which would alter the predicted election outcome. Such self-falsifying predictions, we argued, cannot in general be patched up by anticipating the public reaction to them, for an adjusted prediction would itself have to be adjusted, and so on ad infinitum. The endless prediction–reaction–new prediction cycle so generated appeared to doom any hope one might harbor for making predictions that would be confirmed after public reactions to them.

The reaction paradox lies in the fact that this prediction problem is not as impossible as it first seems. Subject to two weak mathematical conditions—boundedness and continuity—we demonstrated, using Brouwer's Fixed-Point Theorem, that there is always at least one "fixed point" that yields a prediction that is confirmed—not disconfirmed—by public reaction to it. (There may be more than one such point, depending on the reaction function, in which case the pollster's choice could determine the outcome.) We applied this possibility result to the prediction of election outcomes that were presumed to be sensitive to hypothetical bandwagon and underdog effects.

One's ability to take account of these effects, we showed, is predicted on two assumptions, neither of which may be met in practice. The first is that one can make accurate private predictions, which—at least in the case of election predictions—seems fairly well approximated for predictions based on scientific public opinion polls. The second is that the public reaction to any prediction is known, which is generally not the case even for election predictions. If there exists a reaction effect (which has not been established), there is no conclusive evidence that it favors either front-runners or underdogs.

Although the practical implications of the possibility result guaranteed by the Fixed-Point Theorem do not seem great at this time, it does assure us that the problem of public prediction is not, in principle, hopeless. Certainly in the past, the dismantling of conceptual barriers has stimulated empirical efforts of a more applied nature that have led to the development of practical knowledge in new and productive areas.

4

THE PARADOX OF COOPERATION

4.1. INTRODUCTION

In a world ridden with conflict, the lament is often heard that our circumstances would be much improved, and our lives would be happier, if only people could learn to live with each other. To some, underlying this lament is the belief that there are unenlightened people who, were they shown the benefits of cooperation, would quickly come around to the point of view that they indeed have much to gain from friendlier relations and agreements that work to the benefit of all. To one leading exponent of rigorous studies of international conflict, the heart of the problem is that people do not "stop to think":

> Why are so many nations reluctantly but steadily increasing their armaments as if they were mechanically compelled to do so? Because . . . they follow their traditions . . . and instincts . . . and because they have not yet made a sufficiently strenuous intellectual and moral effort to control the situation.[1]

This is a fundamentally optimistic view of the world, for it suggests that with the proper effort—however difficult it may be to achieve—the belligerent intentions of man can be defused and wars can be shown to be unproductive. Others, however, take a more pessimistic view of human nature and—by analogy with other animals—see in human actions an innate aggressiveness. Konrad Lorenz is quite explicit on this point:

> Human behavior, and particularly human social behavior, far from being determined by reason and cultural tradition alone, is still subject to all the laws prevailing in all phylogenetically adapted instinctive behavior. . . . The evil effects of the human aggressive drives, explained by Sigmund Freud as the results of a special death wish,

---

1. Lewis F. Richardson, *Arms and Insecurity: A Mathematical Study of the Causes and Origin of War* (Pittsburgh: Boxwood Press, 1960), p. 12.

simply derive from the fact that in prehistoric times intra-specific selection bred into man a measure of aggression drive for which, in the social order of today, he finds no adequate outlet.[2]

Still a third school of thought can be identified which, while viewing man as innately aggressive and acquisitive, sees his salvation in the creation of institutions capable of enforcing a "social contract." (By contrast, the only hope Lorenz holds out for man is the displacement of his aggressive energy into socially desirable outlets such as sports contests and artistic or scientific endeavors.) Seventeenth- and eighteenth-century political philosophers such as Hobbes and Rousseau believed that an internalized morality offered no escape from the anarchy and brutality of a world in which everybody pursued their self-interests. To rechannel the selfish and amoral interests of individuals toward more productive social ends would require a centralized authority capable of—in Rousseau's phrase—"forcing men to be free." Rousseau distinguished the "will of all," reflecting the selfish interests of individuals, from the socially desirable "general will." To bring these distinct wills into line, he proposed a systematic program of "civil religion" to enlighten the populace on the virtues of submitting to the higher authority of the state.[3]

Although classical political theorists like Hobbes and Rousseau clearly recognized the potential conflict between the interests of individuals and the interests of the community or state—characterized by Hobbes as a "leviathan" because of the great power that would have to be vested in it to overcome formidable opposition by an amoral populace[4]—they nevertheless were unclear about the specific conditions that lead to the formation of the state. If regulated social life is better than a "state of nature," must a populace be strong-armed into submission or indoctrinated through a program of "civil religion"? Or can one achieve social ends without resorting to the use of force or some form of in-doctrination?

Despite a great deal of empirical research on everything from the social behavior of bees to international conflict among nation-states, we do not today have very good answers to these questions. What we do under-stand perhaps better than Hobbes and Rousseau did, however, are the *structural conditions* that give rise to a divergence of individual and group interests.

By focusing on these conditions, of course, we sidestep the question of whether man is innately aggressive. But this question seems unlikely to be resolved in the near future by anthropologists, psychologists, and others

2. Konrad Lorenz, *On Aggression*, trans. Majorie Kerr Wilson (New York: Harcourt, Brace & World, 1966), pp. 237, 243. For a critique of this and related work, see *Man and Aggression*, ed. M. F. Ashley Montagu (New York: Oxford University Press, 1968).

3. See Jean-Jacques Rousseau, *The Social Contract* (New York: Hafner Publishing Co., 1947), particularly book I, chap. VII; book II, chap. III; and book IV, chap. VIII.

4. Thomas Hobbes, *Leviathan* (New York: Liberal Arts Press, 1958).

FIGURE 4.1 PRISONERS' DILEMMA

		SUSPECT 2	
		Do not confess	*Confess*
SUSPECT 1	*Do not confess*	(−1, −1)	(−10, 0)
	Confess	(0, −10)	(−5, −5)

interested in human behavior. Instead of looking for the origins of social conflict in the behavioral makeup of individuals, we shall analyze *situations* in which cooperation among members of a group—independent of the personalities or attitudes of the individuals who compose it—is difficult, if not impossible, to achieve. The *paradox of cooperation* is that, despite the apparent benefits that a set of actors could realize were they to act cooperatively, there may be no means to ensure that these benefits will, in fact, be realized. This situation is epitomized by a simple game we shall describe in section 4.2.

4.2. PRISONERS' DILEMMA[5]

Although the concept of a "game" usually connotes light-hearted entertainment and fun, it carries no such connotation in game theory. Whether a game is considered to be frivolous or serious, its various formal representations all connect its participants, or *players*, to *outcomes*—the social states realized from the play of a game—through the *rules*, or instructions for playing the game. Players need not be single decision makers but instead may represent any autonomous decision-making units that can make conscious choices according to the rules.

One way of representing a game is by a *payoff matrix*, or a rectangular array whose entries indicate the utilities that players associate with all possible outcomes. (*Utilities* are numbers that indicate the degree of preference that players attach to the outcomes.) An outcome is determined when each player selects a *strategy*, which—as described in Chapter 1—is a complete set of instructions specifying what choice a player should make for every contingency that may arise. Unlike the voting situations analyzed in Chapter 1, however, in which a strategy prescribed choices at one or more forks of an outcome tree, the game of Prisoners' Dilemma may be defined by the payoff matrix given in Figure 4.1, in which the first number in the ordered pair of each cell of the matrix represents the payoff to the row player, the second number, the payoff to the column player.

---

5. Material in sections 4.2 and 4.3 is adapted from Steven J. Brams, *Game Theory and Politics* (New York: Free Press, 1975), chap. 1.

More concretely, this game may be described by the following story, attributed to A. W. Tucker. Two persons suspected of being partners in a crime are arrested and placed in separate cells so that they cannot communicate with each other. Without a confession from *at least one* suspect, the district attorney does not have sufficient evidence to convict them for the crime. To try to extract a confession, the district attorney tells each suspect the following consequences of their (joint) actions:

1. If one suspect confesses and his partner does not, the one who confesses can go free (gets no sentence) for cooperation with the state, but the other gets a stiff 10-year sentence—(0, −10) and (−10, 0) in the payoff matrix.

2. If both suspects confess, both get reduced sentences of 5 years—(−5, −5) in the payoff matrix.

3. If both suspects remain silent, both go to prison for 1 year on a lesser charge of carrying a concealed weapon—(−1, −1) in the payoff matrix.

What should each suspect do to save his own skin, assuming that he has no compunction against squealing on his partner?[6] Observe first that if either suspect confesses, it is advantageous for the other suspect to do likewise to avoid his very worst outcome of 10 years in prison (−10). The rub is that the idea of confessing and receiving a moderate sentence of 5 years is not at all appealing, even though neither suspect can assure himself of a better outcome.

A much more appealing strategy for both suspects would be not to confess, if one could be sure that one's partner would do the same. But without being able to communicate with him to coordinate a joint strategy, much less make a binding agreement, this could backfire and one could end up with 10 years in prison. The reason is that the better outcome than (−5, −5) for *both* players, (−1, −1), is unstable, for there is always the temptation for one player to doublecross his partner and turn state's evidence to achieve his very best outcome of being set free (0). Moreover, not only is there this temptation, but if one player thinks that the other player might try to make a sucker out of him, he is left with no alternative but to confess. Thus, both suspects' strategies of confessing *strictly dominate*—that is, are preferable whatever strategy the other player chooses—their strategies of not confessing, though the choice of the former strategy by both suspects results in a relatively undesirable 5 years in prison for each.

The dilemma lies in the fact that when both suspects play it safe by choosing their dominant strategies of confessing, they end up worse off— (−5, −5)—than had they trusted each other and both not confessed— (−1, −1). In a sense, then, it may be rational to play this game irration-

---

6. This is implicit in the utilities, which we assume incorporate moral and ethical considerations as well as more utilitarian factors.

FIGURE 4.2 SYMBOLIC REPRESENTATION OF PRISONERS' DILEMMA

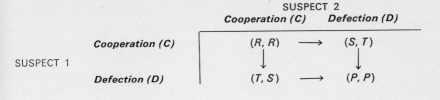

ally—at least if one receives some cooperation from one's partner—by not confessing. But as Anatol Rapoport points out, the choice between cooperation (*C*)—not confessing—and defection (*D*)—confessing—is not strictly a choice between an irrational altruism and a rational selfishness:

> The choice of C is not an act of self-sacrifice but rather an act of trust. But trust is not enough, because even convincing evidence that the other will choose C need not induce C. Not only must one be trusting; one must also be trustworthy; that is, one must resist the temptation to betray the other's trust.
>
> Is it "rational" to be trusting and trustworthy? Here the common usage of the term "rational" sometimes intrudes and beclouds the issue. The usual sense of this question is, "Is it safe to trust people?" But put in this way, the question is clearly an empirical one, to be answered by examining the behavior of a given sample of people in given circumstances.[7]

Before looking at empirical evidence on how this game is actually played, following Anatol Rapoport and Albert M. Chammah we symbolically represent the prospects of the two players in Figure 4.2, where *R* stands for "reward" (for cooperation), *T* for "temptation" (to double-cross the other player), *S* for "sucker's payoff" (to the player who is doublecrossed), and *P* for "punishment" (for playing it safe). A game is a Prisoners' Dilemma whenever $T > R > P > S$.[8]

In Figure 4.2 we have depicted the way in which the symbolic payoffs associated with each pair of strategy choices would successively be chosen if the two players alternately anticipated the choices of each other. For example, if suspect 1 anticipated that suspect 2 would choose his *D* strategy, he would also select his *D* strategy since $P > S$. This means that suspect 1 prefers (P, P) to (S, T), which we indicate by the arrow from

---

7. Anatol Rapoport, *Strategy and Conscience* (New York: Harper & Row, 1964), p. 50.

8. Anatol Rapoport and Albert M. Chammah, *Prisoner's Dilemma: A Study in Conflict and Cooperation* (Ann Arbor, Mich.: University of Michigan Press, 1965), pp. 33–34.

(S, T) to (P, P). It is also evident that he prefers (T, S) to (R, R) since $T > R$.

For suspect 2, (S, T) is preferred to (R, R) since $T > R$; similarly, (P, P) is preferred to (T, S) since $P > S$. It will be observed that the vertical arrows indicate suspect 1's strategy preferences, and the horizontal arrows indicate suspect 2's strategy preferences, for each strategy choice of the other player.[9] The arrows converge on the (P, P) outcome and show the strategies of defection (confessing) by both players to be *in equilibrium:* neither player has an incentive to depart from his D strategy, given that the other player sticks to his. Thus, the "dynamics" of the game, based on the anticipation by the suspects of each other's strategy choices, lead to punishment for both suspects.

One might think that if Prisoners' Dilemma were played repeatedly, perspicacious players could in effect communicate with each other by establishing a pattern of previous choices that would reward the choice of the cooperative strategy. But if the game ends after n plays, it clearly does not pay to play cooperatively on the final round since, with no plays to follow, the players are in effect in the same position that they would be if they played the game only once. If there is no point in trying to induce a cooperative response on the nth round, however, such behavior on the n-1st round would be to no avail since its effect could extend only to the nth round, where cooperative behavior has already been ruled out. Carrying this reasoning successively backwards, it follows that one should not choose the cooperative strategy on *any* plays of the game. (We shall further explore this line of reasoning in Chapter 5.)

Is there any escape from this dilemma? Many social-psychological experiments have been conducted to measure the effects of various parameters on the game's outcome for numerous human subjects. We cannot review all the findings that relate to the conditions under which players cooperate, but some of the most significant include the absolute and relative sizes of payoffs, the number of trials the game is played, the personalities of the players, and the amount of communication between players that permits them to cooperate.[10]

One of the most interesting conclusions that emerges from the experimental research is that neither martyrs nor cynics do well in repeated trials

---

9. This representation of preferred choices by a directed graph is used in Kenneth E. Boulding, *Conflict and Defense: A General Theory* (New York: Harper & Brothers, 1962), chap. 3.

10. The experimental literature on Prisoners' Dilemma is too extensive to cite here. Experimental research until 1965 is discussed in Rapoport and Chammah, *Prisoner's Dilemma;* for a more recent review, see Anatol Rapoport, "Prisoner's Dilemma—Reflections and Observations," in *Game Theory as a Theory of Conflict Resolution,* ed. Anatol Rapoport (Dordrecht, Netherlands: D. Reidel Publishing Co., 1974), pp. 17–34; and for a review of the experimental literature on two-person games generally, see Rapoport, "Experimental Games and Their Uses in Psychology," 4044V00 (Morristown, N.J.: General Learning Corp., 1973); and *Cooperation and Competition: Readings on Mixed-Motive Games,* ed. Lawrence S. Wrightsman, Jr., John O'Connor, and Norma J. Baker (Belmont, Calif.: Brooks/Cole Publishing Co., 1972).

of Prisoners' Dilemma.[11] That is, people willing to trust their opponents and always play their cooperative strategy, come what may, are mercilessly exploited, and persons unwilling to cooperate under any circumstances tend to provoke retaliation by the other player that locks both players into the (P, P) outcome. On the other hand, many players who started out playing their noncooperative strategies were, after several trials, able to break out of the DD trap (both players defect) and achieve the rewards of CC (both players cooperate). In general, it seems, it takes some time for mutual trust to develop between players that enables them to escape the compulsion to assume the worst and shift to their cooperative strategies that result in the mutually beneficial outcome, (R, R).

It is legitimate to ask at this point what relevance Prisoners' Dilemma has for the study of politics. If the seemingly paradoxical features of strategic choice for players in this game were limited only to hypothetical and artificial situations of the kind faced by the two criminal suspects in our example, we could easily pass this game off as an interesting curiosity but not of significance to real problems of social choice. In fact, however, instances of Prisoners' Dilemma have been identified in such diverse areas as agriculture, business, and law. Furthermore, as suggested in section 4.1, the problem it poses lies at the heart of a theory of the state. Political philosophers at least since Hobbes have used the anarchy of a stateless society to justify the need for an enforceable social contract and the creation of government, by coercion if necessary.[12]

The standard example of Prisoners' Dilemma in international relations involves an arms race in which two competing nations may either continue the arms race or desist. If both nations desist (CC), they can devote the resources that they would otherwise spend on armaments to socially useful projects, which presumably would make both better off and still preserve a balance of power between them.[13] If both arm (DD), both will be worse off for their outlays on socially useless weapons systems and

---

11. The terminology "martyrs" and "cynics" is used in Karl W. Deutsch, *The Analysis of International Relations* (Englewood Cliffs, N.J.: Prentice-Hall, 1968) p. 122.

12. For different applications of this game, see Morton D. Davis, *Game Theory: A Nontechnical Introduction* (New York: Basic Books, 1970), pp. 93–103; Daniel P. Maki and Maynard Thompson, *Mathematical Models and Applications* (Englewood Cliffs, N.J.: Prentice-Hall, 1973), pp. 244–247; and Thomas C. Schelling, "Hockey Helmets, Concealed Weapons, and Daylight Saving: A Study of Binary Choices with Externalities," *Journal of Conflict Resolution*, 17 (September 1973), pp. 381–428. Prisoners' Dilemmas have even been uncovered in artistic works, as in the plot of Puccini's opera *Tosca*. See Anatol Rapoport, "The Use and Misuse of Game Theory," *Scientific American*, December 1962, pp. 108–118.

13. One exception to this statement comes to mind for a particular kind of arms expenditure. As argued by Oskar Morgenstern in 1959, once the United States had a strong nuclear *retaliatory* force, it was in her interest for the Soviet Union also to possess one. Otherwise, the Soviet Union would be tempted to initiate a preemptive first strike if she had the slightest fear that the United States might launch an offensive strike that would wipe out her capability to respond. Thus, it was in the interest of both sides to possess a second-strike retaliatory capability. In game-theoretic terms, this would lead to a stable equilibrium, whereas if only one side had the capability to strike back after a first strike (or worse, if neither side did), the situation would be obviously unstable. See Oskar Morgenstern, *The Question of National Defense* (New York: Random House, 1959).

comparatively no stronger militarily. If one nation arms and the other does not (*CD* and *DC*), the nation that arms would develop the military superiority to defeat its adversary and thereby realize its best outcome; the nation that disarms would relinquish control over its fate and thereby suffer its worst outcome. Variants of this example relate to whether or not to adhere to the conditions of a treaty, cheat on weapons inspection agreements, and so on, where it is understood that treaties or agreements are not completely enforceable. Central to all these examples is the question of trust: under what conditions will the players be likely to trust each other sufficiently to risk adopting their cooperative but unstable strategies?

Although the experimental literature furnishes some clues about the kinds of conditions that might generate trust between players, they are not always directly applicable to real-life political situations, such as one finds in international relations.[14] Take the condition of time, for example. Since the start of the Cold War, the United States and the Soviet Union have generally become more conciliatory toward each other and even reached some agreements on limiting the testing and spread of nuclear weapons [e.g., the Treaty Banning Nuclear Weapon Tests in the Atmosphere, in Outer Space, and under Water (1963), and the Treaty on the Non-Proliferation of Nuclear Weapons (1970)]. At least in the recent period of détente, this would seem to indicate that time—as well as more accurate methods for detecting violations of these agreements (see Chapter 8)—has tempered anxieties on both sides about the risks of abrogating agreements. By contrast, after four wars time, if anything, has embittered relations between Israel and her Arab neighbors over roughly the same period. It would thus appear that if a recognition of the benefits of mutual cooperation depends on recurring experiences in Prisoners' Dilemma situations, it is also affected by other factors that are not well understood.

4.3. PRISONERS' DILEMMA AND THE THEORY OF METAGAMES

We can gain further insight into the conditions under which the cooperative outcome (*R, R*) is chosen by players in Prisoners' Dilemma from the *theory of metagames*, which has recently been developed by Nigel Howard.[15] This theory extends the concept of strategy to include one player's responses to possible strategy choices of his opponent, the

---

14. Their inapplicability to one conflict is argued in Malvern Lumsden, "The Cyprus Conflict as a Prisoner's Dilemma Game," *Journal of Conflict Resolution*, 17 (March 1973), pp. 7–32.

15. Nigel Howard, *Paradoxes of Rationality: Theory of Metagames and Political Behavior* (Cambridge, Mass.: MIT Press, 1971). For an extension of the concept of a "metagame" to cover kinds of mutual prediction other than that indicated in the text, see Nigel Howard, " 'General' Metagames: An Extension of the Metagame Concept," in *Game Theory as a Theory of Conflict Resolution*, pp. 261–283.

FIGURE 4.3   SUSPECT 2'S METASTRATEGIES FOR STRATEGIES OF SUSPECT 1

		METASTRATEGIES OF SUSPECT 2			
		C *Regard- less*	**D** *Regard- less*	*Tit-for-tat*	*Tat-for-tit*
STRATEGIES OF SUSPECT 1	**C**	$(-1, -1)$	$(-10, 0)$	$(-1, -1)$	$(-10, 0)$
	D	$(0, -10)$	$(-5, -5)$	$(-5, -5)$	$(0, -10)$

opponent's responses in turn to the first player's conditional choices, and so forth. Because this concept involves choosing a rule to select a strategy conditional upon the strategy choice of one's opponent, it is called a *metastrategy*, which may be thought of as a strategy for selecting a strategy. For example, in Prisoners' Dilemma, a player has two strategy choices: choose C or choose D. These two choices give rise to four meta-strategies:

1. Choose C, regardless of what the other player chooses.

2. Choose D, regardless of what the other player chooses.

3. Choose C if the other player chooses C, choose D if he chooses D (tit-for-tat).

4. Choose C if the other player chooses D, choose D if he chooses C (tat-for-tit).

Given that suspect 2 knew, or believed he could predict, suspect 1's strategy choices in Figure 4.1, we show in Figure 4.3 the outcomes associated with suspect 1's two strategies and suspect 2's four meta-strategies. For example, if suspect 1 chooses strategy C, and suspect 2 always chooses strategy C (i.e., regardless of the choice of suspect 1), the outcome will be $(-1, -1)$ in this expanded game. Note that there is still only one equilibrium point, $(-5, -5)$, from which it is not to the ad-vantage of either player to shift his choice if the other player sticks to his. We have circled this point in Figure 4.3 and note that it is the same equilibrium point as we found in the original game.

Now suppose that suspect 1 has knowledge of, or can predict, the metastrategy choice of suspect 2. If he makes his strategy choice con-ditional on suspect 2's metastrategies, he can formulate his own meta-strategies at a still higher level of analysis. This generates sixteen possible

---

FIGURE 4.4 METAGAME PAYOFF MATRIX OF PRISONERS' DILEMMA

		SUSPECT 2			
		C *Regard- less*	**D** *Regard- less*	*Tit-for-tat*	*Tat-for-tit*
	1. C/C/C/C	(−1, −1)	(−10, 0)	(−1, −1)	(−10, 0)
	2. C/C/C/D	(−1, −1)	(−10, 0)	(−1, −1)	(0, −10)
	3. C/C/D/C	(−1, −1)	(−10, 0)	(−5, −5)	(−10, 0)
	4. C/D/C/C	(−1, −1)	(−5, −5)	(−1, −1)	(−10, 0)
	5. D/C/C/C	(0, −10)	(−10, 0)	(−1, −1)	(−10, 0)
	6. C/C/D/D	(−1, −1)	(−10, 0)	(−5, −5)	(0, −10)
	7. C/D/C/D	(−1, −1)	(−5, −5)	(−1, −1)	(0, −10)
	8. D/C/C/D	(0, −10)	(−10, 0)	(−1, −1)	(0, −10)
SUSPECT 1	9. C/D/D/C	(−1, −1)	(−5, −5)	(−5, −5)	(−10, 0)
	10. D/C/D/C	(0, −10)	(−10, 0)	(−5, −5)	(−10, 0)
	11. D/D/C/C	(0, −10)	(−5, −5)	(−1, −1)	(−10, 0)
	12. C/D/D/D	(−1, −1)	(−5, −5)	(−5, −5)	(0, −10)
	13. D/C/D/D	(0, −10)	(−10, 0)	(−5, −5)	(0, −10)
	14. D/D/C/D	(0, −10)	(−5, −5)	(−1, −1)	(0, −10)
	15. D/D/D/C	(0, −10)	(−5, −5)	(−5, −5)	(−10, 0)
	16. D/D/D/D	(0, −10)	(−5, −5)	(−5, −5)	(0, −10)

---

choices, depending on whether suspect 1 chooses *C* or *D* for each of suspect 2's four metastrategies. If, for example, suspect 1 chooses

(1) *D* whenever suspect 2 chooses *C* regardless,

(2) *D* whenever suspect 2 chooses *D* regardless,

(3) *C* whenever suspect 2 chooses tit-for-tat,

(4) *D* whenever suspect 2 chooses tat-for-tit,

we designate his higher-level metastrategy by *D/D/C/D* in Figure 4.4.

For each of suspect 1's sixteen metastrategies, suspect 2 has four metastrategies, so there are sixty-four possible outcomes in the *metagame*, or game derived from the original game that is defined by the payoff matrix in Figure 4.4. Each of these outcomes corresponds to one of the four outcomes in the original game.

To illustrate how these outcomes are found, consider the outcome at the intersection of suspect 1's metastrategy *D/D/C/D* (row 14 in Figure 4.4) and suspect 2's metastrategy *C* regardless. Because these metastrategies correspond to the choice of *C* by suspect 2 and *D* by suspect 1, which gives outcome (0, −10) in the payoff matrix of the original game in Figure 4.1, the outcome associated with these metastrategies in the payoff matrix of the metagame in Figure 4.4 is also (0, −10).

Now comes the surprise! As indicated in Figure 4.4 by the circled outcomes, there are three equilibria in the metagame, and two are the outcomes $(-1, -1)$ associated with the strategy choices of C by both suspects in the original Prisoners' Dilemma game. In other words, the cooperative outcome $(R, R) = (-1, -1)$ in the original game, which was not in equilibrium, emerges as an equilibrium point in the metagame expansion. The noncooperative outcome $(P, P) = (-5, -5)$ is also an equilibrium point, as it was in the expansion of only suspect 2's strategies in Figure 4.3. All these equilibria are stable in the sense that if both suspects choose metastrategies associated with one of them, neither suspect can do better, and may do worse, by unilaterally switching to a different metastrategy.

What do these new equilibria signify? For suspect 2, the metastrategy tit-for-tat is associated with both of the cooperative equilibria, and it would seem to imply: "I'll cooperate only if you will." For suspect 1, whose reply is conditional on suspect 2's choice, his metastrategy associated with one of the cooperative equilibria $(D/D/C/D)$ was previously discussed; it would seem to imply: "In that case [i.e., if you choose tit-for-tat], I'll cooperate, too." With each suspect's making his cooperation conditional on the cooperation of the other suspect, together they are able to "lock into" the cooperative solution.

One might wonder what the consequence would be of further expanding the payoff matrix to include suspect 1's knowledge of suspect 2's sixteen metastrategies. Would there be still new equilibria? Fortunately, we need not continue the expansion process any longer, for Howard has proved that in an n-person game, an expansion beyond n levels will not reveal any new equilibria, nor will any be lost. Furthermore, it does not matter which player we start the expansion with; if we gave suspect 1 the four conditional strategies at the first level, and suspect 2 the sixteen conditional responses, their roles would be reversed but the same equilibria would be obtained.

We have observed that there are two cooperative equilibria, but we gave an interpretation only to the outcome at the intersection of suspect 2's tit-for-tat metastrategy and suspect 1's $D/D/C/D$ metastrategy. For the same tit-for-tat choice of suspect 2, suspect 1's $C/D/C/D$ metastrategy (row 7 in Figure 4.4) also results in the cooperative equilibrium outcome $(-1, -1)$, but it is not as compelling as the former. The reason is that $D/D/C/D$ dominates $C/D/C/D$—that is, for one metastrategy of suspect 2 (C regardless), suspect 1 fares worse with metastrategy $C/D/C/D$ than with metastrategy $D/D/C/D$: he obtains a payoff of -1 rather than 0. Since $D/D/C/D$ is at least as good and in one contingency better than $C/D/C/D$, it is the dominant equilibrium metastrategy for suspect 1.[16]

From the vantage point of suspect 2, he maximizes his *security level*—

---

16. Metastrategy $D/D/C/D$ also dominates $D/D/D/D$, suspect 1's metastrategy containing his noncooperative equilibrium outcome, but this is not true in all games. In fact, in Chapter 5 we shall give an example of a game in which the metastrategy containing a noncooperative equilibrium outcome dominates the one containing the cooperative equilibrium outcome.

the minimum amount that he can ensure for himself—by choosing either the metastrategy D regardless or the metastrategy tit-for-tat; whatever the choice of suspect 1, his payoff is at least -5. Given that he would prefer an equilibrium with a larger payoff for his opponent, as well as for himself (on the assumption that his opponent would choose his metastrategy containing it), he should choose his metastrategy containing the cooperative equilibria $(-1, -1)$, rather than the noncooperative equilibrium $(-5, -5)$, which dictates the choice of tit-for-tat. Thus, the outcome $(-1, -1)$ at the intersection of metastrategies $D/D/C/D$ and tit-for-tat is (1) in equilibrium; (2) preferred by both players to the noncooperative equilibrium $(-5, -5)$; and (3) the product of undominated metastrategies for both players (in fact, metastrategy $D/D/C/D$ of suspect 1 dominates *all* his other metastrategies).

This is a rather complicated route to take to get to the cooperative solution to Prisoners' Dilemma. Is the reasoning on which it is based justified? Insofar as players can accurately predict each other's strategies and formulate metastrategy choices, the reasoning is logically impeccable. Because such predictions are usually based on some form of communication between the players, however, it seems also fair to say that the dilemma is in essence resolved by permitting preplay communication in a cooperative game. For once the players are free to communicate, they can agree to play their cooperative strategies and—provided there is some means for enforcing their agreement—the dilemma disappears.

In place of insisting that agreements be enforceable, the metagame approach requires foreknowledge of the metastrategy choices of one's opponent. Obviously, if one's forecasting ability or clairvoyance is infallible, one does not need a guarantee that an agreement will not be broken, because one knows this a priori. Hence, given that there is no risk associated with one's choice, the theory of metagames resolves Prisoners' Dilemma by substituting knowledge—or at least expectations (i.e., imperfect knowledge)—of the future for an enforceable agreement needed in its absence. It is reasonable to suppose that some form of communication or bargaining occurs between the players to obtain knowledge or an agreement.

Although the theory of metagames would seem to provide less of an "escape" from a paradox[17] than a recasting of it in different terms, this is

---

17. Anatol Rapoport, "Escape from Paradox," *Scientific American*, July 1967, pp. 50–56. Two other "solutions" to Prisoners' Dilemma are offered by Martin Shubik, but neither seems as relevant to the study of politics as does the theory-of-metagames solution. See Martin Shubik, "Game Theory, Behavior, and the Paradox of the Prisoner's Dilemma: Three Solutions," *Journal of Conflict Resolution*, 13 (June 1970), pp. 181–193; for a solution with repeated plays when the number of plays is uncertain, see Walter W. Hill, Jr., "Prisoner's Dilemma: A Stochastic Solution," *Mathematics Magazine*, 48 (March–April 1975), pp. 103–105. See also Chapter 8 for a "probabilistic" solution based on the ability of each player to predict beforehand the other player's strategy choice.

not a mean achievement.[18] We shall try to demonstrate this point in Chapter 5 with an empirical example. At this juncture, however, we note in passing that probably most actors, at least in international politics, do *not* operate from a metagame perspective. Whether they lack information about an opponent, the ability to forecast his behavior, or simply mistrust him, their focus is not on metastrategies but on strategies, which is after all what they choose in the end.[19] From a game-theoretic perspective, there is hardly anything perverse or irrational in choosing to play it safe, or, if you will, to select the noncooperative strategy of defection in Prisoners' Dilemma. Indeed, the players in *Realpolitik* games who fail to grasp this fact, and the nature of the equilibrium solution, are often the victims of preemptive attacks, losers in arms races, and so forth; it is precisely these players who are irrational for trusting an adversary without good reasons. Although, perhaps, "there should be a law against such games," as Luce and Raiffa wistfully put it,[20] since there is none, it behooves us to try to understand under what circumstances, if any, the logic of the noncooperative solution can be transcended. Clearly, the power of a theory lies in its ability not only to point out paradoxes but to identify solutions as well.

4.4. VOTE TRADING: AN ESCAPE FROM THE PARADOX OF VOTING?

Although it is comforting to find that there may, in principle, be ways of resolving—or circumventing—paradoxes, these "solutions" may not be readily applicable to real-life situations. Worse, a solution may be a

---

18. Neither is it a mean achievement for game theory to have drawn attention to the paradox in the first place, which is less a creation of game theory—it was surely anticipated before its creation—than a limitation of certain situations that the theory helps to clarify.

19. This is the point made in Harris's critique of Rapoport's claim of an "escape from paradox." See Richard J. Harris, "Note on Howard's Theory of Meta-Games," *Psychological Reports*, 24 (1968), pp. 849–850; in rebuttal, see Anatol Rapoport, "Comments on Dr. Harris' 'Note on Howard's Theory of Meta-Games,'" *Psychological Reports*, 25 (1969), pp. 765–766; in counterrebuttal, see Richard J. Harris, "Comments on Dr. Rapoport's Comments," *Psychological Reports*, 25 (1969), p. 825. At this point Howard joined the debate. See Nigel Howard, "Comments on Harris' 'Comments on Rapoport's Comments,'" *Psychological Reports*, 25 (1969), p. 826; A. Rapoport, "Reply to Dr. Harris' Comments on My Comments," *Psychological Reports*, 25 (1969), pp. 857–858; Richard J. Harris, "Paradox Regained," *Psychological Reports*, 26 (1970), pp. 264–266; Anatol Rapoport, "Comments on 'Paradox Regained,'" *Psychological Reports*, 26 (1970), p. 272; and, finally, Nigel Howard, "Note on the Harris-Rapoport Controversy," *Pschological Reports*, 26 (1970), p. 316. A more recent challenge—and defense—of the metagame solution in Prisoners' Dilemma can be found in Mike Robinson, "Prisoner's Dilemma: Metagames and Other Solutions"; Anatol Rapoport, "Some Comments on 'Prisoner's Dilemma: Metagames and Other Solutions'"; and Robinson, "Reply to Rapoport," *Behavioral Science*, 20 (May 1975), pp. 201–205, 206–208, 209.

20. R. Duncan Luce and Howard Raiffa, *Games and Decisions: Introduction and Critical Survey* (New York: John Wiley & Sons, 1957), p. 97.

chimera in the sense that it unwittingly leads one into another kind of paradox. We shall now show this to be the case for vote trading, which has been proposed as a solution to the paradox of voting (described in Chapter 2).

Clearly, one escape from the paradox of voting is to allow members of a voting body to express their intensities of preference for alternatives, rather than limit them to making only qualitative choices, for such a voting system violates certain rationality conditions, as we showed for the rank-order method in section 2.3. Suppose, however, we do not permit a member directly to express his intensities of preference but instead permit him to exchange his vote on a bill whose outcome is of less concern to him for the support of another member on a bill whose outcome is of more concern to him through a vote trade. If members are able to express their intensities through vote trades, can they avoid the paradox of voting guaranteed by the General Possibility Theorem for voting systems in which members are able to rank, but not express intensities for, outcomes?

Contrary to the writings of several theorists, we shall show in the remainder of this chapter that vote trading does not provide an escape from the paradox of voting. Indeed, the very conditions that permit vote trading also ensure that no outcome is preferred by a majority to all others and is, therefore, stable. Furthermore, we shall demonstrate that under certain conditions, vote trading may lead to a kind of n-person Prisoners' Dilemma wherein everybody, as a result of making individually rational trades, ends up worse than before trading. First, however, to provide some background on the controversy surrounding vote trading, we begin by looking at the recent literature that portrays vote trading as by and large socially beneficial and compare it with an older literature in which a more skeptical view is taken about the value of voting trading.[21]

The conventional judgment on vote trading in legislatures is one of severe disapproval. In the United States, at least, the usual idiom is "logrolling," and this word has always had pejorative connotations.[22]

---

21. The remainder of this chapter is based largely on William H. Riker and Steven J. Brams, "The Paradox of Vote Trading," *American Political Science Review*, 67 (December 1973), pp. 1235–1247; the permission of the American Political Science Association to adapt material from this article is gratefully acknowledged.

22. *A Dictionary of Americanisms* (Chicago: University of Chicago Press, 1951), which is probably the most authoritative collection, cites many political examples from 1812 (Ninian Edwards) to 1949 (*Time* magazine), in every one of which the word is clearly used in a pejorative sense. In the quotation from Edwards, logrolling is specifically identified with intrigue; and the climate of intrigue is conveyed by almost all the later quotations. The *Oxford Dictionary* (*A New English Dictionary on Historical Principles* [Oxford: Clarendon Press, 1908]) cites political usage from both sides of the Atlantic from 1823 (*Niles Weekly*) to the end of the nineteenth century, and its quotations also are uniformly pejorative. John Russell Bartlett's *Dictionary of Americanisms* (New York: Bartlett and Welford, 1848) contains a lengthy and righteously indignant explication of the political sense of "logrolling." None of these sources indicates any pejorative connotation at all for the word when it refers to clearing land or building houses. It seems to have acquired the sense of intrigue only when it was transferred from the bartering of labor to the bartering of votes, which demonstrates that the bartering of votes has traditionally been socially disapproved.

The common sense of the language has been reinforced by the judgment of scholars. E. E. Schattschneider, whose study of the writing of the Smoot-Hawley tariff of 1930 is the most detailed examination of a single event of vote trading, concluded his book with the remark: "To manage pressures [i.e., for vote trading] is to govern; to let pressures run wild is to abdicate."[23] Furthermore, it seems likely that the widespread scholarly support for concentrated national leadership—as embodied, for example, in such writings as the report of the Committee on Political Parties of the American Political Science Association, a report to which Schattschneider contributed substantially—was engendered in part at least by a desire to minimize vote trading.[24]

Despite the long-standing unanimity of scholarly and popular judgment, however, it has recently been argued by a number of scholars that vote trading is socially desirable because it allows the expression of degrees of intensity of preference. James M. Buchanan and Gordon Tullock argue that the voter or legislator can improve his welfare "if he accepts a decision contrary to his desire in an area where his preferences are weak in exchange for a decision in his favor in an area where his feelings are stronger." Hence they say: "Bargains among voters can, therefore, be mutually beneficial."[25] The authors recognize that when bargains are concluded "in which the single voter does not participate, . . . he will have to bear part of the costs of action taken."[26] But they nevertheless conclude that these external costs are on the average less than the benefits obtained so that, for the society as a whole, vote trading, or logrolling, is a desirable kind of activity.

Following this argument a small literature on the subject has developed with the same tone. Tullock elaborated his earlier position.[27] James S. Coleman has argued that logrolling is a device both to avoid the Arrow paradox and to arrive at optimal allocations.[28] A number of writers have

---

23. E. E. Schattschneider, *Politics, Pressures and the Tariff* (New York: Prentice-Hall, 1935), p. 293. Schattschneider interpreted the process of tariff writing as an "attempt to set up a beneficently discriminatory set of privileges"—beneficent in the sense that a few particular industries deemed worthy would benefit. This attempt failed, he argued, because the legislation as actually written protected so "indiscriminately . . . as to destroy the logic and sense of the policy" (p. 283). One of our purposes here is to explain the conditions for such failure.

24. Committee on Political Parties of the American Political Science Association, *Toward a More Responsible Party System* (New York: Rinehart, 1950).

25. James M. Buchanan and Gordon Tullock, *The Calculus of Consent* (Ann Arbor, Mich.: University of Michigan Press, 1962), p. 145.

26. Buchanan and Tullock, *Calculus of Consent*, p. 145.

27. Gordon Tullock, "A Simple Algebraic Logrolling Model," *American Economic Review*, 60 (June 1970), pp. 419–426.

28. James S. Coleman, "The Possibility of a Social Welfare Function," *American Economic Review*, 56 (December 1966), pp. 1105–1122.

pointed out, however, that vote trading does not eliminate the Arrow paradox.[29] But these same writers and others have taken pains to argue that it does improve allocations in the direction of Pareto optimality.[30]

We thus have an intellectual confrontation between an older (and popular) tradition and new developments in social science. To try to reconcile this conflict, we shall define the relationship between salience and utility in section 4.5, where we shall also describe the assumptions of our model of vote trading. Then we shall offer an example that demonstrates how, through vote trades which are all individually rational (to be defined subsequently) for pairs of members of a voting body, every member may end up worse off than before. This is what we call the *paradox of vote trading*, which we shall demonstrate can be viewed, in effect, as an *n*-person Prisoners' Dilemma that extends the paradox of cooperation to more than two actors. Finally, we shall assess the significance of the vote-trading paradox in light of some empirical examples.

4.5. DEFINITIONS AND ASSUMPTIONS

In the analysis that follows, we assume that each member of a hypothetical voting body can rank all roll calls in terms of their salience to him. By *salience* we mean the difference that it makes to a member to be in the majority (i.e., win) versus the minority (i.e., lose). More precisely, if $u_i(M)$ is the utility member i associates with being in the majority (M) on a particular roll call—which may not be positive if he votes insincerely, as we shall presently show—and $u_i(N)$ is the utility he associates with being in the minority (N), then we define his salience for that roll call as

$$s_i = u_i(M) - u_i(N).$$

For the two roll calls shown in Table 4.1, the second is more salient to member i than the first (since $s_i = 4$ on roll call 2, $s_i = 2$ on roll call 1), whereas the first is more salient to member j than the second (since $s_j = 3$ on roll call 1, $s_j = 1$ on roll call 2).

Note that even though $s_i > s_j$ on roll call 2, and $s_j > s_i$ on roll call 1, we make no comparisons of salience *between* members. Such interpersonal comparisons of salience, and the utilities associated with salience, we rule out in the absence of any universal standard (e.g., based on money,

29. Dennis C. Mueller, "The Possibility of a Social Welfare Function: Comment," *American Economic Review*, 57 (December 1967), pp. 1304–1311; and Robert Wilson, "An Axiomatic Model of Logrolling," *American Economic Review*, 59 (June 1969), pp. 331–341.

30. See Wilson, "An Axiomatic Model of Logrolling"; Edwin T. Haefele, "Coalitions, Minority Representation, and Vote-Trading Probabilities," *Public Choice*, 8 (Spring 1970), pp. 75–90; and Dennis C. Mueller, Geoffrey C. Philpotts, and Jaroslav Vanck, "The Social Gains from Exchanging Votes," *Public Choice*, 13 (Fall 1972), pp. 55–79.

TABLE 4.1   UTILITY OF POSITIONS AND SALIENCE OF ROLL CALLS FOR TWO MEMBERS

	UTILITY AND SALIENCE					
	Roll call 1			Roll call 2		
MEMBERS	u(M)	u(N)	s	u(M)	u(N)	s
i	1	−1	2	2	−2	4
j	1	−2	3	1	0	1

power, or prestige) that can be presumed for all members in their evaluation of social choices.[31]

In our subsequent analysis, we shall continue the development of the example in Table 4.1 to illustrate our definition of vote trading. First, however, we present the assumptions of our model:

1. A voting body of (initially) three members, $V = \{i, j, k\}$.

2. A set of (initially) six roll-call votes, $R = \{1, 2, 3, 4, 5, 6\}$, on each of which a member has a preference for either one of two *positions* (for or against): if two of the three members agree on a roll call (by voting either for or against), this is the majority position, which we denote by M; we denote the minority position of the third member by N.

3. There are no roll calls on which all three members agree. Winning majorities are thus assumed to be always *minimal winning*, which means that if either member of the two-member majority changes his position on a roll call, this changes the majority outcome on that roll call. Thus, the votes of the majority members on all roll calls are *critical*.

4. Each member of the voting body can rank all roll calls in terms of the importance or *salience* of the outcome to him. As we shall show, the differential salience members attach to the outcomes of different roll calls is the condition that makes vote trades possible.

5. Each member possesses *complete information* about the positions and salience rankings of all other members and can *communicate* with them.

6. The *goal* of each member is, through vote trading, to maximize his utility across all roll calls by being in the majority on the roll calls whose outcomes are most salient to him.

---

31. For a detailed discussion of this important, but often misunderstood, aspect of utility theory, see Luce and Raiffa, *Games and Decisions*, chap. 2.

Clearly, if members value the outcomes on roll calls differently (assumption 4), then it follows from the goal assumption (assumption 6) that a rational member would be willing to give up a preferred position on one roll call to secure a preferred position on another roll call whose outcome is more salient to him. The mechanism by which he accomplishes this we call a *vote trade*. The possibility of a vote trade depends on the presence of two conditions for any pair of members i and j who vote on roll calls 1 and 2:

(a) Member i is in the majority on roll call 1, the minority on roll call 2.

(b) Member j is in the majority on roll call 2, the minority on roll call 1.

A trade occurs when member i (majority position holder) gives his support to member j (minority position holder) on roll call 1 in return for the support of member j (majority position holder) on roll call 2 (on which member i is in the minority).

It is precisely the asymmetry of the positions of the two members on the two roll calls that permits an exchange of support. By assumption 3, such an exchange will alter the majority outcome on each roll call because the switcher (member i on roll call 1, member j on roll call 2) casts a critical vote when the majorities are minimal winning. Under this circumstance, the minority position for which a member (i on roll call 2, j on roll call 1) receives support becomes the majority position when this support is given.

Simple, as these conditions are, they tell us quite a bit about the occurrence of logrolling in real legislatures. It is apparent that, for a trade to be possible, the traders must be on opposite sides on two roll calls. One trader must be in the initial majority on the first roll call and the initial minority on the second. The other trader must be in the initial minority on the first roll call and the initial majority on the second. If these conditions cannot be met, then trading is not possible.

One obvious place it cannot be met is in legislatures with just two disciplined parties. To say that a party is disciplined is to say that all its members are on the same side on any roll call. Hence, if the members of a party are a majority on one roll call, they are a majority on all roll calls. For the conditions to be met, some of the party members must sometimes be in the minority, but they cannot by reason of their being disciplined.

Consequently, in a legislature with just two disciplined parties, logrolling is extremely rare. This is probably one reason why so many American writers from Woodrow Wilson onward have admired the British Parliament, especially when it has approached the two-party situation in which conditions (a) and (b) cannot be satisfied. They should have also admired the state legislatures of New York and Pennsylvania, for example, which party bosses have usually run with an iron hand, because logrolling is equally impossible in them. But it has never been fashionable to admire boss rule.

Of course, once vote trading is banished from the legislature, political compromise goes on someplace else politically antecedent to the legislature. Thus, in state legislatures and city councils with disciplined parties, the compromise takes place in the majority caucus or in the mind of the boss. In England, the Cabinet serves as one place of compromise, and very probably something like vote trading goes on there. Since the Cabinet situation is unstructured in comparison with the situation in the Parliament, however, it is probably hard to identify the trades and compromises that do occur.

A third condition is necessary to ensure that a vote trade is *individually rational* for each member in a pair:

(c) The minority position for which a member receives support changes an outcome more salient to him than the outcome of the roll call on which he switches his vote.

In other words, a trade is individually rational for a pair of members when it not only changes the outcomes of the two roll calls on which they exchange votes but also assures each member a majority position on the roll call whose outcome is more salient to him. As we shall show later, however, the trades of other pairs of members may upset these calculations in such a way that the trades which produce positive gains for each pair of trading members may lower the collective benefits for all members of the voting body. Before discussing the interdependence of vote trades, though, we must distinguish between "sincere" and "insincere" voting.

4.6. SINCERE AND INSINCERE VOTING

By *sincere voting* we mean, as in Chapter 1 (see section 1.2), that a member of a voting body votes directly according to his preferences, which in this chapter translates to mean that a member takes the position on a roll call (for or against) that offers him the greatest utility. This is to be contrasted with *insincere voting*, which is defined as voting against one's interest— that is, for one's less-preferred rather than one's more-preferred position on a roll call—when there is an incentive to do so. Insincere voting includes sophisticated voting, discussed in Chapter 1, but it also includes voting in cooperative situations wherein voters can communicate with other voters and make agreements. Surely one of the main reasons for insincere voting is logrolling, which we analyze in this chapter.

Whatever one thinks of the propriety of this kind of behavior, it may be rational with respect to the goal postulated earlier (see assumption 6). Consider again the situation we assumed earlier of two members, i and j, whose (sincere) positions on roll calls 1 and 2 are such that member i is in the majority on roll call 1, which we denote by $M(1)$, and member j is in the majority on roll call 2, which we denote by $M(2)$. Similarly, let $N(1)$ and $N(2)$ indicate the minority positions on these roll calls, which we assume are the positions, respectively, of members j and i.

TABLE 4.2   POSITIONS AND UTILITIES BEFORE TRADING

MEMBERS	High		Low		TOTAL UTILITY
	Position	Utility	Position	Utility	
i	$N(2)$	−2	$M(1)$	1	−1
j	$N(1)$	−2	$M(2)$	1	−1

SALIENCE

Now let us assume, as was the case in Table 4.1, that roll call 2 is the roll call whose outcome is more salient to member i, and roll call 1 is the roll call whose outcome is more salient to member j. This situation is summarized in Table 4.2, with the utilities associated with the positions of each member, originally given in Table 4.1, also shown. ("Total utility" is simply the algebraic sum of the utilities of each member across the two roll calls.) Given the goal of each member to be in the majority on roll calls most salient to him (assumption 6), member i would prefer to be in the majority on roll call 2 and member j on roll call 1. We shall now show that each member can realize his goal through a vote trade.

To effect such a trade, each member will have to vote insincerely on the roll call whose outcome is of less salience to him. We label the insincere positions of the members on these roll calls as M_d to signify support of a majority with which one disagrees (d). Assuming that the outcomes N and M_d are valued as equally bad—that is, on any roll call $u(M_d) = u(N)$ for each member—the utilities of the new positions of members after the trade, originally given in Table 4.1, are as shown in Table 4.3. The value of the trade can be seen by comparing the total utilities of the members before (Table 4.2) and after (Table 4.3) trading, which increase for both from −1 to +1. The advantages of vote trading are readily apparent—there is a clear gain for both members from the trade—and one can easily understand why the notion of logrolling has been so attractive to contemporary scholars.

Nevertheless, there are some severe limitations. The possibilities of trading are quite restrictedly finite. By reason of assumption 3, a switch is pointless unless the switcher casts a critical vote with respect to his initial majority. Consequently, we have a maximum limit on logrolling: since it takes two critical members to trade, there can at most be as many trades as half the number of issues. In a temporal world, moreover, only a finite number of issues can be juggled at once. In a session of a typical national legislature, there are probably no more than, say, two thousand roll calls, which gives a theoretical maximum of one thousand trades.

TABLE 4.3   POSITIONS AND UTILITIES AFTER TRADING

| MEMBERS | SALIENCE | | | | TOTAL UTILITY |
| | High | | Low | | |
	Position	Utility	Position	Utility	
i	$M(2)$	2	$M_d(1)$	-1	1
j	$M(1)$	1	$M_d(2)$	0	1

But, of course, many issues are trivial so that no trade is worthwhile; many others come up for decision so quickly that the elaborate arrangements of logrolling are not possible; for many others it may be difficult for a member to discover another one with whom conditions (a), (b), and (c) can be satisfied; and, finally, since roll calls come up serially so that many future roll calls cannot be anticipated and so that past roll calls are irrevocably settled, only a small subset of roll calls is available for trading at any one moment. In fact, it would seem, the practical maximum of trades is at most one-tenth of the theoretical maximum. Consequently, in the typical legislature (with, say, one hundred members) in the typical session it may well be that the average member can expect to be involved in at most one trade.

The utilities given in Tables 4.2 and 4.3 are purely illustrative, for individually rational vote trades as we have defined them will always be profitable for the participating members, given the equivalence between the N and M_d positions that we assumed previously. This equivalence assumption is justified by the fact that in the case of both N and M_d, a member's sincere position differs from the prevailing one, expressed in one case by *public nonsupport* of the majority position (i.e., voting with the minority, N) and in the other by *public support* of a majority position with which one privately disagrees (M_d). Although one might regard the hypocrisy of the latter position as distasteful, if not unconscionable, it would seem that whether one's disagreement is public or private, the results are the same: one's preferred position on a roll call is thwarted by the majority, even if it is a majority one publicy supports.

For this reason we consider these positions equivalent in terms of the cardinal utilities associated with each. Indeed, implicit in the goal assumption (assumption 6) is that a member's majorities on roll calls whose outcomes are less salient to him are negotiable, and, in particular, he will be willing to sacrifice preferred positions on these roll calls—and form majorities inimical to his interests—if he can prevail on roll calls whose outcomes are more salient. We assume that these more salient outcomes override any ethical qualms associated with insincere voting—that is, the utilities are a true expression of preferences.

So far so good for the vote-trading members in our previous example: they both come out better after the trade. Their good fortune is not costless to all members, however, for the reversal of the majorities on the two roll calls must occur at somebody's expense—namely, the third member of the voting body.

To see this difficulty, consider the original (sincere) positions of members i and j on the two roll calls given in Table 4.2. By assumption 2, a third member k must take the majority position on both roll calls in order that two members support the majority on each roll call and one member, the minority. Thus, the (sincere) positions of a third member k on roll calls 1 and 2 will necessarily be $M(1)$ and $M(2)$.

Now recall that after the vote trade of members i and j, the old minority positions become the new majority positions because of the switch of member i on roll call 1, and member j on roll call 2, to positions with which they disagree (see Table 4.3). Because of the critical nature of members' votes on roll calls, these switches produce new majorities on the roll calls. These new majorities, which members i and j now together constitute on the two roll calls 1 and 2, recast the previous majority positions of member k on these roll calls into minority positions, $N(1)$ and $N(2)$. Thus, the costs of the favorable trade between members i and j fall on the nonparticipant, member k. This follows from the fact that the number of majority and minority positions must remain constant by assumption 2 (in a three-member body, a 2:1 ratio of M's and N's must be preserved on all roll calls under simple majority rule), so all switches in positions produced by the vote-trading members on each roll call will perforce generate an equal number of involuntary outcome changes (from majority to minority) for the nontrading member. If we assume that member k associates the same utilities with the majority and minority positions on the two roll calls as member i (see Table 4.1), then the vote trade between members i and j drops his total utility from $+3$ to -3, as shown in Table 4.4.

If the gains from a vote trade can be wiped out by external costs (defined in the following paragraph), the enthusiasm of logrolling's proponents may be misplaced. Indeed, it is quite possible to imagine a system in which everyone gains from individual trades—and so has a positive incentive to logroll—and yet everyone also loses if all such trades are carried out. This is the paradox of logrolling to whose illustration we shall turn in section 4.7.

External costs are costs which one bears as a result of the actions of others. They are to be contrasted with internal costs, which result from one's own action. The noise that comes from a pneumatic drill is an internal cost with respect to the driller because it is part of what he must suffer to earn his pay. But to the neighbor at the construction site, the

TABLE 4.4   POSITIONS AND UTILITIES OF LEFT-OUT MEMBER BEFORE AND AFTER TRADING

| | SALIENCE | | | | |
| MEMBER k | High | | Low | | TOTAL UTILITY |
	Position	Utility	Position	Utility	
Before trading	$M(2)$	2	$M(1)$	1	3
After trading	$N(2)$	-2	$N(1)$	-1	-3

noise is an external cost. He must bear it, not in order to get something else, but merely because he is there.

Debate is never-ending about the existence of some external costs. (For example, does the noise of the drill really bother the neighbor or does he see a chance, by complaining of the noise—even though it does not bother him—to blackmail the contractor?) But it seems impossible to doubt the existence of external costs in vote trading. Consider the position of some member who is not party to a trade: since the trade brings about a different winner on a roll call, the nontrader bears an external cost if he were originally in the majority, or he receives an external gain if he were in the original minority. In our example, member k is entirely passive throughout the entire transaction, but two of his positions are reversed from majority to minority.

External costs have mostly been ignored in the writings of those who extol the benefits of vote trading.[32] Yet they must by assumption 3 on critical votes be present: since trading changes the outcomes, there must always be innocent bystanders who suffer. Although the size of their losses in particular cases will depend on the amounts of utility associated with their salience rankings, it is possible to show that in particular cases suffering is general and universal, which is the paradox of logrolling.

In summary, it would appear that the optimal joint strategy of a pair of vote-trading members i and j is to vote insincerely on the roll calls

---

32. An exception is Coleman, "The Possibility of a Social Welfare Function," p. 1121, who notes in passing that the inclusion of such costs requires a "much more extensive calculation," but he does not try to develop it. In a more recent article, Coleman provides an explicit calculation and concludes that vote trading will be generally profitable only under conditions of "absolutely free and frictionless political exchange" that preclude arbitrary decision rules (e.g., majority rule). See James S. Coleman, "Beyond Pareto Optimality," in *Philosophy, Science, and Method: Essays in Honor of Ernest Nagel*, ed. Sidney Morgenbesser, Patrick Suppes, and Morton White (New York: St. Martin's Press, 1969), pp. 415–439; also, Coleman, *The Mathematics of Collective Action* (Chicago: Aldine Publishing Co., 1973), wherein computer-simulation models of vote trading are developed.

whose outcomes are less salient and sincerely on the roll calls whose outcomes are more salient. The trade puts both members on the side of the majority on both roll calls, one of which (the roll call whose outcome is more salient) each member agrees with, the other of which he disagrees with. The external cost which this trade imposes on member k in our example is to change his previous majority positions on both roll calls into minority positions.

4.7. THE PARADOX OF VOTE TRADING: AN N-PERSON PRISONERS' DILEMMA

We now turn to a simple example to demonstrate that vote trades that are individually rational for pairs of members in a voting body may leave all members worse off after the trades. We assume that roll calls are voted upon serially so that future roll calls are not necessarily anticipated when current roll calls are considered. Note that this assumption about the voting process is quite different from the assumption made in the previously cited works of proponents of vote trading, who typically posit that all roll calls are simultaneously before the legislature. In such a system, support can be traded back and forth in all possible ways, but in the present system support can be traded only with respect to the subset of roll calls currently before the legislature or anticipated to come before it.[33] The rationale for this more restrictive assumption is simply that it accords with an important feature of the real world.

To illustrate the paradox of vote trading wherein each member is worse off after trading, consider our voting body $V = \{i, j, k\}$, which consists of three members who vote on six roll calls $R = \{1, 2, 3, 4, 5, 6\}$. Assume

> On roll calls 1 and 2, members i and j have the utilities shown in Table 4.1, with member k having the same utilities as member i.
>
> On roll calls 3 and 4, members j and k have the same utilities, respectively, as members i and j in Table 4.1, with member i having the same utilities as member i in Table 4.1.
>
> On roll calls 5 and 6, members i and k have the same utilities, respectively, as members i and j in Table 4.1, with member j having the same utilities as member j in Table 4.1.

Applying the reasoning given in section 4.6 for the trade between member pair (i, j) on roll calls (1, 2), member pairs (j, k) and (i, k) can also make individually rational vote trades on roll calls (3, 4) and (5, 6), respectively. [This is not the only possible set of trades—one might have member

---

33. What comes before a legislature may very well be a product of vote trades in committees, where typically support is exchanged among members on the provisions of a single bill, rather than on wholly different bills.

pair (i, j) trade on roll calls (5, 6), member pair (j, k) on roll calls (1, 2), and member pair (i, k) on roll calls (3, 4)—but all other complete sets of trades result in the paradox to be described subsequently.] The effect of member i's pairwise trade with member j will be to increase his total utility from -1 (see Table 4.2) to $+1$ (see Table 4.3), or by an increment of $+2$; similarly, member i's pairwise trade with member k will increase his total utility also by an increment of $+2$, giving member i a combined total utility gain of $+4$ after his two vote trades. Members j and k will likewise realize combined total utility gains of $+4$ from their two trades.

The difficulty with each of these three pairwise transactions, however, is that each carries external costs for the one nontrading member. As we saw from Table 4.4, member k's total utility is reduced from $+3$ to -3 by the trade of member pair (i, j) on roll calls (1, 2), giving him a total utility loss of -6. Similarly, members i and j also bear utility losses of -6 from the trade of member pair (j, k) on roll calls (3, 4) (on which member i is left out), and the trade of member pair (i, k) on roll calls (5, 6) (on which member j is left out). When the utility gains of $+4$ from trading on two pairs of roll calls for each member are added to the utility losses of -6 from being left out of trading on one pair of roll calls, one sees that each member suffers a net loss of -2 from all three trades!

What would each member have received had there been no trades at all? Without trading, each member would have suffered a loss of $2(-1) = -2$ on the two pairs of roll calls on which he had individually rational trades (see Table 4.2), but this loss would have been more than offset by the gain of $+3$ on the one pair of roll calls on which he did not trade (see Table 4.4), giving him a total utility of $+1$. If there were trading, on the other hand, each member would suffer a net loss of -2, as we have shown, which would reduce his total utility to -1. This is the *paradox of logrolling*: that rational trades by all members make everyone worse off by reducing each member's total utility (from $+1$ to -1 in our example).

It is not easy to extricate oneself from this situation. For example, it might be said that if members were foresighted, they would refuse to make trades at all, lest the trades lead to the realization of the paradox. Self-restraint is not so easy to achieve, however. Suppose each member makes no trade himself but anticipates a trade between the pair that does not include him. That is, he himself behaves with self-restraint; yet, with a conservative appreciation of what others can do to harm him, he anticipates the worst from them. His expectation will then be a loss of $2(-1) = -2$ on the two pairs of roll calls on which he did not trade, plus a loss of -3 on the pair of roll calls on which he was left out, giving him a total loss of -5.

This is worse than his loss of -1 if he trades; in fact, it is the worst thing that can happen to him. By contrast, his best outcome occurs when he consummates trades with the other two members—giving him a gain $2(+1) = +2$—and the pair of which he is not a member does not trade. By not suffering the external costs of being the left-out member, he thereby

TABLE 4.5 THE PARADOX OF VOTE TRADING AS A THREE-PERSON PRISONERS' DILEMMA[a]

	MEMBER i			
	TRADE		NOT TRADE	
MEMBER k	*Member* j		*Member* j	
	Trade	*Not trade*	*Trade*	*Not trade*
Trade	$(-1, -1, -1)$	$(5, -5, 5)$	$(-5, 5, 5)$	$(1, 1, 1)$
Not trade	$(5, 5, -5)$	$(1, 1, 1)$	$(1, 1, 1)$	$(1, 1, 1)$

[a] Payoffs refer to members (i, j, k), in this order.

realizes a gain of $+3$ on the two roll calls on which he does not trade, giving him a total gain of $+5$.

These results are summarized in Table 4.5. Clearly, each member's strategy of trading dominates his strategy of not trading, even though all members would be better off not trading. For whether the other two members trade or not, a member does at least as well, and sometimes better, by trading. This situation is clearly a natural extension of a two-person Prisoners' Dilemma to three persons, wherein the cooperative strategy is *not* to trade. Yet, each member has an incentive to "defect" by trading. If only one member defects, the cooperative solution $(1, 1, 1)$ is not upset since the defecting member will have nobody to trade with; if two members defect (say, i and j) and trade with each other, the outcome will be $(5, 5, -5)$, and they will make out handsomely; if all three members defect, however, all will have to suffer the noncooperative solution of $(-1, -1, -1)$.

Conceivably, the members might escape the paradox by agreeing to vote sincerely. But if any member suspects that the other two members may not abide by their agreements not to trade, then his best strategy is to trade himself. In this way, it is rational to trade not only to achieve one's best payoff of $+5$ (if the other pair of members does not trade) but also to avoid one's worst payoff of -5 (if the other pair of members does trade) by arriving at a modest loss of -1 (when all members trade). Trading is, therefore, the unconditionally best (i.e., dominant) strategy for members. Thus, with every member forced to trade in order to behave rationally, each may, perversely, come to a worse end than if he abstained from trades and always voted sincerely.

This paradoxical result is not an accidental consequence of the particular cardinal utility numbers used in our example nor of the particular choices of trades to be made. Rather, the paradox persists even if one uses ordinal utility and permits members to rank the roll calls from most to least salient only, without assigning particular cardinal utilities to each outcome.[34] Doubtless, other examples of the paradox can be worked out for legislatures of any size. Our three-member example, moreover, can be embedded in any legislature, and, of course, the three members can be three factions.

One possible way to avoid the paradox is for a pair to form a coalition whose members pledge to trade only with each other. Thereby they may obtain the benefits of trading and avoid the external costs of others' trades. Of course, this solution to the paradox simply denies that conditions (a), (b), and (c) (given in section 4.5), which define an individually rational trade, are operative for all members, but it is one way to cut the Gordian knot. It is comparable to cooperative solutions to Prisoners' Dilemma in which, with preplay communication allowed and the suspects able to make binding agreements, they agree never to confess and thereby thwart the prosecutor. In the absence of enforceable agreements, however, there may be instabilities in such solutions simply because they are not individually rational.[35]

This lack of a stable equilibrium is significant, for it shatters any hope one might harbor that a dominant collective preference can be ensured through vote trading.[36] Indeed, if trades are not considered irrevocable, members always have an incentive to break old trading agreements and make new ones to try to arrive at better outcomes than those given by the initial trades.[37] This fundamental disequilibrium in vote trading—

---

34. For an ordinal example, see Riker and Brams, "The Paradox of Vote Trading," pp. 1242–1244.

35. This example illustrates a possible conflict once again between individual and collective rationality (see section 2.2), though here the concept of collective rationality does not imply the absence of cyclical majorities. Rather, the positions of vote-trading members are collectively rational, or Pareto optimal, if there are no vote trades that would leave no voter worse off and at least one voter better off. Without an enforceable agreement that guarantees the sanctity of the collectively rational outcome $(1, 1, 1)$, every member is best advised to break the agreement. Particularly if each member assumes that every other member is individually rational, all members together may arrive at outcome $(-1, -1, -1)$, which is not collectively rational.

36. For the case in which the preferences of members for outcomes on roll calls can be expressed in terms of cardinal utilities, R. E. Park has shown that there is in general no stable equilibrium if there is a majority that can, through vote trading, improve the payoffs to all its members over those without vote trading. Furthermore, he has shown that if there is a stable equilibrium with vote trading, it must be exactly the same as the outcome without vote trading. See R. E. Park, "The Possibility of a Social Welfare Function: Comment," *American Economic Review*, 57 (December 1967), pp. 1301–1305. But see James S. Coleman, "The Possibility of a Social Welfare Function: Reply," *American Economic Review*, 57 (December 1967), pp. 1311–1317, who argues that Park's assumptions are unrealistically restrictive. For other "negative" results on vote trading, see John A. Ferejohn, "Sour Notes on the Theory of Vote Trading," California Institute of Technology Social Science Working Paper no. 41 (Pasadena, Calif., June 1974).

37. See Riker and Brams, "The Paradox of Vote Trading," pp. 1244–1246.

even in the absence of the paradox—is intimately tied to the fact that the conditions that lead to a paradox of voting also make vote trades possible.[38] In effect, the paradox of voting generates instabilities when voting occurs, whereas the instabilities associated with vote trading manifest themselves before a vote is taken. These instabilities not only preclude a dominant collective preference but, given an appropriate distribution of tastes and external costs, may also lead to a Prisoners' Dilemma-type situation whereby everyone suffers from being individually rational.

To be sure, the logic of metagame theory (see section 4.3) may enable members to extricate themselves from the paradox. In fact, the selection of the cooperative solution by players in some Prisoners' Dilemma games seems to provide prima facie evidence that on occasion players actually choose strategies on the basis of metastrategic calculations (another example of such calculations will be given in Chapter 5, and a probabilistic solution to Prisoners' Dilemma in Chapter 8). But these calculations, and the conditional strategies on which they are based, offer a less persuasive resolution to Prisoners' Dilemma-type situations in n-person games, wherein contingent calculations become far more complex, than in two-person games. As Russell Hardin has shown, this problem is equivalent to the problem of collective action in the theory of collective (or public) goods.[39] As applied to vote-trading situations, it means that every pair of members who can benefit from trading has no incentive to cooperate with other members whose positions they might adversely affect by trading. This makes it impossible for members of a voting body to reach a

---

38. See Peter Bernholz, "Logrolling, Arrow Paradox, and Cyclical Majorities," *Public Choice*, 15 (Summer 1973), pp. 87–95; Bernholz, "Logrolling, Arrow-Paradox and Decision Rules— A Generalization," *Kyklos*, 27 (Fasc. 1, 1974), pp. 41–62; Nicholas R. Miller, "Logrolling and the Arrow Paradox: A Note," *Public Choice*, 21 (Spring 1975), pp. 107–110; and the following exchange in the *American Political Science Review*, 69 (September 1975): David H. Koehler, "Vote Trading and the Voting Paradox: A Proof of Logical Equivalence," pp. 954–960; Bernholtz, "Logrolling and the Paradox of Voting: Are They Really Logically Equivalent? A Comment," pp. 961–962; Joe Oppenheimer, "Some Political Implications of 'Vote Trading and the Voting Paradox: a Proof of Logical Equivalence:' A Comment," pp. 963–966; Koehler, "Vote Trading and the Voting Paradox: Rejoinder," pp. 967–969. Furthermore, the paradox of vote trading is not dependent on the majority rule assumption, as shown in Eric M. Uslaner and J. Ronnie Davis, "The Paradox of Vote Trading: Effects of Decision Rules and Voting Strategies on Externalities," *American Political Science Review*, 69 (September 1975), pp. 929–942, wherein necessary and sufficient conditions for the occurrence of the paradox are also given. For a proposed solution to the paradox, see Gudmund Hernes, "The Paradox of Vote Trading and Markets for Externalities" (Paper delivered at the Annual Meeting of Public Choice Society, Chicago, April 3–5, 1975).

39. Russell Hardin, "Collective Action as an Agreeable n-Prisoners' Dilemma," *Behavioral Science*, 16 (September 1971), pp. 472–481. See also Henry Hamburger, "*N*-Person Prisoner's Dilemma," *Journal of Mathematical Sociology*, 3 (1973) pp. 27–48; and Norman Frohlich, Thomas Hunt, Joe Oppenheimer, and R. Harrison Wagner, "Individual Contributions for Collective Goods," *Journal of Conflict Resolution*, 19 (June 1975), pp. 310–329. A *collective good* is one that, when supplied to some members of a collectivity, cannot be withheld from other members of that collectivity. Thus, a vote trade that changes the majorities on two roll calls is a collective good (or bad, depending on one's preferences) to all members of the voting body.

collective agreement not to trade unless there are sanctions (e.g., group norms) that penalize such actions.[40]

4.8. EMPIRICAL EXAMPLES OF THE PARADOX OF VOTE TRADING

The popular distrust of logrolling probably stems from an intuitive, incomplete, but nonetheless sure comprehension of the vote-trading paradox, or at least of the external costs on which it is based. To make a judgment on the validity of this popular distrust requires, therefore, that one estimate the likelihood that the paradox arises in real legislatures. If it arises frequently, then surely the popular distrust has a reasonable basis. If it arises only rarely, however, then one probably ought to conclude that logrolling is a socially useful technique to approach collectively rational states of the world. Even though there seems no systematic way to investigate real-world frequencies of the paradox, one can specify types of circumstances in which it is likely to occur and then estimate the likelihood of these circumstances.

The crucial element of the paradox is external costs, which of course depend on the specific trade. It is always the case, however, that more people gain than lose on each switch, for the gainers (including the critical member who switches) necessarily constitute a majority of members. Consequently, in a system of trades—and usually for each participant as well—more instances of gain occur than do instances of loss. But gains and losses are not necessarily equal in magnitude, so the paradox occurs when, in a system of trades, members generally lose more when they lose than they gain when they gain. The question then is: under what real-world circumstances might these large losses be expected to occur?

Manifestly, if there is only one trade, the paradox is impossible because the gainers on this trade cannot suffer external costs on another, which does not exist. Consequently, if trades are occasional and isolated and not part of a system of interrelated bargains, losses are probably less than gains for many members of the legislature. This kind of sporadic logrolling is often found in American legislatures, where party discipline is not usually very strong, but it is not the kind so earnestly recommended by the several scholars cited earlier in this chapter (pages 93–94). Rather,

---

40. For an interesting example in which effective sanctions were not (and probably could not) be imposed, and the attempt to concert action therefore failed, see J. Ronnie Davis and Neil A. Palomba, "The National Farmers Organization and the Prisoner's Dilemma: A Game Theory Prediction of Failure," *Social Science Quarterly*, 50 (December 1969), pp. 742–748. For other examples and a general analysis of the "free-rider" problem in the theory of collective goods, see Mancur Olson, Jr., *The Logic of Collective Action: Public Goods and the Theory of Groups* (Cambridge, Mass.: Harvard University Press, 1965); Norman Frohlich, Joe A. Oppenheimer, and Oran R. Young, *Political Leadership and Collective Goods* (Princeton N.J.: Princeton University Press, 1971); and Jeffrey Richelson, "A Note on Collective Goods and the Theory of Political Entrepreneurship," *Public Choice*, 16 (Fall 1973), pp. 73–75.

the kind they recommend is that in which members engage in a constant round of bargaining in order to arrive at optimal outcomes over the whole set of issues in the legislative session. Unfortunately, it is exactly this kind of logrolling that probably increases the likelihood of the vote-trading paradox.

If one can separate out his reformist concerns, this is what Schatt-schneider seems to have perceived about the writing of the Smoot-Hawley tariff. Each member who joined the tariff combination for a price on some issue (usually a tariff on something manufactured in his district) gained an advantage for himself and his constituents. Such a large number joined, however, that protection was made indiscriminate—nearly everybody got something. Thereby, international trade was discouraged and disrupted—to the disadvantage of everybody in the society. To the extent that the Smoot-Hawley tariff deepened and extended the Great Depression in the 1930s, even the gainers probably suffered more than they gained.

One can see the same process at work in, for example, the rivers and harbors bills of the twentieth century when they ceased to have the character of vital internal improvements that they had had in the nineteenth century. A majority gains from the pork in such barrels, else the bills would not pass. But there are also losses, external costs. Once taxes are paid, the net gains of the gainers are probably pretty small. And if the projects are for the most part economically useless (e.g., locks on a canal that only a few pleasure boats use), then opportunity costs probably exceed the gainers' gains; if the projects are positively harmful (e.g., dikes on a river that would otherwise support wetlands and a higher water table), then their absolute losses almost certainly exceed the gainers' gains.

Still other possible cases come easily to mind. A long-term example is the system of income tax exemptions and deductions, which are so generally distributed that they actually provide savings for only an unidentifiable few and at the same time probably assess very high costs against nearly everybody in the form of distortions of the market for many goods. Another and even longer-term example is the proliferation of army bases throughout the country, each providing a small economic benefit to its neighborhood, but by their inefficiency considerably increasing in sum the military cost for everybody.

As these examples suggest, the bills and circumstances likely to occasion paradoxes are those that bring together an interrelated set of issues, many of which are of interest to only a few legislators. Tax bills, internal improvement bills, redistributions of income, to cite but a few cases, seem especially prone to providing the kind of situation in which the paradox can easily arise. Since these kinds of bills and business occupy a good part of any legislature's time, it must be concluded that the paradox of vote trading is a real fact of political life. One suspects that, because of it, logrolling leads more often away from, rather than toward, collectively rational social allocations.

With a bow in the direction of reformers, both those who recommend and those who excoriate logrolling, it might be asked whether or not occurrences of the paradox can be prevented. The answer is, probably not, short of highly unpalatable restrictions. Legislatures do occasionally adopt self-denying ordinances, like the so-called closed rule in the U.S. House of Representatives, a rule that prohibits amendments from the floor on which additional votes might be traded. Although this perhaps prevents the grosser and more thoughtless types of logrolling, the anticipation of it probably forces the trading back off the floor into committee. Given all the rational pressures for trading, it is not really to be expected that a policy of self-denial will work. Stronger measures, like a system of responsible and disciplined parties, may well make trading impossible in the legislature, but they certainly cannot prevent it in the executive branch or in the party caucus.

It seems, then, that so long as we have the open kind of legislature in which any pair of members can trade, trading cannot be eradicated. Although its distributive effects may be beneficial to some or all members, the instances of logrolling in Congress previously discussed suggest that this is frequently not the case. Speaking normatively, we would have to conclude that the paradoxical consequences of logrolling are unpalatable and one probably ought to try—by such devices as closed rules and popular condemnation—to discourage the kinds of logrolling that generate paradoxes.

4.9. SUMMARY AND CONCLUSION

We began this chapter by contrasting the views of different theorists on the origins of social conflict. Focusing on the structural conditions that make cooperation difficult to achieve, we showed that in the game of Prisoners' Dilemma it is (individually) rational for players not to co-operate, despite the fact that through cooperation all players can achieve the (collectively) rational outcome that results in higher payoffs for all. Since the strategies associated with this outcome are not in equilibrium, however, each player is tempted to "defect" to obtain an even greater payoff. We referred to this conflict between individual and collective rationality as the paradox of cooperation.

To transcend the self-defeating logic of individual rationality, the theory of metagames specifies the conditional strategies by means of of which players may arrive at the cooperative solution and, in addition, ensure its stability. In the case of Prisoners' Dilemma, each player must be ready to cooperate if he expects the other player also to cooperate, but he must be ready to exact retribution if he expects the other player to act recalcitrantly. In other words, the players must be both firm and forbearing—firm when their adversary is firm, forbearing when he is forbearing—and convey this image to him as well. This obviously requires that the players be able to communicate with each other, implicitly or explicitly, but not necessarily that they be parties to a binding and enforceable contract. What agreement or understanding they do reach, in effect, is rendered enforceable by the expectation that each player will be willing to abide by the terms of the unwritten contract and enforce it, if necessary, by defecting himself. This reduces the risks to the players of choosing their cooperative strategies.

More specifically, the metarational cooperative outcome for two players 1 and 2 was found by (1) expanding player 2's strategies into four metastrategies in anticipation of player 1's original strategies and (2) subsequently expanding player 1's original strategies into sixteen metastrategies in anticipation of player 2's four metastrategies. Given the possibility of communication between the players, this expansion offers a means for describing the sequential and dynamic buildup of players' expectations, which typically are formed from their words and actions in bargaining and negotiation processes.

Metagame theory prescribes what these expectations must be to lead to the cooperative solution. By introducing players' expectations about the environments in which they interact, it provides one approach to specifying more precisely the bargaining processes that lead to different outcomes in games like Prisoners' Dilemma (another problematic game will be described in Chapter 5).

Metagame theory offers a less compelling resolution to the paradox of cooperation when there are more than two players and the number of conditional strategies is consequently much greater. As an illustration of such a larger game, we discussed vote trading in legislatures, wherein members vote insincerely on less salient roll calls in exchange for support from other members on more salient roll calls. Because vote trading provides a means, albeit limited, for voters to register their intensities of preference across a set of issues when the voting procedure itself permits them to express only approval or disapproval for individual issues, its supporters have argued that it offers an escape from the paradox of voting, which characterizes all ordinal ranking procedures satisfying Arrow's conditions. We contrasted this view with that of an older (and more skeptical) school of thought that deplores vote trading—or logrolling, as it is popularly known—because of its presumed ill effects on the public good.

To try to clarify and resolve these different viewpoints, we developed a simple model of vote trading. We showed by way of an example that the external costs of vote trading can wipe out the private gains of members on pairwise trades and leave everyone worse off after the trades. We called this phenomenon the paradox of vote trading and showed it to be rooted in an n-person Prisoners' Dilemma in which the noncooperative strategy of trading dominates the cooperative strategy of not trading for all members. Thus, for at least some assignments of utilities to outcomes by members, there may be no stable equilibrium that is collectively rational. Moreover, because, as we indicated (but did not prove), a paradox of voting underlies vote-trading situations, vote trading does not violate the conditions assumed in the proof of Arrow's General Possibility Theorem (see section 2.3), which are all necessary for the occurrence of the paradox.

Certainly if one interprets vote trading as simply one way in which support develops around some issues and not others, its effect is no different in principle from that which occurs when provisions are added to and subtracted from bills that gain some supporters and lose others. In the end, of course, when members of a voting body must decide on whether they will vote for or against a bill, they cannot express their intensities of preference. In the absence of a mechanism that permits voters to register their intensities of preference in the actual voting process, their choices necessarily remain qualitative and the conditions of the General Possibility Theorem are not violated by vote trading.[41]

Several examples of issues in which interests are relatively private, and for which support can therefore more readily be exchanged, were suggested as those most likely to engender vote trading and, under certain conditions, the paradox. Devices that limit vote trading on such issues have in some cases been institutionalized (e.g., the closed rule in the U.S. House of Representatives), which may discourage rampant trading and its most deleterious effects. These restrictions, however, usually do not prevent vote trading entirely but simply push it back to more private settings (e.g., committees), where exchanges occur in a smaller market among fewer traders.

Our analysis in this chapter has shown that cooperation may not be easy to achieve in games like Prisoners' Dilemma in which the individually and collectively rational outcomes do not coincide. In the next chapter, we shall extend this analysis to other games that highlight further problems connected with the determination of rational choice.

---

41. Kenneth J. Arrow makes a similar argument in responding to critics in *Social Choice and Individual Values*, 2d ed. (New Haven, Conn.: Yale University Press, 1963), p. 109.

5
THE PARADOX OF INDUCEMENT

5.1. INTRODUCTION

In Chapter 1 we showed that if voters possess straightforward (dominant) strategies, they should always choose them because, by definition, they are unconditionally best. To be sure, these strategies offer no guarantee that one's best outcome will be chosen. In fact, if communication is allowed and coalitions can form in a cooperative game, one's very worst outcome may be chosen, as we illustrated in section 1.9.

Nevertheless, there is something compelling about a dominant strategy, especially in a noncooperative game in which players cannot communicate and everybody is therefore on his own, so to speak. Certainly the fact that the defection (D) strategy dominates the cooperative (C) strategy for both players in Prisoners' Dilemma (see section 4.2) makes it strategically appealing, despite the relatively low returns that accrue to the two players when both choose D. Moreover, even in repeated plays of Prisoners' Dilemma, the appeal of the DD strategies would seem to lose none of its logical force, as we showed in section 4.2.

Now the theory of metagames offered one way in which the DD trap might be circumvented if the players could communicate and alternately predict the conditional strategy choices of each other. Given that the players restrict their attention only to metastrategies that contain equilibria—since at least one player would have an incentive to depart from all outcomes associated with other metastrategies—we argued in section 4.3 that suspect 1 in Prisoners' Dilemma would prefer his tit-for-tat strategy, containing the cooperative equilibrium $(-1, -1)$, to his D regardless metastrategy containing the noncooperative equilibrium $(-5, -5)$. For similar reasons, suspect 2 would prefer one of his metastrategies ($D/C/C/D$ or $D/D/C/D$) containing the cooperative equilibrium; since $D/C/D/D$ dominates $D/C/C/D$, the former metastrategy, we suggested, would have greater appeal.

Yet, there are circumstances in which the metastrategies associated with a metagame equilibrium may not have the appeal that they do in Prisoners' Dilemma. As in Prisoners' Dilemma, a cooperative solution may be preferred to a noncooperative solution by the players, but there may be good reasons for rejecting it, even at the level of metagame-theoretic analysis. For despite the equilibrium properties of an outcome, or the fact that the strategy of a player associated with it is dominant, the anticipation of this strategy choice by other player(s) may motivate the first player to choose another (dominated) strategy that leads to a preferred outcome for himself. A *paradox of inducement* occurs when a player must choose an apparently irrational dominated strategy to avoid a less-preferred outcome that is induced by the anticipation that he will choose his dominant strategy.

Exactly what form such inducement may take will be illustrated by two examples, one real and one hypothetical. In the real example, we shall model the Cuban missile crisis as a two-person game and demonstrate, through a metagame-theoretic analysis, that if the dominant metastrategy of one player is anticipated, this leads to the very best outcome for the *other* player. To prevent this from happening, it would appear that the first player should *not* choose his dominant strategy. In the hypothetical example, which concerns the campaign strategies of candidates over a series of primaries in an *n*-person game, we shall show that the logic of cooperation may be contravened by the initially aggressive behavior of one candidate who tries to induce subsequent compliant responses on the part of the other candidates.

5.2. CHICKEN AND THE CUBAN MISSILE CRISIS

Next to Prisoners' Dilemma, the game of Chicken probably better captures the difficulties that two actors in politics face in reaching agreements than any other two-person game.[1] Like Prisoners' Dilemma, Chicken is a *nonzero-sum* game, because the payoffs to the players associated with each outcome do not necessarily sum to zero. One player can gain and the other player can lose different amounts, or both players can gain or lose at the same time. Although in two-person zero-sum games the players have no common interests—what one player wins must necessarily be what the other player loses—in two-person nonzero-sum games the players typically have both competitive and complementary interests. For this reason, such games are sometimes referred to as *mixed-motive* games.

Chicken takes its name from a rather gruesome sport that apparently originated in the 1930s and was later popularized by a film about California

---

1. For a classification of the seventy-eight distinct two-person games in which each player has two strategies, see Anatol Rapoport and Melvin Guyer, "A Taxonomy of 2 × 2 Games," *General Systems: Yearbook of the Society for General Systems Research*, 11 (1966), pp. 203–214; and Melvin Guyer and Henry Hamburger, "A Note on 'A Taxonomy of 2 × 2 Games,'" *General Systems: Yearbook of the Society for General Systems Research*, 13 (1968), pp. 205–208. A different taxonomy of 2 × 2 games, based on their vulnerability to deception, is developed in Steven J. Brams, "Deception in 2 × 2 Games," forthcoming. The material that follows in this section is adapted from Steven J. Brams, *Game Theory and Politics* (New York: Free Press, 1975), chap. 1.

FIGURE 5.1   CHICKEN

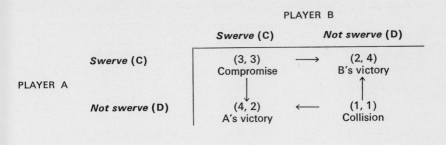

PLAYER B

		Swerve (C)	Not swerve (D)
PLAYER A	Swerve (C)	(3, 3) Compromise ⟶	(2, 4) B's victory
	Not swerve (D)	(4, 2) A's victory ⟵	(1, 1) Collision

teenagers in the 1950s, *Rebel without a Cause*. As two teenage drivers approach each other at high speed on a narrow road, each has the choice of swerving and avoiding a head-on collision, or continuing on the collision course. As shown in the payoff matrix of Figure 5.1, there are four possible outcomes:

1. The player who does not swerve when the other does gets the highest payoff of 4 for his courage (or recklessness).

2. The player who "chickens out" by swerving when the other does not is disgraced and receives a payoff of 2.

3. If both players lack the will to continue on the collision course to the bitter end, they both suffer some loss of prestige, obtaining payoffs of 3, but not as much as if only one player had played it safe by swerving.

4. If both players refuse to compromise, then they hurtle to their mutual destruction, which may be fine for martyrs but not for the players in this game, who (posthumously) receive the lowest payoffs of 1 each.

As with Prisoners' Dilemma, Chicken is defined by the ranking of outcomes, not the actual numerical payoffs that we use for convenience in Figure 5.1.[2]

This game bears some resemblance to Prisoners' Dilemma, except that the worst outcome for both players in Chicken occurs when both players "defect" from cooperating. This is the next-worst outcome for both players in Prisoners' Dilemma; the worst is incurred by the player who defects (*D*) when his opponent cooperates (*C*). Unlike the situation in Prisoners' Dilemma, two outcomes—not one—are in equilibrium, *CD* and *DC*. Like Prisoners' Dilemma, both players, by choosing *C*, can do better than *DD*, but the *CC* outcome is unstable since, given the choice of

---

2. The ranking of outcomes in Chicken simply reverses the payoffs we have used: "4" is the best outcome, "3" next best, and so on.

the C strategy by one player, the other player has an incentive to choose his D strategy, as indicated by the arrows in Figure 5.1.[3]

Chicken serves as a good analogue for some situations in international politics wherein threats to use military force figure prominently in bargaining strategies among nations.[4] Perhaps the most potentially devastating confrontation between major powers ever to occur was that between the United States and the Soviet Union in October 1962. This confrontation, in what has come to be known as the Cuban missile crisis, was precipitated by Soviet installation in Cuba of medium-range and intermediate-range nuclear-armed ballistic missiles capable of hitting a large portion of the United States.

The goal of the United States was to obtain immediate removal of the Russian missiles, and United States policy makers seriously considered two alternative courses of action to achieve this end:

1. A naval blockade (B), or "quarantine" as it was euphemistically called, to prevent shipment of further missiles, followed by possibly stronger action to induce the Soviet Union to withdraw those already installed.

2. A "surgical" air strike (A) to wipe out the missiles already installed, insofar as possible, followed possibly by an invasion of the island.

The less provocative blockade option was eventually chosen, which left open to Soviet leaders essentially two alternatives:

1. Withdrawal (W) of their missiles.

2. Maintenance (M) of their missiles.

These alternative courses of action for both players are shown in Figure 5.2; the probable outcomes for each pair of strategy choices by both players are also indicated.

Needless to say, the strategy choices and probable outcomes as presented in Figure 5.2 provide only a skeletal picture of the crisis as it developed over a period of thirteen days. Both sides considered more than the two alternatives we have listed, and several variations on each. The Russians, for example, demanded withdrawal of American missiles from Turkey as a quid pro quo for withdrawal of their missiles from Cuba, a demand ignored by the United States. Furthermore, there is no way to verify that the outcomes given in Figure 5.2 were "probable," or valued in a manner consistent with the game of Chicken. For example, if the

---

3. Karl W. Deutsch labels *CC* the "rational solution," but it is certainly not so in a game-theoretic sense because of its instability. See Deutsch, *The Analysis of International Relations* (Englewood Cliffs, N.J.: Prentice-Hall, 1968), p. 120.

4. Many examples of the use of military power as a bargaining tool can be found in Thomas C. Schelling, *Arms and Influence* (New Haven, Conn.: Yale University Press, 1966).

FIGURE 5.2   PAYOFF MATRIX OF CUBAN MISSILE CRISIS

SOVIET UNION

		Withdrawal (W)	*Maintenance* (M)
UNITED STATES	*Blockade* (B)	(3, 3) Compromise	(2, 4) Soviet victory, U.S. defeat
	Air strike (A)	(4, 2) U.S. victory, Soviet defeat	(1, 1) Nuclear war

Soviet Union had viewed an air strike on their missiles as jeopardizing their vital national interests, the AW outcome may very well have ended in nuclear war between the two sides, giving it the same value as AM. Still another simplification relates to the assumption that the players chose their actions simultaneously, when in fact a continuous exchange in both words and deeds occurred over those fateful days in October.

Nevertheless, the basic conception most observers have of this crisis is that the two superpowers were on a "collision course," which is actually the title of one book recounting this nuclear confrontation.[5] Most observers also agree that neither side was eager to take any irreversible step, such as the teenage driver in a game of Chicken might do by defiantly ripping off his steering wheel in full view of his adversary, thereby foreclosing his alternative of swerving. Although in one sense the United States "won" by getting the Russians to withdraw their missiles, Khrushchev at the same time extracted from Kennedy a promise not to invade Cuba, which seems to indicate that the eventual outcome was a compromise solution of sorts. Moreover, even though the Russians responded to the blockade and did not make their choice of a strategy independently of the American strategy choice, the fact that the United States held out the possibility of escalating the conflict to at least an air strike would seem to indicate that the initial blockade decision was not considered final—that is, the United States considered its strategy choices still open after imposing the blockade.

5. Henry M. Pachter, *Collision Course: The Cuban Missile Crisis and Coexistence* (New York: Frederick A. Praeger, 1963). Other books on this crisis include Elie Abel, *The Missile Crisis* (Philadelphia: J. B. Lippincott Co., 1966); Graham T. Allison, *Essence of Decision: Explaining the Cuban Missile Crisis* (Boston: Little, Brown and Co., 1971); Robert F. Kennedy, *Thirteen Days: A Memoir of the Cuban Missile Crisis* (New York: W. W. Norton & Co., 1969); *The Cuban Missile Crisis*, ed. Robert A. Divine (Chicago: Quadrangle Books, 1971); and Abram Chayes, *The Cuban Missile Crisis: International Crises and the Role of Law* (New York: Oxford University Press, 1974).

FIGURE 5.3 PARTIAL METAGAME PAYOFF MATRIX OF CUBAN MISSILE CRISIS

		SOVIET UNION			
		W Regard-less	**M** Regard-less	*Tit-for-tat*	*Tat-for-tit*
	B/B/B/B	(3, 3)	((2, 4))	(3, 3)	(2, 4)
UNITED STATES	A/B/B/A	(4, 2)	((2, 4))	(3, 3)	(4, 2)
	A/A/B/A	(4, 2)	(1, 1)	((3, 3))	(4, 2)
	A/A/A/A	((4, 2))	(1, 1)	(1, 1)	((4, 2))

What can the theory of metagames tell us about how a cooperative solution was achieved in this crisis, despite the instability of this outcome in the game of Chicken? One's first response might be that there is nothing paradoxical about the compromise reached because this crisis was not really a noncooperative game. There was extensive formal and informal communication between the two sides during the crisis, it might be argued, which explains how the two adversaries were able to arrive at the cooperative outcome even though a binding and enforceable agreement was never concluded.

The assertion that open lines of communication, and particularly the "hot line" between Washington, D.C. and Moscow, attenuated the crisis seems certainly true, but this is not a very complete or satisfying explanation. To be so, an explanation should indicate at least what the general nature of the communication must have been to assure each side that it could trust the other. Otherwise, simply "talking," letting the conflict cool down, would always put an end to such crises, which is patently not the case.

If we expand the game of Chicken in the same manner as we did Prisoners' Dilemma in Chapter 4, we can derive a 16 × 4 payoff matrix that gives the metagame representation for Chicken. We have not illustrated in Figure 5.3 all sixteen metastrategies of the United States, but four that contain equilibria (equilibria associated with other strategies are simply repetitions of the five shown in Figure 5.3). As we showed in section 4.3 for Prisoners' Dilemma, neither player has an incentive unilaterally to depart from these equilibria, which would presumably be the basis for any solution viewed as stable by both sides. It will be observed that four of the five equilibria, which are circled, end in victories for the United States or the Soviet Union; only the outcome at the intersection of United States metastrategy $A/A/B/A$ and the Russian metastrategy tit-for-tat results in the compromise outcome (3, 3).

In analyzing the Cuban missile crisis, Nigel Howard, whose representation of the players' strategies and metastrategies differs somewhat from ours, draws three conclusions:[6]

1. *For the compromise outcome (3, 3) to be stable, both sides must be willing to risk nuclear war.* This is surely the meaning of the Russian metastrategy of tit-for-tat. Since the only American response to this choice that results in a cooperative equilibrium outcome is $A/A/B/A$, which stipulates American cooperation (blockade) only if the Russians choose tit-for-tat, the American metastrategy $A/A/B/A$ can also be viewed as a tit-for-tat policy, though one step removed (i.e., conditional on the Russian selection of tit-for-tat).

2. *If one side but not the other is willing to risk nuclear war, that side wins.* For example, if the Russians choose metastrategy M regardless, the only American metastrategies that result in equilibrium outcomes, $B/B/B/B$ and $A/B/B/A$, are those that involve the American response of B, which produce Soviet victories.

3. *If neither side is willing to risk nuclear war, no stable outcome is possible.* For example, if the Russians choose metastrategy W regardless, and the American response is $B/B/B/B$, the outcome is compromise, (3, 3), but it is not in equilibrium: the Russians could do better by unilaterally switching to M regardless, the Americans, by unilaterally switching to $A/A/A/A$.

Thus, it would appear that a policy of deterrence, by which each side promises retaliation for any untoward acts by the other side, is not only desirable from the viewpoint of both players but stable as well. This analysis suggests that if we live in an age of "balance of terror," the only way to ensure the maintenance of this balance is through the pursuit of retaliatory policies by both sides.

Superficially, this conclusion would seem to contradict the fact that the compromise outcome in the original game occurred when neither side was willing to risk nuclear war. It will be recalled, however, that this compromise outcome was unstable, as are all but one of these outcomes in the metagame shown in Figure 5.3. The stable compromise outcome in the metagame occurs when each side refuses to give in unless the other side also does—it is better to incur nuclear war than be blackmailed. On the other hand, if one player thinks his opponent is really not bluffing, but means business, then the analysis recommends (when interpreted normatively) that he respond by giving in—approach the brink but not overstep it, as implied in the strategy of "brinkmanship"—rather than by provoking his opponent into a situation that terminates in a collective suicide pact.

6. Nigel Howard, *Paradoxes of Rationality: Theory of Metagames and Political Behavior* (Cambridge, Mass.: MIT Press, 1971), p. 184.

In sum, what the theory of metagames reveals is the effect on the outcome of players' expectations—and sometimes knowledge, as sequential moves in the game occur—about an opponent's strategy choices. This effect may be considerable and salutory, changing a desirable but unstable outcome into a stable one from which the players will not be motivated to depart. Typically, these expectations are inferred from, and perceived through, a variety of communication channels, which means that the road to the cooperative solution in Chicken—as well as Prisoners' Dilemma—must be paved with more than the good intentions of one side. If anything, good intentions alone will probably ruin any possibility of a stable peace.

Metagame theory specifies rather precisely, if indirectly, the *content* of the communications, and the *nature* of the bargaining, necessary to reach compromise.[7] At least in the two games that we have used metagame theory to analyze—Prisoners' Dilemma and Chicken—the players must convey tough (but not totally inflexible) images that indicate their readiness to cooperate but, if necessary, also to apply sanctions. A content analysis of the messages exchanged between the United States and the Soviet Union tends to support the proposition that both sides held similar perceptions of the threatening and conciliatory actions of each other during the Cuban missile crisis,[8] which is perhaps at least a partial explanation of why we are still around to tell about this momentous confrontation.

The fact that both sides went to great lengths to clarify their positions of what would be acceptable to resolve the crisis indicates that the communication of intentions—relating to both concessions and threats—played a prominent role in the final settlement. These exchanges enabled each side to estimate more accurately the probable reactions of the other side to the range of alternative actions that they considered taking, which underscores the relevance of metagame analysis elucidating the conditional choices through which the expectations of players are tied to outcomes. As Theodore Sorenson described American deliberations, "We discussed what the Soviet reaction would be to any possible move by the

---

7. In this regard it offers a more "dynamic" picture of the *processes* that lead to various outcomes than does classical game theory, which also does not offer any way of unifying cooperative and noncooperative solution concepts within a single framework. For other attempts to transcend the limitations of the original theory to include a theory of bargaining (and arbitration), see R. Duncan Luce and Howard Raiffa, *Games and Decisions: Introduction and Critical Survey* (New York: John Wiley & Sons, 1957), pp. 119–152; Robert L. Bishop, "Game-Theoretic Analysis of Bargaining," *Quarterly Journal of Economics*, 77 (November 1963), pp. 559–602; and Morton D. Davis, *Game Theory: A Nontechnical Introduction* (New York: Basic Books, 1970), pp. 77–107, 139–172. More generally, see Martin Shubik, *Games for Society, Business and War: Towards a Theory of Gaming* (Amsterdam: Elsevier Scientific Publishing Co., 1975).

8. Ole R. Holsti, Richard A. Brody, and Robert C. North, "Measuring Affect and Action in International Reaction Models: Empirical Materials from the 1962 Cuban Crisis," *Journal of Peace Research*, 1 (1964), pp. 170–189.

United States, what our reaction with them would have to be to that Soviet reaction, and so on, trying to follow each of those roads to their ultimate conclusion."[9]

5.3. THE INDUCEMENT PARADOX IN THE CUBAN MISSILE CRISIS

Based on the interlocking expectations of the two sides, metagame analysis would appear to explain quite well how a compromise solution was reached in the Cuban missile crisis: each side's tit-for-tat expectations about what the other's behavior would be became sufficiently reassuring after a series of exploratory moves that a settlement satisfactory to both sides could in the end be reached. Testifying to the durability of this outcome is its stability for more than a decade, which—in the absence of a binding and enforceable agreement—lends support to the proposition that it is the product of metastrategy, not strategy, choices.

What happens, however, when communication and bargaining processes do not lead to reinforcing expectations? If a player is truly in the dark about his opponent's intentions, then what Howard calls the "sure-thing" metastrategy would seem best.[10] This choice, which for the United States is metastrategy $A/B/B/A$ (second row in Figure 5.3), is at least as good as, and in at least one contingency better than, any other metastrategy for the United States. Since a sure-thing (meta)strategy dominates all other (meta)strategies of a player, it is a dominant choice.

This metastrategy also maximizes the security level of the United States—the worst outcome that can occur from its choice of a metastrategy—by ensuring that the outcome (1, 1) will not be chosen. Metastrategy $B/B/B/B$ also insures against the selection of outcome (1, 1), but it is dominated by $A/B/B/A$: if the Russians choose W regardless or tat-for-tit, $A/B/B/A$ leads to a better outcome for the United States and therefore is preferred. Yet, should the Russians anticipate the choice of $A/B/B/A$ on the part of the United States, this anticipation has the unfortunate effect (for the United States) of inducing them (the Russians) to choose M regardless and thereby consummate a Soviet victory [outcome (2, 4) in the second row of Figure 5.3].

In general, such inducement is possible when (1) one player has a sure-thing, or dominant, (meta)strategy and (2) the best equilibrium for one player is not the best for the other. This is not the case in the original Prisoners' Dilemma game (Figure 4.1): both players have dominant strategies, so there is no need for either player to take account of the other's strategy choice. Similarly, in the metagame of Prisoners' Dilemma

---

9. Quoted in Holsti, Brody, and North, "Measuring Affect and Action in International Reaction Models," p. 188.

10. Howard, *Paradoxes of Rationality*, p. 27.

(Figure 4.4), though suspect 1 has a dominant metastrategy $(D/D/C/D)$, his best equilibrium $[(-1, -1)]$ is also best for suspect 2, whose metastrategy tit-for-tat is associated with it.

A problem arises, however, when one player can make an independent "best" choice which the other player can exploit. This will occur when one player has a sure-thing (meta)strategy, as is $A/B/B/A$ for the United States in the Cuban missile crisis (see Figure 5.3). Since this metastrategy leads to an outcome for the United States as good as or better than any other metastrategy—whatever metastrategy the Soviet Union chooses—the normal game-theoretic prescription would be that the United States should adopt it.

But following this prescription, Howard argues, is to be a "sucker" who capitulates entirely to the other side.[11] For if the Russians believe that the United States will adopt its (presumably rational) sure-thing metastrategy $A/B/B/A$, then they can ensure their very best outcome, (2, 4), by adopting M regardless.

This apparent breakdown in rationality is not confined to the game of Chicken. Howard proves that it characterizes all two-person nonzero-sum games in which there is conflict between equilibrium outcomes, one being favored by one player and the other by the other player [(2, 4) and (4, 2) in Chicken]. In the metagames of all such games, one player has a sure-thing strategy that induces the best possible equilibrium outcome for the *other* player.[12]

Howard is harsh in his condemnation of the "sure-thing" rational player, particularly in foreign affairs: "He is really proposing a policy of complete appeasement, which would make his country a doormat for others in any international conflict." It is precisely for this reason that

"idealism," "unselfishness," "honor," "loyalty," and so forth, should appear as elements in a country's foreign policy: by appealing to such unselfish motives, a country can more effectively bluff and bully others into capitulation —or, to put it another way, can more effectively resist the temptation to capitulate in the face of others' bluffs.[13]

This is an interesting argument, but it is not at all clear that an avoidance of sure-thing strategies will enable a country "more effectively [to] bluff and bully others." On the contrary, pursuing a sure-thing strategy, but getting an opponent to believe otherwise, would be not only a safer strategy but would also permit one to escape from the paradox of inducement through deception rather than by forsaking a "sure thing." This, of course, leaves open the question of how one successfully deceives

11. Howard, *Paradoxes of Rationality*, p. 181.
12. Howard, *Paradoxes of Rationality*, Theorem 9, pp. 180–181.
13. Howard, *Paradoxes of Rationality*, p. 181.

an opponent. But, as Howard recognizes, deception—successful or not—is not precluded by the rules of a game, which do not require that the truth be told or believed.[14]

In the absence of a rational theory of deception to complement Howard's "inducement theory," there seems little basis for ruling out any particular strategy choice, real or deceptive.[15] This seems especially true in games of incomplete information (see section 7.4 for examples), in which strategy and metastrategy choices are obviously vulnerable to manipulation.

Even in games of complete information, it is probably premature to condemn (meta)strategy choices that not only maximize one's security level but also dominate all others. If these choices induce inferior outcomes, and are therefore to be avoided, could not this avoidance itself be anticipated and a still less acceptable outcome—perhaps for both players—be the result?

This point is made forcefully by John C. Harsanyi in a sharp exchange with Howard over Harsanyi's book review of *Paradoxes of Rationality*.[16] Harsanyi admits to a mathematical error he made in criticizing Howard's theorem relating sure-thing strategies to the other player's best outcome, but he contends that this mistake does not rescue Howard's inducement theory.[17]

To support this contention, Harsanyi considers the game shown in Figure 5.4. Noting that the game has two equilibria, (A, X) and (B, Y)—the former more favorable to player 1, and the latter to player 2—he points out that Howard's theory would prescribe that player 1 should *not* adopt his sure-thing strategy, B. For if he did, player 1 would in effect be accepting the equilibrium outcome less favorable to him $[(B, Y)]$ as the outcome of the game. Harsanyi then describes his own point of view:

. . . in my own view, the only rational course open to Player 1 is exactly to accept (B, Y) as the outcome. This is so because in this game *one* of the two players *must* make a concession: *either* Player 1 must accept the payoff vector (2, 1) *or* Player 2 must accept the payoff vector (1, 2)—if they are to avoid (0, 0), which would be

14. Howard, *Paradoxes of Rationality*, p. 100.

15. The results of current research on deceptive strategies will be reported in Steven J. Brams, *Theory of Political Deception*, forthcoming. Examples of deceptive strategies in three-person—three-alternative voting games are described in Chapter 7.

16. John C. Harsanyi, review of Howard, *Paradoxes of Rationality*, in *American Political Science Review*, 67 (June 1973), pp. 599–600.

17. For the full exchange, see N. Howard, "Comment on a Mathematical Error by Harsanyi," *International Journal of Game Theory* 2 (1973), pp. 251–252; Howard's comment and Harsanyi's rejoinder in "Communications." *American Political Science Review*, 68 (June 1974), pp. 729–731; and, finally, the rebuttal and counter-rebuttal by Howard and Harsanyi in "Communications," *American Political Science Review*, 68 (December 1974), pp. 1692–1695.

FIGURE 5.4   HARSANYI'S EXAMPLE

PLAYER 2

		X	Y
PLAYER 1	A	(2, 1)	(0, 0)
	B	(2, 1)	(1, 2)

---

worse than either, and which in any case would not represent an equilibrium situation. But Player 1 is in a *much weaker* bargaining position than Player 2 is; therefore there is nothing unreasonable in suggesting that *he* has to make the concession.[18]

To show up the weakness of player 1's bargaining position, Harsanyi calculates the *expected payoff* of each of player 1's two strategies, which is the sum of his payoffs associated with the outcomes in each row times the probability that they will occur. If p is the probability that player 2 chooses strategy X, and $(1 - p)$ the probability that he chooses strategy Y, then player 1's expected payoff from the choice of strategy A is

$$E(A) = 2p + 0(1 - p) = 2p,$$

and his expected payoff from the choice of strategy B is

$$E(B) = 2p + 1(1 - p) = p + 1.$$

Subtracting,

$$E(B) - E(A) = p + 1 - 2p = 1 - p,$$

we see that strategy B always yields a higher expected payoff than strategy A except when $p = 1$ (and the expected payoffs are equal). By this calculation, only if player 1 suspects player 2 will *never* adopt strategy Y should he consider choosing strategy A.

From the perspective of player 2, if q is the probability that player 1 chooses strategy A, and $(1 - q)$ is the probability that he chooses strategy B, then player 2's expected payoff from the choice of strategy X is

$$E(X) = 1q + 1(1 - q) = 1,$$

and his expected payoff from the choice of strategy Y is

$$E(Y) = 0q + 2(1 - q) = 2 - 2q.$$

Subtracting,

$$E(Y) - E(X) = 2 - 2q - 1 = 1 - 2q,$$

we see that strategy Y yields a higher expected payoff whenever $q < \frac{1}{2}$. Thus, player 2 should choose strategy Y "even if he thinks there is a

---

18. Harsanyi, in "Communications" (June 1974), p. 731; italics in original.

substantial positive probability q that player 1 will use A (viz. so long as q is not larger than one half)."[19]

What outcome is suggested by these calculations? Given that player 1 can *never* obtain a greater expected payoff by choosing strategy A, it is reasonable to suppose that he will always choose strategy B [with probability $(1 - q) = 1$]. But this implies $q = 0$, which in turn implies that player 2 should choose strategy Y. Together, these choices result in the selection of the equilibrium outcome (1, 2).

To be sure, this outcome is less favorable to player 1 than equilibrium outcome (2, 1), but it would seem foolish for him to choose strategy A and risk the possibility that outcome (0, 0) will be selected. Of course, were player 2 absolutely assured that player 1 would choose his sure-thing strategy B, player 2 could choose strategy Y with impunity and obtain his very best outcome. In competitive political situations, however, absolute assurances are hard to come by; yet, to the extent that they are associated with sure-thing strategies, player 1's deviation from this choice would be harmful (to both players) had this choice been anticipated by player 2 and had he therefore chosen strategy Y. For this reason, Harsanyi's argument that player 1 "play it safe" (i.e., choose strategy B) is persuasive.

On the other hand, given the validity of our metagame analysis of the Cuban missile crisis, the United States did *not* choose its sure-thing metastrategy $A/B/B/A$, for this metastrategy does not contain the co-operative equilibrium (3, 3), which we argued in section 5.2 was the outcome of this game. If the metagame representation is accurate, the United States could have chosen what Howard calls its "retaliatory" metastrategy, $A/A/B/A$, only—because this metastrategy alone leads to the cooperative equilibrium. Thus, it would seem that this crisis was settled by a mutual respect for a tit-for-tat kind of thinking by both sides, as we suggested in out earlier analysis.

Whether the metastrategies chosen in the Cuban missile crisis were dictated by an awareness of the inducement paradox, which rewards victory to the player without the sure-thing metastrategy when the player who has it chooses it, is not clear. What does seem clear from the evidence presented earlier is that both sides engaged in metastrategic calculations. But these calculations—in and of themselves—are insufficient in a game like Chicken to explain which one of the equilibrium outcomes is likely to be chosen. To explain why a particular choice was made, we must try to correlate the metastrategies with the nature and content of the communication between the players, as we attempted to do in the case of the Cuban missile crisis.

In summary, we have outlined Howard's argument, using the Cuban missile crisis as a real-life example, that inducement considerations may— quite unexpectedly—steer players away from sure-thing strategies and metastrategies. We have also presented Harsanyi's counterargument,

---

19. Harsanyi, in "Communications" (June 1974), p. 731.

using a hypothetical example, that players neglect their sure-thing strategies at their own peril. Both these arguments apply at the level of games and metagames, but only the metagame representation of Chicken— as well as of Prisoners' Dilemma—admits the possibility that the "compromise" outcome is stable (i.e., in equilibrium).

Although neither Howard's nor Harsanyi's argument seems conclusive at this stage, it would appear that the inducement paradox is more real the more players *believe* they possess complete information about each other's preferences (or expectations). For then they will be more willing to predict the (meta)strategy choices of each other rather than simply choose sure-thing strategies (if they possess them).

But a willingness to predict makes one more vulnerable to deception. Information (or misinformation) that encourages predictions, therefore, also facilitates one player's taking deliberate actions that cause the other player to react in such a way as to lead to a preferred outcome for himself (first player), which is the essence of inducement.

If, however, the players believe they can glean little from each other's statements or behavior, or doubt the veracity of the information they do obtain, then they will be less willing to predict each other's behavior and—as a consequence of this greater uncertainty—less subject to being influenced in a particular direction. In this case, therefore, the sure-thing strategy would seem more advisable, though this conclusion itself might be anticipated and exploited.

To try to clarify the inducement question further, we shall next consider a hypothetical *n*-person game that can be used to model a sequential series of election campaigns. Because this game is rather complicated, we shall make no attempt to develop its metagame representation.

5.4. THE SEQUENTIAL-PRIMARY GAME[20]

The hurdle all serious presidential aspirants face in the United States is to gain the nomination of one of the two major political parties. At least in recent times, this has usually necessitated that an aspirant enter a series of state primary elections to establish his popular appeal among party voters in different states. If successful, he usually has a better chance of winning his party's nomination at its national convention.[21]

---

20. The game described in this section is based largely on Reinhard Selten, "The Chain Store Paradox," Institute of Mathematical Economics, University of Bielefeld, Working Paper no. 18 (Bielefeld, West Germany, July 1974). My adaptation of Selten's ingenious example from a business to a political context retains the game's essential features, but my analysis of its paradoxical aspects in section 5.5 differs from Selten's.

21. There are exceptions. Estes Kefauver racked up a string of victories in Democratic primaries in 1952 but lost the nomination to Adlai Stevenson. Since 1952, however, no presidential candidate of either major party, unless he were an incumbent president or vice-president, has won his party's nomination without entering and winning in the primaries first.

Sometimes a person will enter a state primary with no serious hope or intention of capturing his party's presidential nomination. Instead, his purpose is to deny a state's convention votes to a major candidate—at least on the first ballot of the convention—or slow down or stop a developing bandwagon that has the potential to sweep the major candidate on to subsequent primary victories and the convention nomination (see section 3.8 for a discussion of bandwagon and underdog effects).

The person most frequently cast into the "spoiler" role is a prominent state politician, often the governor, who runs as a so-called favorite son in his state. Whether his purpose in running is to deny his party's presidential nomination to a particular candidate or—as is often claimed—to maximize his state's later influence in the party convention, he does this by withholding, at the early stages of the convention proceedings, his state's convention votes from all of the major candidates at the party convention. After observing how support develops for the various candidates and assessing their prospects for eventually winning the presidential nomination, he is in a better position to throw his support to one candidate at a crucial stage and thereby augment his importance in the decision-making process (and perhaps maximize his own later rewards).[22]

The game we envision is one in which there is a single major party candidate who announces his intention to enter all the state primaries. We may imagine that his vote-getting power has not been well established in different parts of the country (perhaps because of his religion or race), and his primary campaigns are designed to demonstrate his nationwide appeal. This was John Kennedy's strategy in his 1960 presidential bid; his Catholicism was the big unknown that he wanted to prove would not impede his chances of winning, if he were nominated by his party, the general election.

We assume that the only opposition the leading candidate, whom we designate player A, faces is from favorite sons possibly running against him in each of the state primaries. Concretely, assume that there are 20 primaries, numbered from 1 to 20, each occurring on a different day.[23] Designate the potential favorite sons in each primary as players k, $k = 1, 2, \ldots, 20$, where player 1 is the potential favorite son in the first primary to occur, player 2 is the potential favorite son in the second primary to occur, and so forth. There are thus 21 players in this game, the leading candidate A and the 20 potential favorite sons.

22. For a mathematical model of this process, see Steven J. Brams and José E. Garriga-Picó, "Bandwagons in Coalition Formation: The 2/3's Rule," *American Behavioral Scientist*, 18 (March–April 1975), pp. 472–496.

23. Twenty-three of the fifty states held primaries in the 1972 presidential election, but not all fell on different days (the maximum was four primaries on one day). For the names of the primary states and the dates of their primaries, see Nelson W. Polsby and Aaron B. Wildavsky, *Presidential Elections: Strategies of American Politics*, 3rd ed. (New York: Charles Scribner's Sons, 1971), Appendix A, p. 317.

FIGURE 5.5 DECISION TREE IN ONE PRIMARY ELECTION

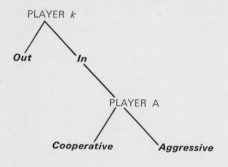

The game proceeds as follows. After candidate A announces his intention to enter all 20 primaries, each of the 20 potential favorite sons in each state faces the following decision: to run against candidate A in his state (*in*) or not to run (*out*). (This is why we refer to favorite sons as "potential.") Each of the potential favorite sons, however, does not make his decision until his state primary comes up in the sequence of primaries. In particular, except for player 1, each player k awaits the results of the races (if any) in the $k - 1$ primaries preceding his.

Player A faces the following decisions. If player k does not run in his state (out), player A runs unopposed. In this case, player A does not have to choose a campaign strategy. If player k does contest his primary (in), player A must choose between two campaign strategies: *cooperative* or *aggressive*. He faces this choice in the case of each player k who decides to run in his state. In Figure 5.5 we have summarized in a *decision* (or *game*) *tree* the sequence of choices that all players k, and player A, make in every primary election (read from top to bottom).

Now we must specify the payoffs associated with these strategy choices. Recall that the game runs over all 20 primaries in a definite sequence, but we shall not try to specify the payoffs to all players after each primary. Instead, we have indicated in the payoff matrix in Figure 5.6 the payoffs to player A and player k, associated with each of their strategy choices, *as if* the game were played between two players in only one primary. Naturally, new players will enter the game over the sequence of 20 primaries. And, depending on the outcomes of the previous primaries, the payoffs to player A will accumulate, changing his possible outcomes after each primary in the ongoing game. But more on this later.

The consequences of the strategy choices of players A and k in each primary can be summarized as follows:

1. If player k does not enter his primary, he receives a payoff of 1.

FIGURE 5.6   PAYOFFS TO THE TWO PLAYERS IN ONE PRIMARY ELECTION

		PLAYER A	
		Cooperative	*Aggressive*
PLAYER k	*In*	(2, 2)	(0, 0)
	Out	(1, 5)	(1, 5)

2. If player k does enter his primary, he does better than had he not entered if player A is cooperative (payoff of 2), worse if player is aggressive (payoff of 0).

3. Player A does best when player k does not enter his primary (payoff of 5), less well if he is cooperative when player k enters (payoff of 2), and worst if he is aggressive when player k enters (payoff of 0).

"Cooperative" and "aggressive" refer to how vigorously player A pursues his campaign against player k. Underlying the payoffs associated with these campaign strategies is the assumption that since an aggressive campaign is costly not only to player A, who wages it, but also to player k, who must respond to it, both players come out worse off—even if the election results are unaffected—when player A is aggressive.

If player k is "out," a cooperative or aggressive campaign makes no difference in the payoffs to both players (see Figure 5.6). In this case, therefore, the nature of player A's campaign is irrelevant. We may interpret this to mean, consistent with the game tree shown in Figure 5.5, that player A makes effectively no choice—at least not one that results in different consequences for the players—when any player k does not run in his primary.

We make two assumptions, one about information and one about communication, in the sequential-primary game. First, player k's decision to enter or not to enter his primary, when his turn comes up in the sequence, is immediately made known to all other players. If player k contests his primary, the players are also informed of whether player A chooses a cooperative or aggressive strategy in his campaign. In particular, the potential favorite sons who have yet to decide whether to enter their primaries will be informed of the kind of campaign player A waged in the primaries preceding their own.

The second assumption we make is that though all players have knowledge of the strategies chosen at each stage of the game, and the resulting payoffs to the participants, they cannot communicate with each other. This latter assumption precludes bargaining, side payments, and binding agreements among the players that could inspire the formation of coalitions in a cooperative game.

As a noncooperative game of perfect information, what are the optimal strategies of each player? For the potential favorite sons, do these depend on what position they occupy in the sequence of primaries? We shall explore these and related questions in section 5.5.

5.5. THE INDUCEMENT PARADOX IN THE SEQUENTIAL-PRIMARY GAME

Recall the logic of repeated plays of Prisoners' Dilemma (see section 4.2), in which we reasoned backwards from the last trial. If we pursue a similar line of reasoning in the sequential-primary game, we may start by considering the twentieth primary. If the last potential favorite son chooses not to run in this primary, he gets a payoff of 1. Of course, he could do better (payoff of 2) if he entered his primary and candidate A chose his cooperative strategy. But he may also end up with a payoff of 0 if candidate A wages an aggressive campaign.

Consider this primary from the vantage point of candidate A. Since there are no primaries to follow, he does not have to concern himself with how his behavior in this primary might influence the strategy choices of his possible opponents in future primaries. If the twentieth potential favorite son should run against him in this primary, therefore, he need concern himself only with how to maximize his payoff in this primary. This he accomplishes by choosing his cooperative strategy, which gives him a payoff of 2 rather than 0 if he wages an aggressive campaign. But now, given that it is in the interest of candidate A to cooperate in the last primary, it is also in the interest of the twentieth potential favorite son, knowing this, to run in his primary and also realize a payoff of 2.

Having settled on "in" and "cooperative" as their mutually advantageous strategies in the twentieth primary, what strategies should player A and player 19 choose in the nineteenth primary? Clearly, they can ignore any possible effects that their strategy choices will have on the twentieth primary because, as we have argued, *the optimal choices in this primary* (*the twentieth*) *do not depend on the primaries which preceded it* (*including the nineteenth*). Thus, the nineteenth primary can be treated *as if* it were the last primary, and the previous reasoning applied. This would dictate once again the choices of "in" and "cooperative" by players 19 and A, respectively.

Carrying this reasoning successively backwards, *all* players k should enter their respective contests, and player A should *always* respond with his cooperative strategy. The payoff to each player k would then be 2, and the payoff to player A, summed across the sequence of 20 primaries, would be $20(2) = 40$.

Note that this is the same argument that we developed in the case of repeated plays of Prisoners' Dilemma to justify the suspects' always choosing their noncooperative strategies. It may strike one as puzzling that, with a change in the game but not the logic, we can now make the case for cooperation. Yet, a glance at Figure 5.6 will show that the cooperative strategy for player A in one election of the sequential-primary game is dominant, whereas the noncooperative strategy is dominant for both suspects in Prisoners' Dilemma. Extending play of these games over time does not affect the desirability of the respective dominant strategies.[24]

Yet something seems amiss, at least in the case of the sequential-primary game. Is it really in the interest of player A always to cooperate in each primary—and realize a payoff of only 2—when he can more than double his payoff (to 5) by inducing potential favorite sons not to challenge him? Once again, as in the metagame of the Cuban missile crisis, the question of a player's (A's) inducing more for himself by departing from his apparently best game-theoretic strategy ("cooperative") confounds the analysis.

Although the backwards induction argument supporting the "in" and "cooperative" strategies of players 1, 2, . . . , 20 and player A, respectively, is logically unassailable, its weakness is that the assumptions on which it is built are, in reality, probably untenable. The crux of the argument is the assumption, stated in the foregoing analysis of the nineteenth and twentieth primaries, that "optimal choices in [one] primary do not depend on the primaries which preceded it." In effect, considering one primary *de novo*—as if it were a single game—does not admit the history of previous plays in the sequence. But this history may be just as important to predicting player A's actions as his "rational" choice on the last round, looking to the future. Since there is no future play, the problem of what constitutes a rational choice is, by the induction argument, reduced to a trivial question: what constitutes the best choice for players if the game is played only once?

Since the game as we have defined it encompasses a sequence of primaries, and the players have perfect information about the choices made in each primary over the course of play, it seems implausible that they would ignore this information. Yet, this is exactly what the induction argument asks us to believe. Indeed, if the players had no information about the strategy choices of the players who preceded them, the induction argument could be applied to the twentieth primary, and recursively to preceding primaries, just as before.

---

24. There is, of course, a difference between playing a game a number of times against a single player, as in repeated plays of Prisoners' Dilemma, and playing against different players, as in the sequential-primary game. In the former, players may be able to establish from their pattern of strategy choices the conditions under which they will cooperate, which in some Prisoners' Dilemma experiments has engendered a significant amount of cooperation. When playing against different players in independent trials, however, the cooperative strategy in Prisoners' Dilemma is inherently riskier, and hence the cooperative solution is more difficult to achieve. This would seem to reinforce the reasoning—which we develop subsequently in the text—that player A should always campaign aggressively, since no interpersonal relationship between two players, based on repeated plays, can evolve.

In fact, however, we assumed that the players *do* have perfect information, and it is this information that player A can exploit. By assuming an aggressive posture initially, he can easily suffer the consequences of payoffs of 0 in several early primaries and still come out ahead in the end.

It is unclear how many primaries it would take for potential favorite sons to become convinced that they almost certainly will lose more than they will gain if they enter their primaries. In fact, candidate A could afford to campaign aggressively in as many as the first twelve primaries, and succeed in deterring potential favorite sons from running in the remaining eight primaries only, for his payoff,

$$12(0) + 8(5) = 40,$$

to match that which he would obtain if all potential favorite sons ran and he responded with his cooperative strategy in each case [giving him a payoff of $20(2) = 40$].

It seems unlikely that it would take as many as twelve primaries for candidate A to establish the credibility of his aggressive response. More likely, six or fewer primaries would probably suffice—especially if they were strung together in the beginning of the sequence—to discourage future challengers. Assuming this to be the case, candidate A would come out substantially better off by punishing, rather than appeasing, all challengers (except player 20). This, of course, is the logic of deterrence, which can be applied not only to the analysis of political competition but also to business pricing policies (Selten's example), nuclear defense strategy (see section 5.6), and so forth.

If we consider each primary contest in the sequential primary game separately (see Figure 5.6), we showed previously that player A has a dominant strategy ("cooperative"), but player k does not. If player A chooses his dominant cooperative strategy, however, player k can exploit this choice to achieve his very best outcome (payoff of 2). This is precisely the problem that Howard asserted the United States faced in choosing its sure-thing strategy in the metagame version of the Cuban missile crisis (see section 5.3): it would induce the best outcome for the other player (Soviet Union). To prevent this, he advised against choosing one's sure-thing strategy.

The new twist in the sequential-primary game is that player A can communicate, *through his actions in the course of the game*, that he will not be "suckered" into choosing his cooperative strategy that allows player k to consummate his very best outcome (and results in a less-preferred outcome for player A). In other words, this game permits player A to *counterinduce* the other players—through his actions—since it is played sequentially.

By comparison, the choice of metastrategies in the Cuban missile crisis permits counterinducement only through the buildup of expectations before final choices are made. This requires that each player communicate information about his own intentions since, as we have shown, the specification of metastrategies in Chicken does not imply the choice of a particular outcome. Whereas in the sequential-primary game player A is able to signal his intentions through a pattern of repeated moves *within* the game, in the Cuban missile crisis the player with the dominant metastrategy cannot counter—except through possible messages and actions *outside* the metagame—the other player's best response to his own dominant choice. Hence, though the problem for the player with the dominant (meta)strategy is the same in both the Cuban missile crisis and the sequential-primary game, player A in the sequential-primary game, by repeatedly invoking his aggressive strategy in each primary contest, has a more explicit way of clearly establishing his intentions and, as a consequence, dealing with this problem.

5.6. SUMMARY AND CONCLUSION

Two games were described in this chapter to illustrate the possible effects that the (expected) choice of a strategy by one player may have on inducing the other player(s) to respond in a particular way. The surprising result was that dominant or sure-thing (meta)strategies, normally considered to be superior to a player's other (meta)strategies, may actually work to the advantage of the other player(s); in fact, its choice may allow other player(s) to realize their very best outcome(s). This we called the paradox of inducement and showed that it bedeviled the strategy choices of players in both two-person and n-person games.

Our first example of this paradox was based on the two-person game of Chicken. The metagame expansion of this game, which we applied to the analysis of American and Soviet strategies in the Cuban missile crisis, elevated the cooperative solution to equilibrium status (as it also did in Prisoners' Dilemma). We showed that this solution was a product of each side's tit-for-tat retaliatory metastrategies; in addition, we presented some evidence that indicated these were the actual terms each side presented to the other.

Had one side adopted its sure-thing metastrategy in this crisis, following Howard we showed how it could induce victory for the other side. As a consequence, Howard argues that it is in general disastrous for players to make sure-thing choices, given that these choices can be anticipated and exploited by one's opponent. We presented Harsanyi's rebuttal to this argument, based on the calculation of expected payoffs, and suggested it to be more persuasive the more complete information that players believe they have about each other's preferences.

To establish that the inducement paradox also carried over to n-person games, we offered an example of a 21-person game in which a presidential candidate, player A, faces several potential favorite sons in a series of state primary contests that occur in a specified sequence. The potential favorite sons must decide whether to run against candidate A in their states, and, if they do, candidate A must decide whether to wage a cooperative or aggressive campaign.

Using an induction argument developed in Chapter 4 to analyze repeated plays of Prisoners' Dilemma, we demonstrated that candidate A should always choose his cooperative strategy. But this argument seemed to fly in the face of common sense, which led us to question its underlying assumptions. In particular, we suggested that because the induction argument took account of only what could happen in the future, it neglected a history of behavior that player A's actions might establish. Since the players were assumed to have perfect information about all moves made in the game, it seemed eminently reasonable that potential favorite sons would be deterred from entering their primaries if candidate A's behavior were consistently aggressive, though candidate A, by being aggressive, did stand the chance of getting less than the payoff of 40 he could guarantee for himself if he were always cooperative.

Why does the induction argument (for cooperation) seem to fail in the case of the sequential-primary game but seem more plausible (for non-cooperation) in the case of repeated plays of Prisoners' Dilemma? Since *both* players have dominant strategies in Prisoners' Dilemma,[25] neither player can be induced to try for something better: each player's dominant strategy ("confess") is unconditionally best, which yields the non-cooperative solution when both players choose it.[26] But in each primary contest in the sequential-primary game, only player A has a dominant strategy, so his choice can induce a response on the part of the other players. Although waging aggressive campaigns may not work to player A's short-run benefit, it may prove profitable in the long run, as we illustrated. Thus, to avoid the inducement paradox that the existence of his dominant strategy creates, it may be to player A's advantage to suffer initial losses by forsaking his dominant strategy.

This kind of play rationalizes the role that threats may play in games in which inducement is possible. In fact, one significant conclusion we draw from our analysis of inducement games is that the use of threats may lead to the moderation, rather than the aggravation, of conflict. This may occur either through the clarification of intentions, which seems to have

---

25. Both players have dominant strategies in other two-person games, but Prisoners' Dilemma is the only such game that has a "strongly stable," yet "deficient," equilibrium (since each player can do better without hurting—in fact, helping—the other player if the cooperative outcome is chosen). See Rapoport and Guyer, "A Taxonomy of 2 × 2 Games," pp. 207–208.

26. In the metagame of Prisoners' Dilemma, however, there seem good reasons for players to choose their metastrategies that lead to a cooperative equilibrium (as we showed in section 4.3), but this solution presupposes that there is sufficient communication to permit the buildup of certain expectations. Naturally, if such communication should develop in repeated plays of Prisoners' Dilemma, then the cooperative solution will seem less risky, and hence be more attractive, to the players in this case, too.

led to the cooperative solution of the Cuban missile crisis after each side communicated its tit-for-tat retaliatory policy and accepted the fact that the other side held to a similar policy; or it may occur through a series of actions that communicate this intent more explicitly, which is the lesson we take from our analysis of the sequential-primary game.

In the realm of international relations, the policy of nuclear deterrence, pursued by both superpowers since World War II, has been justified in similar terms. If the resultant "balance of terror" has prevented World War III, however, it has not prevented the superpowers from trying to maintain the credibility of their threats through the use of conventional military forces and subversion in many parts of the world.

This, unfortunately, may be the price each side pays to avoid an erosion in its alliance commitments. For threats, by their very nature, may on occasion have to be backed up by a show of force. Needless to say, the effects of force will not be benign for all parties.

The apparent contradiction in the use of force to prevent its usage on a more massive scale (e.g., in a nuclear war) is simply another way of stating the paradox of inducement. Once players abandon sure-thing strategies—for example, a policy of appeasement that involves giving in to the threats of an opponent to avoid war—they must choose among riskier alternatives (e.g., limited war). But precisely because they are riskier, these choices must be made credible, which implies some measure of retribution if certain threats are ignored. In the case of the superpowers, this presents them with a real quandary if they do not want the "balance of terror," at best rather delicate, to break down.[27]

So far, it seems, this quandary has been settled in favor of trying to maintain the nuclear balance, and, at the same time, selectively employing nonnuclear options. Rooted in the paradox of inducement, there seems no easy way out of this quandary for the superpowers or other actors caught in it. Yet, at the very least it deserves to be better understood, even if we cannot offer a solution at this time.

---

27. See Albert Wohlstetter, "The Delicate Balance of Terror," *Foreign Affairs*, 37 (January 1959), pp. 211–234; and, more generally, Thomas C. Schelling, *The Strategy of Conflict* (Cambridge, Mass.: Harvard University Press, 1960).

6

THE ALABAMA
PARADOX

6.1. INTRODUCTION

Of all the paradoxes discussed in this book, the so-called Alabama paradox is unique for two reasons: (1) it was discovered in the course of a routine empirical calculation, whereas all the other paradoxes treated here appear to be the products of logical analysis or theoretical calculations, which were only later applied to empirical phenomena; and (2) it has been all but forgotten in recent times, though the problem to which it is related has been the subject of controversy, sometimes raging, since the ratification of the United States Constitution almost two hundred years ago. In fact, I have yet to find a political scientist (including an Alabaman) who ever heard of the Alabama paradox. Neither is it mentioned in any recent American government textbooks that I have reviewed, which underscores a point made in the Preface: the overemphasis in the political science literature (especially textbooks) of the here and now—and the concomitant neglect of genuine problems far more deserving of serious analysis.

Briefly, the Alabama paradox was discovered in the following way. After the census of 1880, Congress had to decide on a new apportionment for the House of Representatives. The method of apportionment in use at that time involved the following calculations, given a House of fixed size.

1. The population of the United States (with some qualifications, to be spelled out subsequently), as determined from each decennial census, was divided by the House size to give an average district size for a representative in the House.

This chapter is based largely on M. L. Balinski and H. P. Young, "The Quota Method of Apportionment," *American Mathematical Monthly*, 82 (August–September 1975), pp. 701–730; and M. L. Balinski and H. P. Young, "A New Method for Congressional Apportionment," *Proceedings of the National Academy of Sciences*, 71 (November 1974), pp. 4602–4606. Direct quotations of historical figures, unless otherwise indicated, are taken from these articles, which give full citations of original sources. I am grateful to the authors for bringing the apportionment problem to my attention and for their very helpful advice.

2. The population of each state was next divided by this average district size to give the exact number of representatives to which each state was entitled. Typically, this calculation yielded some whole number, plus a fractional remainder, for each state.

3. Each state was assigned a number of representatives at least equal to its whole number in the preceding calculation. If this whole number were zero (i.e., if the state were entitled by this assignment to no representative), it was automatically assigned one representative.

4. After this whole number assignment, the seats remaining (if any) were allocated to the states entitled to at least one representative—by the whole number assignment procedure—with the largest fractional remainders. Starting with the state with the largest fractional remainder, then going to the state with the next largest, and so forth, an extra seat was assigned to states until the designated House size was reached and all seats were allocated.

This, of course, is only one of many possible methods for assigning representatives to states, but, as we shall show, it has several reasonable properties. One property, however, that was totally unanticipated came to light in the following calculation made by the Census Office in 1881: when the size of the House was set at 299 representatives, Alabama was entitled by this apportionment method to 8 seats; when the House size was set at 300 representatives, it was entitled to only 7 seats!

This incredible result created a tremendous political furor, and a search for explanations, which did not die down for decades. Only after thirty years, in 1911, was the method of apportionment finally changed to preclude the *Alabama paradox*—that is, one in which the number of seats to which a state is entitled cannot decrease if the size of the House is increased. But this method, as well as the method in use today, has some serious defects of its own, as we shall show.

We shall begin by specifying what apportionment is (and is not) and by defining some concepts that will facilitate our later analysis. Next we shall illustrate several apportionment schemes that have been tried or proposed, giving a brief history of each. All, it will be demonstrated, give results inconsistent with certain criteria of fairness and representativeness to be discussed. Finally, we shall describe a new method that has been proposed which not only satisfies all the stipulated criteria but is the only method to do so.

6.2. THE APPORTIONMENT PROBLEM

Before specifying what the "apportionment problem" is, it is useful to indicate what apportionment is *not*—but what it is often confused with, nonetheless. Apportionment does not refer to the drawing of district boundaries, which has been a subject of considerable recent interest since court decisions beginning in 1962 affirmed the "one man, one vote" principle. This is generally known as the *districting* or *reapportionment problem*, and analysis in this area has generally been directed at developing techniques for equalizing the populations of districts, within contiguous and compact boundaries (i.e., techniques that avoid gerrymandering), *in* a state, given that the number of representatives apportioned to a state has already been determined.

The determination of this number for all states constitutes the *apportionment problem*, and we need look no further than Article I, Section 2, of the United States Constitution to find out how it first arose:

> Representatives and direct taxes shall be apportioned among the several States which may be included within this Union, according to their respective numbers, which shall be determined by adding to the whole number of free persons, including those bound to service for a term of years, and excluding Indians not taxed, three fifths of all other persons.

This section was later amended, with the references to "direct taxes" and "free persons" deleted, by the Fourteenth Amendment (1868), Section 2, to read:

> Representatives shall be apportioned among the several States according to their respective numbers, counting the whole number of persons in each State, excluding Indians not taxed.

Article I, Section 2, further specifies:

> The actual enumeration shall be made . . . every . . . ten years in such a manner as they [Congress] shall direct. The number of Representatives shall not exceed one for every thirty thousand, but each State shall have at least one Representative. . . .

Thus, although the Constitution stipulates that each state is entitled to at least one representative, beyond this minimum requirement it is not at all clear what "apportioned . . . according to their respective numbers" means.

To formulate the apportionment problem somewhat more precisely, assume that p is the total population to be counted for purposes of apportionment, and h is the number of house seats to be apportioned. Assume further that p_i is the population of each state i, where $\sum_i p_i = p$, and a_i is the number (always a nonnegative integer) of seats apportioned to each state i, where $\sum_i a_i = h$. Then the *exact quota*, or number of representatives each state is "due" if representatives were capable of being divided exactly, is

$$q_i = p_i(h/p),$$

where h/p is the fraction of the total population each seat "ideally" represents—that is, the fractional share each person possesses of his representative—which is the inverse of the "ideal" district size, p/h. This fractional share, h/p, multiplied by the population of each state, p_i, yields, in effect, the "ideal" number of representatives that should be apportioned to each state.

Since states cannot be represented by fractional representatives, and q_i will not in general be an integer, this ideal cannot be met by letting $a_i = q_i$ for every state i. Instead, it is convenient to define *lower quota*, $\underline{q_i}$, to be the largest integer less than or equal to q_i, and *upper quota*, $\overline{q_i}$, to be the smallest integer greater than or equal to q_i. Put another way, lower and upper quota are the integers obtained from rounding "down" or "up" the exact quota q_i. We shall speak of an apportionment method as

1. *Satisfying lower quota* if, for every a_i it gives, $a_i \geq \underline{q_i}$.

2. *Satisfying upper quota* if, for every a_i it gives, $a_i \leq \overline{q_i}$.

3. *Satisfying quota* if, for every a_i it gives, it satisfies both lower and upper quota.

It should be noted that an *apportionment method*, or rule for apportioning the seats in a house to states, may give more than one *apportionment solution* $(a_1, \ldots, a_s)$, where s is the number of states. This phenomenon may occur in the case of "ties," wherein two or more states are "entitled" to an extra seat but only one can receive it for a given house size h. We shall illustrate later an apportionment method that yields more than one apportionment solution.

To provide some historical perspective on the controversy that sprang up almost immediately over the proper interpretation of the constitutional mandate "apportioned . . . according to their respective numbers," we begin by illustrating three apportionment methods, one proposed by Thomas Jefferson, another by Alexander Hamilton, and a third by Daniel Webster. After pointing out some difficulties with these methods, we shall consider some more recent methods that attempt to circumvent these difficulties. The difficulties all relate to the fact that a state must be represented by a whole number of representatives; they have nothing to do with the minimum requirements for the House—that each state must have at least one representative—which is a topic we take up at the end of the chapter.

6.3. THE JEFFERSON METHOD

After the ratification of the Constitution in 1789, it did not take long for the Founding Fathers to become embroiled in a controversy over the meaning of the crucial phrase "according to their respective numbers." The first census was taken in 1790, and in 1792 Congress passed an apportionment act that allotted a total of 120 seats to the fifteen states then in the Union. (The apportionment of 65 seats to the original thirteen states was specified in Article I, Section 2, of the Constitution.)

George Washington sought the advice of both his Secretary of State, Thomas Jefferson, and Treasury Secretary Alexander Hamilton, on the proposed apportionment. Hamilton recommended that Washington sign the bill (we shall give his reasons in section 6.5), but Jefferson counseled against signing it, warning, "No invasions of the Constitution are fundamentally so dangerous as the tricks played on their own numbers, apportionment."

Washington sided with Secretary of State Jefferson, after having "maturely" considered the bill, and cast the first presidential veto against it. (As perhaps an indicator of the depth of feeling this subject aroused right from the start, Washington's veto of this bill was one of only two vetoes he cast in his eight years as president.) In his veto message, Washington explained:

> First . . . there is no one proportion or division which, applied to the respective numbers of the States, will yield the number and allotment proposed by the bill. Second . . . the bill has allotted to eight of the states more than one [representative] for thirty thousand.

The "proportion or division" to which Washington referred is what Jefferson called a "divisor," which he used to justify an alternative apportionment method:

> It will be said that, though, for taxes, there may always be found a divisor which will apportion them among the States according to numbers exactly, . . . yet, for *representatives*, there can be no such common ratio, or divisor which . . . will divide them exactly without a remainder or fraction. I answer, then, that taxes must be divided *exactly*, and representatives as *nearly* as the *nearest ratio* will admit; and the fractions must be neglected. . . .

In other words, Jefferson sought a divisor λ such that (1) each state i would receive $a_i = p_i/\lambda$, where p_i/λ is, analogous to lower quota, the largest integer less than or equal to p_i/λ; and (2) $\sum_i p_i/\lambda = h$, the total number of seats to be apportioned. Each state i therefore would receive an apportionment a_i that is an integer (hence, fractions could be "neglected"), and the apportionments to all states would sum to h.

One might hope that for $\lambda = p/h$, the "ideal" district size, it will always be the case that the resulting a_i by the Jefferson criterion sum to h. This hope, however, is illusory. Consider the hypothetical legislature in Table 6.1, in which $h = 26$ seats must be apportioned among five states whose total population is 26,000. In this case, the "ideal" $\lambda = 26,000/26 = 1,000$. Dividing the populations by 1,000 and rounding down, however, one obtains the apportionment shown in the fourth column of Table 6.1, which sums to $h = 25$, not 26, representatives.

TABLE 6.1   JEFFERSON METHOD

STATE i	POPULATION p_i	$\lambda = 1,000$		$\lambda = 906.1$	
		$\mathbf{p}_i/\lambda$	$\mathbf{a}_i$	$\mathbf{p}_i/\lambda$	$\mathbf{a}_i$
A	9,061	9.061	9	10.000	10
B	7,179	7.179	7	7.923	7
C	5,259	5.259	5	5.804	5
D	3,319	3.319	3	3.663	3
E	1,182	1.182	1	1.304	1
Total	26,000	25.000	25	28.694	26

Evidently, λ must be "adjusted" downward so that it allots just one more representative to one of the states but the a_i's for all the other states remain the same. It does not take much calculation to show that state A will be the first for which p_i/λ increases to the next higher integer value (10) as λ decreases, and this threshold will be reached at $\lambda = 906.1$ (since state A's population of 9.061, when divided by 906.1, is exactly 10). Thus, the apportionment solution by the Jefferson method, which involves choosing the threshold λ, gives state A 10 seats, as shown in the last column of Table 6.1.

The Jefferson method is also known as the *method of greatest divisors* and was used in a somewhat haphazard way for apportionments based on the censuses of 1790 through 1830. Instead of Congress's setting a House size h and adjusting λ after each census, however, a λ was chosen through a series of political bargains so as not to deprive any state of House seats that it had held in previous apportionments. The a_i's were then determined by $a_i = \underline{p_i/\lambda}$, which, of course, is not properly a "method" in the sense of providing a rule for apportioning seats, given a particular h.

6.4. THE WEBSTER METHOD

In 1832 Daniel Webster, then a member of the Census Committee of the Senate, contended that the Jefferson method's neglect of fractional remainders deprived the New England states (and Massachusetts, in particular) of representatives, which in toto got two fewer seats than New York, which had 40,000 fewer inhabitants.[1] To counter this loss, Webster proposed an apportionment method which has much in common with the Jefferson method—except for one significant difference:

---

1. DeAlva Stanwood Alexander, *History and Procedure of the House of Representatives* (Boston: Houghton Mifflin Co., 1916), p. 6.

TABLE 6.2   APPORTIONMENTS WITH "IDEAL" λ: NO STABLE SOLUTION

STATE i	POPULATION p_i	$\lambda = 10$		$\lambda = 9.804$	
		p_i/λ	a_i	p_i/λ	a_i
A	16	1.6	2	1.632	2
B	16	1.6	2	1.632	2
C	16	1.6	2	1.632	2
D	16	1.6	2	1.632	2
E	16	1.6	2	1.632	2
F	920	92.0	92	93.839	94
Total	1,000	100.0	102	102.000	104

Let the rule be that the population of each state shall be divided by a common divisor, and, in addition to the number of members resulting from such division, a member shall be allowed to each state whose fraction exceeds a moiety [one-half] of the divisor.

In effect, what Webster proposed was that a "common divisor" λ be found such that, after rounding p_i/λ either up (fractional remainder equal to or greater than one-half) or down (fractional remainder less than one-half) for each state i, the sum of the resulting a_i's for all states be h:

$$h = \sum_i \underline{p_i/\lambda + \tfrac{1}{2}},$$

where $\underline{p_i/\lambda + \tfrac{1}{2}}$ is, analogous to lower quota, the largest integer less than or equal to $p_i/\lambda + \tfrac{1}{2}$. Recall that the Jefferson method, in contradistinction, stipulates that a λ be found such that, after preserving only the integer portion of p_i/λ (i.e., always rounding down p_i/λ, whatever the fractional remainder), the sum of the resulting a_i's for all states be h:

$$h = \sum_i \underline{p_i/\lambda}.$$

There may be many possible λ's that give an apportionment $(a_1, \ldots, a_s)$ for a given h under Webster's proposal. Webster stipulated, however, that the apportionment be "as near as may be . . . the nearest approach to the relative equality of representation among states." One approaches such equality by choosing a λ as close to the "ideal" district size, p/h, as possible.

That $\lambda = p/h$ may not yield the required h can be seen from the example in Table 6.2. If $h = 100$, then this "ideal" $\lambda = 1,000/100 = 10$ gives apportionments to each state that sum to 102, rather than 100, representatives. But then letting $\lambda = 1,000/102 = 9.804$ to obtain a new "ideal"

TABLE 6.3 WEBSTER METHOD

STATE i	POPULATION p_i	$\lambda = 1,000$		$\lambda = 957.2$	
		p_i/λ	a_i	p_i/λ	a_i
A	9,061	9.061	9	9.466	9
B	7,179	7.179	7	7.500	8
C	5,259	5.259	5	5.494	5
D	3,319	3.319	3	3.467	3
E	1,182	1.182	1	1.235	1
Total	26,000	26.000	25	27.162	26

district size for a house with 102 representatives, the resulting apportionments sum to 104, a still greater number of representatives. Although this example is somewhat artificial, it does illustrate the important point that the apportionment solutions obtained from the choice of an "ideal" λ are thoroughly unstable.

For technical reasons, there may not even be a "closest" λ that yields the required h. Instead, we shall specify as the rule for the Webster method that the *largest* λ be chosen such that rounding p_i/λ up or down (according to whether the fractional remainder is equal to or greater, or less, than one-half) for all states i gives resulting a_i's that sum to h.

For our earlier example, we have illustrated in Table 6.3 the apportionment by the Webster criterion for the "ideal" $\lambda = 26,000/26 = 1,000$. As with the Jefferson method (see Table 6.1), we see that the a_i's sum to 25, which is not the designated house size of 26. Thus, for $\lambda = 1,000$, the requirement that $\sum_i a_i = h$ for both the Webster and Jefferson methods is not fulfilled in our example.

As with the Jefferson method, we must "adjust" λ downward so that it allots just one more representative to one of the states but the a_i's for all the other states remain the same. A little calculation shows that as λ is decreased, the first state whose fractional remainder increases to one-half, which thereby entitles that state to an extra seat, is state B.

To determine the exact value of λ at which state B's p_i/λ equals 7.5, we solve the equation $7,179/\lambda = 7.5$, which gives $\lambda = 957.2$. For this value of λ, we have shown in Table 6.3 the values of p_i/λ for all states, and the resulting a_i's according to the Webster method, that yield $h = 26$. Note that this solution $(a_1, \ldots, a_s)$ according to the Webster method differs from the Jefferson solution shown in Table 6.1: the Jefferson method gives state A the extra seat; the Webster method gives state B the extra seat.

Under both the Jefferson and Webster methods, there may exist no λ's that—because of ties—yield the required h. Consider the example shown in Table 6.4, in which both states B and C have the same population as

TABLE 6.4 WEBSTER METHOD WITH TIES

STATE i	POPULATION p_i	$\lambda = 1,000$		$\lambda = 957.2$	
		p_i/λ	a_i	p_i/λ	a_i
A	9,061	9.061	9	9.466	9
B	7,179	7.179	7	7.500	8
C	7,179	7.179	7	7.500	8
D	1,399	1.399	1	1.462	1
E	1,182	1.182	1	1.235	1
Total	26,000	26.000	25	27.163	27

state B did in the previous example, with state D's population correspondingly diminished so that $p = 26,000$ remains the same as before. By the Webster method, when $\lambda = 1,000$, $h = 25$; but now the value of λ that we showed earlier is just sufficient to give state B 1 extra seat (957.2) also allots to state C 1 extra seat, making $h = 27$.

Since h jumps from 25 to 27 at the threshold value of λ, there exists no λ that yields $h = 26$. Obviously, a similar example—involving, for instance, a tie between states A and B, both with populations of 9,061—could be constructed for which, under the Jefferson method, there would exist no λ that yields $h = 26$. The possibility of ties is not usually a serious practical problem, but it may create a situation for the Jefferson and Webster methods in which no λ exists that gives the required h.

The Webster method, also known as the *method of major fractions*—an allusion to fractions greater than one-half—was used in 1842 to apportion the House based on the 1840 census.[2] As happened in applications of the Jefferson method before it, however, an h was not first determined and then the method applied. Rather, political considerations again dictated that no state lose seats when the size of the House increased, so the choice of an appropriate λ itself continued to be included in the calculation of the number of seats to which each state was entitled.

6.5. THE HAMILTON METHOD

The method of apportionment that Alexander Hamilton proposed was described in section 6.1: (1) give each state i its lower quota $\underline{q}_i$; (2) order the fractional remainders of states from greatest to smallest; (3) give one additional seat to each state in this order until h is reached and there are

---

2. As perhaps a reflection of the times, a central issue in the debate preceding adoption of the Webster method was the "constitutionality" of fractions. See Alexander, *History and Procedure of the House of Representatives*, p. 7.

no additional seats to allocate. As with the Jefferson and Webster methods, however, ties may upset this calculation if two or more states—not necessarily with the same populations but with equal fractional remainders —are both entitled to the last remaining seat.

If ties in fractional remainders render a solution for a particular house size impossible, this problem can be obviated by an additional rule that specifies, for example, that one state will be selected at random to receive the last extra seat. Similarly, a random selection device could also be used to determine which state would get the extra seat under the Jefferson and Webster methods for "jumps" in h when there exists no λ for an intermediate value.

When consulted by Washington on whether to sign the first apportionment bill incorporating his proposal, Hamilton described and justified it as follows:

> It is inferred from the provisions of the Act that the following process has been pursued. (I) The aggregate number of the United States are divided by 30,000, which gives the total number of representatives, or 120. (II) This number is apportioned . . . by the following rule: as the *aggregate* numbers of the *United States* are to the *total number* of representatives found as above, so are the *particular numbers of each state* to the number of representatives of such state. But (III) as this process leaves a residue of eight out of the 120 members unapportioned, these are distributed among those states which upon that second process have the largest fractions or remainders. . . . And hence results a strong argument for its constitutionality.

But Jefferson attacked the bill's failure to specify in sufficient detail a method for arriving at an apportionment. Although the bill specified a particular apportionment, based on the 1790 census, which was consistent with Hamilton's description of the method quoted earlier, it was silent on how "residuary representatives," unallocated after each state's lower quota was satisfied, would be assigned *in the future*. As Jefferson noted:

> The bill does not say that it has given the residuary representatives *to the greatest fractions*; though in fact it has done so. It seems to have avoided establishing that into a rule, lest it might not suit on another occasion. Perhaps it may be found the next time more convenient to distribute them *among the smaller states*; at another time *among the larger states*; at other times according to any other crochet which ingenuity may invent and the combinations of the day give strength to carry . . . whereas the other construction [Jefferson's] reduces the apportionment always to an arithmetical operation, about which no two men can ever possibly differ.

Despite the failure of the Hamilton method to gain acceptance when Hamilton first proposed it, it was incorporated in the apportionment act of 1850 sponsored by Representative Samuel F. Vinton of Ohio. It became known as the *Vinton method of 1850* and remained the law through the apportionment based on the census of 1900.

6.6. THE ALABAMA PARADOX

The first real challenge to the validity of the Hamilton method came with the discovery of the Alabama paradox in 1881. Its discovery occurred after the chairman of the Committee on the Census directed the Census Office in the Department of Interior to compute various apportionments, based on the census of 1880, for House sizes between 275 and 300 members. Discovery of the paradox created a storm of protest that culminated in a House debate in 1901 after further manifestations of the paradox were revealed in apportionment figures based on the census of 1900.

Representative John C. Bell of Colorado had particular reason to be upset by what he called "this atrocity which [mathematicians] have elected to call a 'paradox' . . . this freak [which] presents a mathematical impossibility." For every House size between 350 and 400 members, the Hamilton method gave Colorado, based on the 1900 census, 3 seats— except for a House size of 357 members, for which the Hamilton method gave Colorado only 2 seats. Yet, it was precisely a House size of 357 members that a majority coalition, led by Representative Albert J. Hopkins of Illinois, chairman of the Census Committee, favored.

Representative Charles E. Littlefield of Maine also had reason to be upset, for by the apportionment act of 1891 Maine had received 4 seats, but in a newly apportioned House of 357 members it would receive only 3. To compound the confusion,

> Maine loses on 382. She does not lose when the House is increased to 383, 384, or 385. She loses again with 386, and does not lose with 387 or 388. Then she loses again on 389 and 390, and then ceases to lose.

A few days later Chairman Hopkins replied:

> It is true that under the majority bill Maine is entitled to only three Representatives, and, if Dame Rumor is to be credited, the seat of the gentleman who addressed the House on Saturday last is the one in danger. . . . [He] takes a modest way to tell the House and the country how dependent the State of Maine is upon him. . . . Maine crippled! Maine, the State of Hannibal Hamlin, of William Pitt Fessenden, of James G. Blaine. . . . That great State crippled by the loss of Littlefield! Why, Mr. Speaker, if the gentleman's statement be true . . . , I can see much force in the prayer he uttered here when he said, "God help the State of Maine" [laughter] !

The upshot of the House debate in 1901 was a compromise solution of sorts whereby Congress retreated to a position it had taken earlier. The

6.5 THE ALABAMA PARADOX

STATE i	POPULATION p_i	$h = 25$		$h = 26$		$h = 27$	
		q_i	a_i	q_i	a_i	q_i	a_i
A	9,061	8.713	9	9.061	9	9.410	9
B	7,179	6.903	7	7.179	7	7.455	8
C	5,259	5.057	5	5.259	5	5.461	6
D	3,319	3.191	3	3.319	4	3.447	3
E	1,182	1.137	1	1.182	1	1.227	1
Total	26,000	25.000	25	26.000	26	27.000	27

apportionment act of 1901 set the House size at 386, a figure that ensured that no state would lose any seats.

The extracts from the House debate previously quoted may seem amusing now, but it was deadly serious business for representatives who were threatened with the loss of their seats. The reality of the Alabama paradox can perhaps best be appreciated by a simple example, using the same population figures from our previous illustrations of the Jefferson and Webster methods.

In Table 6.5 we have given the exact quotas q_i for house sizes of 25, 26, and 27 members. For each of these values of h, we have also given the apportionment solutions using the Hamilton method. After each state is assigned its lower quota, 2 "residuary representatives" are allocated to states A and B for $h = 25$, 1 to state D for $h = 26$, and 2 to states B and C for $h = 27$. The existence of the paradox is confirmed by assignments to state D, which starts off with 3 seats when $h = 25$, then goes to 4 seats when $h = 26$, and subsequently drops to 3 seats when $h = 27$.[3]

We shall call an apportionment method *house monotone* if it can never lead to the Alabama paradox: whenever the size of a house is increased by one member, no state can lose any of its seats. Clearly, if each state keeps at least the number of seats it had prior to every *one-member* increase in house size, house monotonicity implies that a state can *never* lose seats, whatever amount by which house membership is increased.

---

3. Even stranger than the Alabama paradox is what has been dubbed, amusingly, the "super" Alabama paradox by Edward V. Huntington, the founder of the modern mathematical theory of apportionment (whose work is described in section 6.7). Holding the total population of all states constant, but now permitting changes in the populations of states in going from h to $h + 1$, Huntington constructs a hypothetical three-state example in which, when the size of a house increases from h to $h + 1$, the one state to *lose* a seat is the state that *gains* in population (the other two states lose). See Edward V. Huntington, *Methods of Apportionment in Congress*, U.S. Senate, 76th Cong., 3rd sess. (Washington, D.C.: Government Printing Office, 1940), pp. 28–29.

Although there is nothing in the Constitution that specifically prohibits apportionment methods admitting the Alabama paradox—it was hardly anticipated by the Founding Fathers—the solutions resulting from such methods do seem fundamentally undemocratic. This, however, is not because any state is particularly hurt or helped by this method, which satisfies quota: every state gets at least its lower quota of representatives and not more than its upper quota.[4] Rather, the paradox highlights an arbitrariness in the criterion for assigning extra seats stemming from the fact that it is not a state's fractional remainder, but the *ranking* of its remainder in some ordering, which determines its eligibility for an extra seat. Although the fractional remainders of all states i will increase—if the integer portions (q_i) do not—when the size of the house is increased, the remainders either (1) may not increase uniformly or—if the $\underline{q}_i$ of some states i do increase after the new apportionment—(2) there may be fewer extra seats to distribute.

Whether the ranking of states eligible for an extra seat changes, or there are fewer extra seats to distribute, the effect is the same: one formerly eligible state may no longer be eligible. This means that in going from h to $h + 1$, the distribution of extra seats to the states with the highest fractional remainders may also involve a redistribution of old seats as well. It is hard to think of a rationale rooted in democratic political theory that could be used to justify an eligibility criterion, basically number-theoretic in nature, which redistributes seats in this manner.

One might hope that the basic idea of the Hamilton method could be saved, but the Alabama paradox avoided, through some modification of the criterion for assigning extra seats. For example, if the states were ordered not according to their fractional remainders, $(q_i - \underline{q}_i)$, but rather according to these values relativized by population, $(q_i - \underline{q}_i)/p_i$, would the resulting apportionment method be house monotone? The answer is "no." In fact, Balinski and Young show that all attempts in this direction are futile; they have proven that there is no "generalized Hamilton method" that is house monotone.[5]

At this point we note that all apportionment methods (Jefferson, Webster, and Hamilton) so far discussed give different apportionment solutions to our running example for $h = 26$ (see Tables 6.1, 6.3, and 6.5). Even if we rule out the Hamilton method because it leads to the Alabama paradox, this still leaves open the question of which of the two

---

4. Besides quota, it can be shown that the Hamilton method minimizes certain objective functions of statistical error [e.g., $\sum_i (a_i - q_i)^2$]. Other methods that we shall discuss minimize other functions, but none seems to hold any a priori claim as incorporating the "best" goodness-of-fit measure. Moreover, the sum of errors across states, whatever the goodness-of-fit measure used, gives a total or average that does not necessarily reflect how individual states are affected, which may be an important political consideration.

5. Balinski and Young, "The Quota Method of Apportionment." The proof of this result is given in the unpublished, but not the published, version of this paper.

other apportionment solutions, given by the Jefferson and Webster methods, is in any sense "better."

Unfortunately, this question cannot be answered by comparing only these two methods. As we shall show in section 6.7, there are yet other apportionment methods that avoid the Alabama paradox (as do the Jefferson and Webster methods) but lead to still different apportionment solutions.

6.7. THE HUNTINGTON METHODS

As we have already indicated, the House continually sidestepped the question of fixing a House size h, preferring instead to manipulate h so that no state would lose seats (except when the total size of the House actually decreased, which it did temporarily after the censuses of 1840 and 1960). Following the apportionment act of 1911, however, the House's membership had ballooned to 433 members. With the admission into the Union in 1912 of New Mexico and Arizona, which each got 1 seat, it now had 435 members. Except for a brief period after Alaska and Hawaii gained statehood in 1958 and 1959, and the size of the House was temporarily increased to 437, House membership has remained constant at 435 ever since.

Extreme dissatisfaction with the Alabama paradox, and the Hamilton method that produced it, led to the readoption of the Webster method in the 1911 apportionment act. This method was championed by an economist at Cornell University, W. F. Willcox, who gave it the name "method of major fractions" and also developed a constructive procedure for calculating apportionment solutions for any h, thus making it truly an apportionment method.

In 1921 Edward V. Huntington, a mathematician at Harvard University, suggested a new approach to the question of apportionment. The class of all house-monotone methods, he argued, could be evaluated in terms of a "fundamental question":

Between any two states there will practically always be a certain inequality which gives one of the states a slight advantage over the other. A transfer of one representative from the more favored state to the less favored state will ordinarily reverse the *sign* of this inequality, so that the more favored state now becomes the less favored, and *vice versa*. Whether such a transfer should be made or not depends on whether the *amount* of inequality between the two . . . is less or greater than it was before; if . . . reduced . . . , it is obvious that the transfer should be made. The fundamental question therefore at once presents itself, as to how the *"amount of inequality"* between two states is to be measured.

Thus, after settling on a measure of the "amount of inequality" between pairs of states, we may ask, for each pair, if the transfer of one representa-

TABLE 6.6   MEASURES OF INEQUALITY

METHOD	MEASURE OF INEQUALITY[a]
Smallest Divisors (SD)	$a_j - a_i(p_j/p_i)$
Harmonic Mean (HM)	$p_i/a_i - p_j/a_j$
Equal Proportions (EP)	$p_i a_j/p_j a_i - 1$
Major Fractions (MF)/Webster	$a_j/p_j - a_i/p_i$
Greatest Divisors (GD)/Jefferson[b]	$a_j/(p_j/p_i) - a_i$

[a] For $p_i/a_i \geq p_j/a_j$.
[b] Also known as the method d'Hondt.

tive from one state to the other reduces this amount. If it does not for every pair of states, then the apportionment solution is, in a sense, stable.

How do we measure the "amount of inequality"? Huntington offered five different measures, listed in Table 6.6, for any pair of states i and j. Although there are still other possible measures of inequality, either they are equivalent to the five listed in Table 6.6 or they do not guarantee the existence of a stable solution. Thus, we may confine our attention to only these methods.

As is indicated in Table 6.6, two of the measures of inequality, Greatest Divisors (GD) and Major Fractions (MF), coincide with the criteria used in the Jefferson and Webster methods. For the other three methods, we have indicated in Table 6.7 the (unique) apportionment solution that each gives for $h = 26$ in our previous example. The new solutions, it will be observed, differ not only from each other but also from the solutions provided by the Jefferson (GD) and Webster (MF) methods, given in Tables 6.1 and 6.3.

Before considering which, if any, of the five methods might deserve certification as "the best," let us illustrate how an apportionment solution can be found from a measure of inequality. Take, as an example, Equal Proportions (EP), which is the method favored by Huntington. If $x \geq y$, define the *relative difference* between x and y as the proportion by which x exceeds y: $(x - y)/y$.

Now consider two states i and j. Previously, we interpreted the numbers p_i/a_i and a_i/p_i to represent, respectively, "average district size" and "average share of representatives" for state i. Then the relative difference of *either* average district size or average share of representatives between states i and j, where $p_i/a_i \geq p_j/a_j$, is

$$\frac{p_i/a_i - p_j/a_j}{p_j/a_j} = \frac{a_j/p_j - a_i/p_i}{a_i/p_i} = \frac{p_i a_j}{p_j a_i} - 1,$$

TABLE 6.7   APPORTIONMENT SOLUTIONS FOR THREE HUNTINGTON METHODS

STATE i	POPULATION p_i	QUOTA q_i ($h = 26$)	SD	HM	EP
A	9,061	9.061	9	9	9
B	7,179	7.179	7	7	7
C	5,259	5.259	5	5	6
D	3,319	3.319	3	4	3
E	1,182	1.182	2	1	1
Total	26,000	26.000	26	26	26

which is the measure of inequality for EP shown in Table 6.6. If the transfer of one representative from state j to state i reduces this measure of inequality, then the EP method prescribes that it should be made.

Assume that the transfer is made so that the new apportionments (indicated by primes) for state i and state j are, respectively,

$$a_i' = a_i + 1; \, a_j' = a_j - 1.$$

Assume the average share of representatives now favors state j, that is,

$$\frac{p_j}{a_j'} \geq \frac{p_i}{a_i'}$$

as a result of this transfer, so the measure of inequality between states i and j becomes

$$\frac{p_j a_i'}{p_i a_j'} - 1 = \frac{p_j(a_i + 1)}{p_i(a_j - 1)} - 1.$$

We say that the original apportionment (a_i to state i, a_j to state j) is *stable* if no transfer is justified, i.e., if any transfer from state j to state i makes i advantaged, j disadvantaged, and the measure of inequality after the transfer greater than or equal to the measure before the transfer:

$$\frac{p_j(a_i + 1)}{p_i(a_j - 1)} - 1 \geq \frac{p_i a_j}{p_j a_i} - 1,$$

or

$$\frac{p_j^2}{(a_j - 1)a_j} \geq \frac{p_i^2}{a_i(a_i + 1)},$$

$$\frac{p_j}{\sqrt{(a_j - 1)a_j}} \geq \frac{p_i}{\sqrt{a_i(a_i + 1)}},$$

for states i and j.

It is not difficult to find an apportionment that satisfies the above inequality for all pairs of states i and j. Clearly, when $h = 0$, $a_k = 0$ for all states k. For $h \geq 0$, an apportionment for $h + 1$ is obtained by assigning the additional seat to any one state k for which the *rank index*, $p_k/\sqrt{a_k(a_k + 1)}$, is greatest. (The rank index may be thought of as the *amount of deviation* of state k from the *norm of equality* either in (1) district size—$p_i/a_i = p_j/a_j$ for all states i and j—or (2) share of representatives—$a_i/p_i = a_j/p_j$ for all states i and j.) It can be proved that the apportionment solutions so obtained at $h + 1$, and, continuing the process, at $h + 2$, $h + 3, \ldots$, satisfy the Huntington stability criterion, and—except for ties—are unique.

Does EP avoid the Alabama paradox? It is evident that if an apportionment method is house monotone, exactly one state's delegation increases by one seat when h goes to $h + 1$. For, except in the case of ties, there is just one state for which the rank index is greatest, and which, under EP, would thereby get the extra seat.

In the event that two or more states have the same maximum rank index, they would all be eligible for the extra seat. The method, however, prescribes that only one of the eligible states be chosen (e.g., randomly) as the recipient of the extra seat.

Since representatives cannot be taken away from states that already have them at h, the assignment of a new seat to one state at $h + 1$ precludes the Alabama paradox. But since the same assignment procedure was followed at h, $h - 1, \ldots$, 1, by induction the paradox could not have occurred earlier. Therefore, EP is house monotone.

For similar reasons, all the methods proposed by Huntington are house monotone, though each is based on a different measure of inequality and gives rise to a different rank index. Each method also implies the existence of a divisor λ, whose calculation we illustrated in the case of the Jefferson (GD) and Webster (MF) methods.

Of Huntington's five methods—sometimes called the five "modern workable methods"—that avoid the Alabama paradox, why did Huntington favor EP? In a rather nice bit of circular reasoning, he argued:

It is generally agreed that Congress, consciously or unconsciously, has had two principal aims in view: First, to equalize the "congressional districts" among the several States; and secondly, to equalize the "individual shares" among the several States. What the modern mathematical theory has done is to establish clearly the relations between these two aims and the five possible methods listed above.

The mathematical facts are as follows: The method of smallest divisors and the method of greatest divisors fail on both these aims; the method of major fractions fails on the first aim; the method of harmonic mean fails on the second aim; the method of equal proportions achieves both aims.[6]

---

6. Huntington, *Methods of Apportionment in Congress*, p. 2.

Of course, once one accepts as a premise that the particular measure of inequality on which EP is based is the proper one, then this automatically rules out the four other house-monotone methods. But what makes the EP measure a priori best?

Huntington advances another argument in support of EP, namely, that it occupies "a neutral position with respect to emphasis on smaller and larger states." That is, if we rank the five methods in the order in which they tend to favor small states, SD ranks first, followed by HM, EP, MF, and GD, which is also the order in which the methods are listed in Table 6.6. A glance at Tables 6.7, 6.3 (for $h = 26$), and 6.1 (for $h = 26$) confirms this relationship: SD gives state E an extra seat (above its lower quota); HM gives state D an extra seat; EP gives state C an extra seat; MF (Webster) gives state B an extra seat; and GD (Jefferson) gives state A an extra seat. Except for an American penchant for compromise, there seems no justification for blessing medium-size states with extra seats by selecting the middle-ranking method, EP.

Huntington's "neutrality" argument, nonetheless, was invoked by the authors of two reports of the National Academy of Sciences, one issued in 1929 and one in 1948. In each case, a panel of eminent mathematicians endorsed EP as the best (compromise) method.[7]

The Committee on Reapportionment of Congress of the American Political Science Association (APSA), composed of distinguished political scientists, also gave its support to EP in a 1950 report. Concurring in the judgment of the APSA committee, Galloway remarks:

> After 150 years of discussion and debate the procedure for re-apportioning Representatives in Congress has developed until now a reapportionment based on a sound statistical approach is assured after each decennial census. Through the cooperation of legislator and technician the fundamental adjustment of representation to population has been made the subject of a scientific procedure, thereby eliminating an important source of possible discontent with the workings of our Government.[8]

This judgment, as we shall see, might have been premature.

Despite these heady recommendations of mathematicians and political scientists, there has been substantial opposition to EP. In 1929, Senator Arthur Vandenberg, who favored the Major Fractions (MF) method advocated by Willcox and used in 1911, wrote Huntington:

> The basic problem is not mathematical at all. . . . I contend as a constitutional axiom that . . . a group of individuals should have as nearly as may be the same weight in choosing Representatives in

---

7. George B. Galloway, *History of the United States House of Representatives*, U.S. House, 89th Cong., 1st sess. (Washington, D.C.: Government Printing Office, 1965), p. 23.

8. Galloway, *History of the United States House of Representatives*, p. 23.

the House whether they happen to live in the large States or the small States. Doctor Willcox declares that [MF] is the only method in the long run that secures this end. . . . There is constitutional warrant for [MF]. . . . I stood for [MF] . . . then came the unfortunate detour.

The "unfortunate detour" to which Senator Vandenberg refers is a dispute over the accuracy of the 1920 census figures, which, it was alleged, undercounted rural areas (because of a bad winter) and were further distorted by postwar migrations. This dispute, coupled with endless quarreling over the best method of apportionment, blocked congressional agreement on a new apportionment for the 1920s.

Still unable to decide on the apportionment method to be used, Congress in 1928 provided that future apportionments be computed by the method used in the previous apportionment (MF was used in the preceding 1911 apportionment act) and EP, and that the results of each method be presented to Congress for consideration. Fortuitously, MF and EP resulted in identical apportionments of the House based on the 1930 census. Hence, no choice between methods was forced upon Congress, and the controversy over apportionment abated.

It was not to lie dormant for long, however. After the census of 1940, Willcox, still an advocate of MF, offered a new argument against EP in 1941:

It is my conviction that the mathematical aspects of apportionment have been greatly exaggerated. . . . The first and most important reason [for rejecting EP] is the difficulty in understanding it. . . . [Senator Vandenberg] did state that the correspondence he had had with the advocates of [EP] had given him a chronic headache.

Whatever the merits of this and other arguments, they seem not to have been decisive when the following discrepancy was revealed between the application of MF and EP to the 1940 census figures: MF gave Arkansas 6 seats and Michigan 18 seats, whereas EP gave Arkansas 7 seats and Michigan 17 seats; the apportionments of all the other states were the same by both methods.

It seems safe to assume that because the Democrats controlled Congress, and Arkansas was at that time a safe Democratic state, whereas Michigan was predominantly Republican, EP was chosen over MF in order to give Arkansas the extra seat. This assumption is supported by the fact that the 1941 House vote for EP was strictly along party lines, except for the Democrats from Michigan, who voted for MF.

6.8. THE QUOTA REQUIREMENT

We indicated in section 6.6 that the Hamilton method satisfies quota but is vulnerable to the Alabama paradox. On the other hand, none of the

TABLE 6.8   HUNTINGTON METHODS: DO NOT SATISFY QUOTA

STATE i	POPULATION p_i	QUOTA q_i ($h = 100$)	EP	MF
A	5,117	51.17	51	52
B	4,400	44.00	43	45
C	162	1.62	2	1
D	161	1.61	2	1
E	160	1.60	2	1
Total	10,000	100.00	100	100

Huntington methods, which include the Jefferson and Webster methods, admits the Alabama paradox. In this section, we shall show by way of examples that the Huntington methods suffer at least as bad a failing as the Alabama paradox: they do not in general satisfy quota.

To illustrate this failing of the two Huntington methods, MF and EP, that were applied to the censuses of 1930 and 1940, consider the hypothetical example shown in Table 6.8. The (exact) quota for state B is 44 representatives, but EP awards it only 43 (less than lower quota) and MF awards it 45 (more than upper quota). Similarly, none of the other three Huntington methods gives state B its (exact) quota of 44 representatives.

Huntington recognized this problem—in fact, he gave the example shown in Table 6.8—but he considered the imposition of a quota requirement "unworkable."[9] Yet, to many analysts, an apportionment method that does not satisfy quota is tantamount to a violation of the constitutional mandate that representatives be apportioned to states "according to their respective numbers." When a real-life instance of this problem came to light in a proposed apportionment bill in 1832, Daniel Webster, in a speech on the Senate floor, objected vigorously:

> The House is to consist of 240 members. Now, the precise portion of power, out of the whole mass presented by the number of 240, to which New York would be entitled according to her population, is 38.59; that is to say, she would be entitled to thirty-eight members, and would have a residuum or fraction; and even if a member were given her for that fraction, she would still have but thirty-nine. But the bill gives her forty . . . for what is such a fortieth member given? Not for her absolute numbers, for her absolute numbers do not entitle her to thirty-nine. Not for the sake of apportioning her members to her numbers as near as may be because thirty-nine is a nearer apportionment of members to numbers than forty. But it is

9. Huntington, *Methods of Apportionment in Congress*, p. 34.

given, say the advocates of the bill, because the *process* which has been adopted gives it. The answer is, no such process is enjoined by the Constitution.

The proposition that no state should receive fewer than the integer portion of its exact quota, nor more than this number rounded up—that is, that its apportionment should satisfy quota—has been reiterated innumerable times since 1832. Not until recently, however, has it been recognized that a state's "precise portion of power" may depart considerably from its proportion of votes. We reserve discussion of this question, however, until Chapter 7.

Although none of the Huntington methods satisfies quota, one (SD) satisfies lower quota and one (GD) satisfies upper quota. But the three methods that fall "in between" these, and which Huntington considered the best candidates for adoption, satisfy neither lower quota nor upper quota. In particular, EP, the method touted by Huntington, can give apportionments *arbitrarily* far from quota.[10]

One does not need artificial examples, like that given in Table 6.8, to demonstrate this problem with EP. In fact, Balinski and Young offer two plausible projections of the future populations of the fifty states in 1984 that produce EP apportionments that are well off quota, in both directions, for several states.[11] Assuming a total United States population of 221,138,415, and a House size of 435 members, they show, for example, that a 0.48 percent *increase* in the population of California from 21,839,542 (quota = 42.960) to 21,944,556 (quota = 43.167)—with similarly small shifts in the populations of the other states such that the total population remains constant—*decreases* California's apportionment from 45 to 41 representatives using EP.[12]

This example illustrates two properties of EP. First, the method satisfies neither lower quota (42 for California in the first projection, 43 in the second) nor upper quota (43 in the first projection, 44 in the second). Second, given that the total population remains constant, *increasing* the population of one state (and changing the populations in one or more other states as well) may actually *decrease* the apportionment to the (now larger) state.

This latter property is related to the so-called *population paradox*, whereby an increase in the total population of all states may result in

---

10. Balinski and Young, "The Quota Method of Apportionment," p. 712.

11. Balinski and Young, "The Quota Method of Apportionment," p. 713, Table 5.

12. From this example Balinski and Young draw the conclusion that "EP is very unstable: small shifts in population can lead to large shifts in apportionment." Balinski and Young, "The Quota Method of Apportionment," p. 712. This example, however, illustrates a more bizarre property of EP, namely, the second property described in the paragraph in the text below, which gives EP solutions the overtones of a paradox. The quota method proposed by Balinski and Young, and discussed in section 6.9, also has this property. Since solutions under the quota method satisfy quota, however, the effects of population shifts on apportionment solutions are circumscribed under this method.

there being fewer house seats to apportion for some fixed divisor λ (average district size), however fractional remainders are treated.[13] Whereas in the population paradox no state whose population increases gains seats (the loss in house seats is entirely attributable to those states that lose population, though the total population of all states increases), the paradox suggested by the Balinski-Young projections using EP is that a state may lose (gain) seats at the same time that it gains (loses) population, though the total population of the country remains constant. In other words, a state's population is not the sole determinant of its apportionment; the populations of other states are also a factor.

Other "paradoxes" could probably be uncovered that characterize house-monotone methods. Instead of pursuing the pathological aspects of the apportionment problem further, however, it is useful at this point to ask a more constructive question: is there any method that satisfies both quota and house monotonicity, the desiderata that emerge from our discussion of unacceptable features of an apportionment method? It is, in fact, possible to satisfy both desiderata and thereby avoid the dilemma of a choice between one or the other evil, as we shall next show.

6.9. THE QUOTA METHOD

Probably the main reason the apportionment problem has been almost forgotten for more than a generation is that every apportionment since EP was mandated in 1941 has satisfied quota. This, of course, is only an accident of recent census figures for states since there is nothing inherent in the method that precludes a nonquota solution. If and when this occurs, one can be quite sure that a hue and cry will be raised by the aggrieved state(s).

That such a result need not occur can now be guaranteed by a new apportionment method proposed by Balinski and Young, which they call, appropriately enough, the *quota method*.[14] Like all Huntington methods, the quota method is house monotone, but it differs from these methods, as we shall illustrate, by never allowing a state's apportionment to fall below its lower quota or climb above its upper quota. Hence, the method satisfies quota.

To illustrate how an apportionment solution can be found using this method, consider the five-state example shown in Table 6.9. Clearly, if $h = 0$, $a_i = 0$ for all states i. When h is increased to $h + 1$, the quota method—like the Huntington methods—asks the following question: which state "most deserves" the next seat? The answer in the case of the

---

13. Huntington, *Methods of Apportionment in Congress*, pp. 18–19.

14. Balinski and Young, "A New Method for Congressional Apportionment"; Balinski and Young, "The Quota Method of Apportionment."

TABLE 6.9 THE QUOTA METHOD

STATE i POPULATION p_i APPORTIONMENTS a_i FOR VARYING HOUSE SIZES h

STATE i	POPULATION p_i									
A	441	0	1	1	2	2	3	3	4	4	4
B	210	0	0	1	1	1	1	1	1	2	2
C	161	0	0	0	0	1	1	1	1	1	2
D	128	0	0	0	0	0	0	1	1	1	1
E	60	0	0	0	0	0	0	0	0	0	0
Total	1,000	0	1	2	3	4	5	6	7	8	9

quota method is the state i which maximizes $p_i/(a_i + 1)$—that is, the state whose average district size would be greatest after the award of the next seat, when it would have $(a_i + 1)$ seats.

Unlike the Huntington methods, however, the quota method imposes a restriction on which states the criterion $p_i/(a_i + 1)$ is applied to so as to prevent a state from receiving an extra seat that puts its apportionment above upper quota. More precisely, if a state i had a_i seats at $h - 1$, it is said to be *eligible at h* for its $(a_i + 1)$st seat if and only if it can receive the hth seat without exceeding upper quota. Thus, in our example in Table 6.9, if $h = 1$, the exact quotas $q_i = p_i(h/p) = p_i/1,000$ for each state i are: $q_A = 0.441$, $q_B = 0.210$, $q_C = 0.161$, $q_D = 0.128$, $q_E = 0.060$. Since the upper quotas for all states are 1 (i.e., each fraction "rounds up" to 1), all states are eligible at $h = 1$ to receive the first seat. The state that maximizes $p_i/(a_i + 1) = p_i/(0 + 1) = p_i$ is simply the state with the largest population, A.

At $h = 2$, the exact quotas $q_i = p_i(h/p) = p_i/500$ are: $q_A = 0.882$, $q_B = 0.420$, $q_C = 0.332$, $q_D = 0.256$, $q_E = 0.120$. Since by the previous apportionment at $h = 1$ state A has 1 seat, it would exceed its upper quota of 1 were it to receive the second seat. Hence, it is ineligible; of the four remaining states, state B maximizes $p_i/(a_i + 1)$: 210/1 exceeds 161/1 for state C; 128/1 for state D; and 60/1 for state E. Thus, state B receives the second seat.

At $h = 3$, the exact quotas $q_i = p_i(h/p) = p_i/333$ are: $q_A = 1.323$, $q_B = 0.630$, $q_C = 0.483$, $q_D = 0.384$, $q_E = 0.184$. Since by the previous apportionment at $h = 2$ state B has 1 seat, it would exceed its upper quota of 1 were it to receive the third seat. But state A would not exceed its new upper quota of 2 were it to receive the third seat, so now it is eligible once again (along with states C, D, and E), and state B is ineligible. In fact, not only is state A newly eligible at $h = 3$ but it also maximizes $p_i/(a_i + 1)$: 441/2 = 220.5 exceeds 210/1 for state C; 128/1 for state D; and 60/1 for state E. Thus, state A receives the third seat, which is its second, before states C, D, and E receive their first seats.[15]

Continuing in this manner, we can fill in the additional columns of Table 6.9, shown for $h = 0, 1, \ldots, 9$. At each h there is always at least one eligible state and, except for ties, one that maximizes $p_i/(a_i + 1)$. If two or more eligible states are tied for the maximum $p_i/(a_i + 1)$, only one is chosen (e.g., randomly) to receive the next new seat.

What properties does the quota method satisfy? Like the Huntington methods, it is obviously house monotone since no state is ever forced to give up a seat when a new seat is assigned. The restriction of new assignments to eligible states also ensures that the method satisfies upper quota. Less apparent is the fact that the method satisfies lower quota,[16] too, and hence satisfies quota.

The quota method satisfies a third, technical condition called *consistency*, which means roughly that the "contest" between two eligible states for an additional seat is dependent only on which has "priority" over the other—based on their populations and current apportionments—and not on the populations of other states.[17] All Huntington methods, none of which imposes an eligibility restriction, are consistent in this sense because the claim to an extra seat is determined unambiguously by the rank index. No method except the quota method, however, *simultaneously* satisfies the three conditions of consistency, house monotonicity, and quota. Thus, as Balinski and Young prove, it is the unique method that meets the two major objections that have been raised against all other methods—that they admit the Alabama paradox (Hamilton) or yield nonquota solutions (Huntington methods)—and is, in addition, consistent.

Without the consistency condition, an apportionment method that satisfies the conditions of house monotonicity and quota could give rise to several possible apportionment solutions, even without ties. The imposition of the consistency condition thus has a twofold effect: (1) it reduces the number of acceptable house-monotone–quota *solutions* to one; and (2) it limits the number of *methods* for generating these to one.

---

15. This cannot occur under Huntington's EP method since maximization of the rank index $p_i/\sqrt{a_i(a_i + 1)}$ implies that every state receives one seat before any state receives two. (This is because if $a_i = 0$ for any state i, its rank index is ∞, thereby entitling it to the next seat.) Thus, EP automatically satisfies the constitutional requirement that every state in the House have at least one representative, given that there are at least as many seats to be apportioned as states, but it may result in an apportionment far off quota. For this reason, it seems preferable first to construct a method that possesses the properties desired (e.g., quota) and then show how these properties can be preserved, insofar as possible, when specified minimum requirements are imposed as constraints on apportionment solutions. This is the approach taken in section 6.10 in generalizing the quota method to reflect arbitrary minimum requirements—not necessarily the same—for all states.

16. The criterion that the next seat be awarded to the eligible state that maximizes $p_i/(a_i + 1)$ ensures this property. For a proof, see Balinski and Young, "The Quota Method of Apportionment," p. 715.

17. Cf. this condition with Arrow's Independence from Irrelevant Alternatives condition, whose spirit is the same, discussed in section 2.3.

6.10. THE QUOTA METHOD WITH MINIMUM REQUIREMENTS

Although the Constitution specifies that the states shall be apportioned "according to their respective numbers," it qualifies this statement by providing that "each State shall have at least one Representative." The French Constitution requires a minimum of two *députés* per *département*; other systems provide for other minimum requirements, not necessarily the same for all units represented.

Sometimes restrictions are imposed on the maximum number of representatives a unit is entitled to, but these can readily be conceptualized as minimum requirements. For example, the County Charter of Nassau County, New York, has in the past prohibited the representative of any town or city on the County Board of Supervisors from having more than half of the total votes on the Board of Supervisors, even though one city (Hempstead) has more than half of the population.[18] Translated into minimum requirement terms, this restriction says that all municipalities except Hempstead must together have at least half the votes on the Board.

The aforementioned examples make it clear that if the quota method is to be applicable generally to representative systems, it should be able to accommodate a variable set of minimum requirements. Specifically, if a constitution or some other set of rules stipulates that state i (or some group of states) must receive at least r_i representatives, where r_i is a nonnegative integer, then it would be desirable that the quota method reflect this requirement.

Unfortunately, the very idea of quota—that state i is entitled to q_i representatives because of its population, wealth, or whatever—may be inconsistent with the notion of minimum requirements. This inconsistency certainly occurs when $r_i > \overline{q_i}$, or the requirement for state i exceeds the maximum number of seats it would be entitled to under the quota method (i.e., its upper quota).

Adopting a purist view, we can simply rule this case out as incompatible with the idea of quota and say that, under such circumstances, the quota method is inapplicable. Taking a more practical view, on the other hand, we can accommodate this case by defining *generalized upper quota* $\tilde{q}_i$, given minimum requirements $(r_1, r_2, \ldots, r_s)$ for states 1 through s, as the maximum of r_i or $\overline{q_i}$ for each state i. That is, if $r_i > \overline{q_i}$, then $\tilde{q}_i = r_i$; if $r_i < \overline{q_i}$, then $\tilde{q}_i = \overline{q_i}$; and if $r_i = \overline{q_i}$, then both criteria give the same number for $\tilde{q}_i = \overline{q_i} = r_i$.

In the case of our earlier example, with minimum requirements r_i as specified in Table 6.10, $\tilde{q}_i = \overline{q_i} = r_i$ for states D and E; and $\tilde{q}_i = \overline{q_i}$ for states A, B, and C. Since there is no state for which $r_i > \overline{q_i}$ in this example, there is no conflict between the purist and practical points of view.

---

18. John F. Banzhaf III, "Weighted Voting Doesn't Work: A Mathematical Analysis," *Rutgers Law Review*, 19 (Winter 1965), pp. 317–343.

TABLE 6.10   THE QUOTA METHOD WITH MINIMUM REQUIREMENTS

STATE i	POPULATION p_i	QUOTA q_i ($h = 26$)	REQUIRE-MENT r_i	$\tilde{q}_i$	q_i	a_i
A	9,061	9.061	6	10	8	8
B	7,179	7.179	6	8	6	7
C	5,259	5.259	5	6	5	5
D	3,319	3.319	4	4	4	4
E	1,182	1.182	2	2	2	2
Total	26,000	26.000	23	30	25	26

Neither is there a conflict in the case of the U.S. House of Representatives, wherein $r_i \leq \overline{q}_i$ for all states i, since the upper quotas of even the very smallest states match the one representative minimally required. However, two of the three states whose exact quotas were less than 1 by the 1970 census (Alaska and Wyoming; the third state is Vermont) would not qualify, on the basis of their populations, for even one seat under the quota method *without* minimum requirements.

To generalize the concept of lower quota to incorporate minimum requirements involves a recursive procedure based on the following idea:

Suppose that the exact quota $[q_i]$ of state i at h is less than or equal to r_i. Then state i certainly deserves no more than r_i seats, while it is required to have at least r_i seats. A fair method would, therefore, allot to i exactly r_i seats. Subtracting such seats from h there is left a smaller house which is to be allocated to the remaining states. Using this smaller house compute the exact quotas for the remaining states and give r_i to any whose exact quota is at most r_i, and so forth.[19]

To illustrate this idea, consider again the example given in Table 6.10 with specified minimum requirements r_i. In defining *generalized lower quota* q_i for each state i, we shall simultaneously determine at each step apportionments a_i, which by definition are *bracketed* by q_i and $\tilde{q}_i$ (i.e., $q_i \leq a_i \leq \tilde{q}_i$). This procedure can be described in three steps for our example:

1. If $r_i \geq \overline{q}_i$, the requirement for state i is at least as great as its upper quota. For such states i, generalized lower quota q_i is defined to be equal to generalized upper quota $\tilde{q}_i$, which we earlier assumed is equal to r_i. Since $q_i = \tilde{q}_i$ must bracket all quota apportionments, the quota apportionments for states where $r_i \geq \overline{q}_i$ (D and E in our example) must necessarily be

---

19. Balinski and Young, "The Quota Method of Apportionment," p. 717.

$a_i = q_i = \hat{q}_i = r_i$. Given $a_D = r_D$ and $a_E = r_E$, states D and E can be eliminated from further consideration.

2. This leaves 20 seats to be apportioned among states A, B, and C, subject to the requirements. For $h = 20$, the new quotas q_i' for these states are: $q_A' = 8.429$, $q_B' = 6.678$, $q_C' = 4.892$. Since $r_C = \overline{q_C'} = 5$, $q_C = \hat{q}_C'' = 5$. Hence, $a_C = 5$ by the reasoning given in step 1, thus eliminating state C from further consideration.

3. This leaves 15 seats to be apportioned between states A and B, subject to the requirements. For $h = 15$, the new quotas q_i'' for these states are: $q_A'' = 8.369$, $q_B'' = 6.631$. Now the lower quotas for states A and B ($q_A'' = 8$, $q_B'' = 6$) are equal to or greater than the requirements ($r_A = 6$, $r_B = 6$). Since the requirements, therefore, impose no constraints on the apportionment solutions for these states, their generalized lower quotas are defined to be equal to simply their lower quotas: $q_A = q_A'' = 8$, $q_B = q_B'' = 6$. Following the procedure for calculating quota apportionment solutions without minimum requirements outlined in section 6.9, we can easily show that the apportionments for states A and B are $a_A = 8$ and $a_B = 7$ by the quota method (i.e., state B gets the "extra" fifteenth seat).

The quota apportionments a_i for all five states in our example, subject to the minimum requirements r_i, are given in the last column of Table 6.10. Despite the fact that the requirements do not exceed the upper quotas for any state i ($r_i \leq \overline{q_i}$), this apportionment solution differs considerably from that given by the quota method when there are no minimum requirements (as well as when $r_i = 1$ for all states i), which is $a_A = 10$, $a_B = 7$, $a_C = 5$, $a_D = 3$, $a_E = 1$. The minimum requirements given in Table 6.10 help the two smallest states, D and E; the state to be hurt at their expense is the largest state, A, which loses two seats when the minimum requirements are imposed.

Only if every state's exact quota is equal to or greater than its minimum requirement can one be assured that the requirements will have no effect on apportionment solutions based on the quota method. If they do have an effect, as in our example, the quota method can be extended to give house-monotone–consistent solutions which, subject to the requirements, satisfy quota in the generalized sense (i.e. are bracketed by generalized lower and upper quota).

As with the quota method without minimum requirements, there is no other method that satisfies the three conditions of house monotonicity, generalized quota, and consistency and incorporates the minimum requirements as well. This includes the original quota method applied directly to the states, after the minimum requirements have been met, to apportion the remaining seats at h, $h + 1$, $h + 2$, and so forth. Since this latter method involves simply adding to an arbitrary number of seats (i.e., the minimum requirements) an apportionment solution, it can lead— depending on the requirements—to an apportionment in which a smaller state has more representatives than a larger state.[20] In no sense can such an apportionment be considered a quota solution.

6.11. SUMMARY AND CONCLUSION

Practically unknown to contemporary political scientists, apportionment methods, and anomalies encountered in their application, have been the subject of recurring controversy since the founding of the Republic. Although this controversy has lain dormant for a generation, it seems likely to be rekindled by recent research that questions the fairness of the current method used to apportion representatives to states in the U.S. House of Representatives.

Three apportionment methods were tried between 1790 and 1910, and all were found to be wanting. The Jefferson method, used until the census of 1840, involved choosing a divisor as close to the average district size as possible that, when used to divide the populations of all states, yielded a house of specified size when the integer portions of the quotients (i.e., the exact quotas for each state) were summed. This method, also known as the method of greatest divisors, was abandoned when Daniel Webster succeeded in convincing a majority of Congress that it discriminated against the New England states.

The method Webster proposed to replace the Jefferson method, and that was used to apportion the House based on the 1840 census, also involved finding a divisor that yielded an agreed-upon House size. The Webster method differed from the Jefferson method in prescribing that the exact quotas of states be rounded up if their fractional remainders equaled or exceeded one-half, and be rounded down otherwise. This method, also called the method of major fractions, was not—as the Jefferson method before it—applied to the apportionment of a House after its size was fixed. Rather, adjustments were made through appropriate increases in the size of the House (and corresponding changes in the divisor) such that no state was ever forced to give up a seat it had previously held when the size of the House was increased.

The method of apportionment originally proposed by Hamilton to Washington in 1792 was adopted for the apportionment based on the 1850 census. This method, which came to be known as the Vinton method of 1850, involved giving to each state its lower quota of representatives (i.e., the integer portion of its exact quota) and allocating the remaining seats to the states with the largest fractional remainders.

The Hamilton method gave rise to the Alabama paradox in 1881 when

---

20. This can occur only if the requirements are *biased*: if state *i* is larger than state *j* ($p_i > p_j$) for some *i* and *j*, then $p_j/r_j > p_i/r_i$, i.e., the number of persons per *required* representative in the smaller state is greater than that in the larger state. If the requirements are biased, the definition of the set of eligible states must be modified in applying the generalized quota method. For details, see Balinski and Young, "The Quota Method of Apportionment," p. 719.

it was discovered that, if the size of the House were increased from 299 to 300 members, Alabama would lose a seat it already had. This discovery, which dumbfounded politicians and caused a political uproar, threatened to deprive not only Alabama of a seat but other states as well when subsequent manifestations of the paradox were uncovered in proposed apportionments based on the censuses of 1890 and 1900.

In fact, however, necessary adjustments were made in the size of the House so that no state ever lost a seat because of the Alabama paradox. Repeated instances of it generated sufficient opposition to the Hamilton method (and suggested modifications of it), nevertheless, so that it was replaced by the Webster method, in newly resurrected form, after the census of 1910, when the size of the House was finally stabilized.

In the 1920s, Huntington showed that there were five possible methods, including the Jefferson and Webster methods, that avoided the Alabama paradox. He favored the method he baptized "equal proportions" (EP), because, among other reasons, it tended to favor neither large nor small states but, instead, medium-size states; he regarded this as a compromise solution. EP gave the same apportionment solution as the Webster, or major fractions (MF), method for the 1930 census (there was no new apportionment following the 1920 census), but EP and MF gave different apportionment solutions for the 1940 census. EP was selected for evident political reasons in 1941 and has been used ever since.

Like all the five Huntington methods, EP has one major defect: it does not satisfy quota. That is, it may assign to one or more states fewer representatives than its lower quota (exact quota rounded down) or more representatives than its upper quota (exact quota rounded up). In developing a set of methods that are house monotone (i.e., avoid the Alabama paradox), Balinski and Young have shown that Huntington sacrificed the quota requirement, which they argue must be the point of departure for any proper interpretation of the constitutional phrase "apportioned . . . according to their respective numbers."

The constitutional requirement that every state be assigned at least one representative means that it may be impossible to satisfy quota in a strict sense. Balinski and Young instead have proposed an apportionment method that satisfies the quota property modified so as to include possible minimum requirements of a system. They call their method the quota method and demonstrate that it is the only apportionment method to satisfy quota, house monotonicity, and consistency, which is a technical property.

Since the quota method uniquely satisfies the three postulated conditions, it incorporates, in a sense, as much as can be asked of an apportionment method; any additional conditions one might consider desirable are either equivalent to these three or inconsistent with them. If the former is the case, the quota method necessarily satisfies these additional conditions; if the latter is the case, one or more of the original conditions would have to be jettisoned to allow for the new conditions.

The consistency condition seems the only one that one might want to replace, but it is not clear by what. In any event, if both the house monotonicity and quota conditions were retained, any alternative to the quota method that satisfies some alternative third condition could produce only marginally different apportionment solutions (i.e., they would not differ by more than one seat per state).

Although the quota method would produce only marginal changes in the present 1970 apportionment based on EP (seven states with 2–6 representatives would each lose one seat to seven states with 8–39 representatives), the changes could be much more substantial, as Balinski and Young illustrate, if the EP apportionment solution did not satisfy quota (which EP has, by accident, satisfied since the 1930 census). This seems a compelling practical reason for adoption of the quota method; in addition, this method seems both legally justified by the language of the Constitution and historically to reflect the beliefs of the Founding Fathers about what apportionment means.

Despite its apparent virtues, the quota method may not, even if adopted, end the apportionment controversy. One reason is that a state's share of House seats does not necessarily mirror its voting power, which may be what one really wants reflected in a representative body. In Chapter 7, after defining two concepts of voting power, we shall describe some paradoxes associated with applications of these concepts to weighted voting bodies.

7

THREE PARADOXES
OF POWER

7.1. INTRODUCTION

"Power" is probably the most suggestive concept in the vocabulary of political scientists. It is also one of the most intractable concepts, bristling with apparently contradictory meanings and implications. One implication of most definitions of power is that the greater the proportion of resources (e.g., votes) that an actor controls, the greater is his power. Another implication is that the fewer conflicts an actor has with other actors, the greater is his power.

In this chapter we shall show that these implications, under certain conditions, are simply not true. To illustrate their falsity, we shall first show that a chairman in a voting body, whom we assume can cast a tie-breaking vote in addition to a regular vote, may be at a disadvantage vis-à-vis the regular members when the preference rankings of outcomes by the members all differ. In particular, if voting is sophisticated, the social choice of a voting body may rank higher on the preference scales of some—or even all—the regular members than it does on the chairman's preference scale, despite his extra tie-breaking vote.

We call this phenomenon the *paradox of the chairman's position*. Although we show that a chairman may be able to realize a more favorable outcome by deceiving the other members, the effectiveness of such a counterstrategy depends on his being better informed than the other members and being able to make his deception believable.

To render the paradoxical relationship between votes and power more precise, we next define two indices of voting power due to Banzhaf and Coleman. The application of these indices to hypothetical voting bodies reveals that an actor's voting power may actually be greater when he controls a smaller, rather than a larger, proportion of the votes in a weighted voting body (one in which the members may cast different numbers of votes). More specifically, we show that the addition of one or more new members to a weighted voting body can increase the voting power of some of the old members, despite the fact that the votes of the old members, individually and collectively, constitute a smaller proportion of the total number of votes in the enlarged body. Empirical examples of this phenomenon, which we call the *paradox of new members*, are given, along with its expected frequency of occurrence in small and moderate-size voting bodies.

The third paradox that we describe in this chapter is one in which quarreling members in a voting body, by refusing to join the same winning coalition, may increase rather than decrease their own voting power. Such situations in which quarreling redounds to the benefit of the quarrelers, which we call the *paradox of quarreling members*, suggest that conflict is not necessarily related to a diminution in an actor's voting power. Finally, we conclude with a discussion of some of the theoretical and empirical ramifications of the paradoxes for the study of power.

7.2. THE PARADOX OF THE CHAIRMAN'S POSITION

Consider the three-voter–three-alternative (or outcome) example discussed at length in Chapter 1, wherein the preference scale of the passers is (O, A, N), the preference scale of the amenders is (A, O, N), and the preference scale of the defeaters is (N, A, O). Assume that the voting procedure used is the plurality procedure (see section 1.8) and that the passers have more votes than either of the other two voters, but not enough to win by themselves if the other two voters agree on a single outcome. Alternatively, the passers may be considered to have the same number of votes as the other two voters but, in the event of a three-way tie, can act as the chairman and break ties. In either event, it would appear that the passers have some kind of edge over the other two voters.

If voting is sincere, this will obviously be true since each voter will vote for the alternative that ranks first on his preference scale. With the passers having the advantage in the case of a three-way split, they will be able to ensure the selection of their first-choice outcome, O.

Curiously, however, their apparent advantage in voting power over the other two voters may disappear if voting is sophisticated. As we showed in section 1.8, for the preference scales of the three voters we have assumed, the equilibrium outcome under the plurality procedure is A, which is the second most-preferred choice of the passers. It is also the second most-preferred choice of the defeaters, but it is the most-preferred choice of the amenders. Thus, under sophisticated voting, the amenders, not the passers, have the edge—insofar as they obtain their first choice—for the preference scales of the three voters we have assumed.

This result is not as curious as it seems when one observes that a majority of voters (amenders and defeaters) prefers the sophisticated outcome A to the sincere outcome O. Since outcome O, the chairman's (passers') first choice, is not the choice preferred by a majority, this fact can be foreseen by the other voters, who can thwart the chairman by voting sophisticatedly.

We see, then, that even in situations in which all three voters have different first preferences—which we shall call *conflict situations*—the chairman's edge in voting power may be for naught if voting is sophisticated. Indeed, the sophisticated outcome (A) would remain unchanged in our example if the amenders or defeaters, rather than the passers, were given the chairman's tie-breaking vote, which demonstrates that this institutional prerogative of a chairman may be entirely ineffectual in such situations.

If the result of sophisticated voting in a conflict situation is not the chairman's first choice—as in our example—then his position certainly does not work to his advantage. We characterize the illusory nature of his extra voting power in such situations as the *paradox of the chairman's position*.

How often will the preference scales of the three voters in conflict situations be such that the chairman, despite his possessing a tie-breaking vote, will not get his first choice if voting is sophisticated? Recall from section 2.3 that there are $6^3 = 216$ distinct ways in which three voters can order three outcomes. The situation illustrated by our example will occur when (1) the first choice of the chairman—outcome O in our example—is the second choice of one of the two other voters, whose first choice—outcome A in our example—and last choice—outcome N in our example—are, respectively, the second and last choices of the chairman; and (2) the third voter's preference scale is the reverse of the chairman's. Thus, once the chairman has chosen a preference scale [e.g., (O, A, N)], which he can do in six ways, a second voter has a choice between only two preference scales [e.g., (A, O, N) or (N, A, O)], and the third voter is restricted to the scale not chosen by the second voter. Hence, given three voters, there are $6 \times 2 \times 1 = 12$ ways in which they can choose preference scales that yield a sophisticated outcome (in this situation) that is not the chairman's first choice. If we assume that all preference scales of the voters are equiprobable, the probability that this situation will occur is therefore $\frac{12}{216} = 0.056$. This, it will be recalled, is the same probability of occurrence of cyclical majorities in three-voter–three-outcome situations (see section 2.5).

Are there other conflict situations in which the chairman's tie-breaking vote either leads to the choice of his second-ranking outcome, or otherwise is of no help if voting is sophisticated? Under the plurality procedure, we showed in section 1.8 that if the preference scales of the passers and defeaters are (O, A, N) and (N, A, O), respectively, but the preference scale of the amenders is (A, N, O) instead of (A, O, N), then the sophisticated outcome will be indeterminate: depending on the voting strategies of the amenders and defeaters (the passers have a straightforward strategy —vote for O), the outcome could be O or A or N. As in the previous situation, 12 of the 216 possible cases fall into this pattern.

Although the first choice of the passers—outcome O in our illustration —*might* be chosen in such a situation, the passers can do nothing with their tie-breaking vote to *ensure* this choice if voting is sophisticated. In fact, if the voters are able to communicate and coordinate their choices of strategy, outcome A, the second choice of the passers, is the only outcome that is invulnerable to all two-voter majority coalitions; if coalitions could form, therefore, it is reasonable to suspect that it would be chosen (see section 1.9). Once again, despite the different first preferences of all three voters, the chairman's tie-breaking vote does not help him to secure his most-preferred outcome.

There is one other conflict situation in which the first preferences of the three voters diverge but the chairman's tie-breaking vote does not ensure the selection of his first-choice outcome under the plurality procedure if voting is sophisticated. This is the already familiar situation of cyclical majorities [e.g., passers—(O, A, N); amenders—(A, N, O); defeaters—(N, O, A)], which, as we previously indicated, comprise another 12 of the 216 cases. In these cases, the chairman's most-preferred outcome is *never* chosen under the plurality procedure if voting is sophisticated. The reason is that the other two voters not only most prefer a different outcome to the chairman's first choice but, by voting sophisticatedly, they can also ensure an outcome that is better for both of them (i.e., is the first choice of one voter and the second choice of the other voter). In this situation, the chairman's tie-breaking vote is not only not helpful but positively harmful: it guarantees that his worst outcome will be chosen if voting is sophisticated!

We have shown that in three distinct conflict situations, comprising 36 of the 216 possible three-voter–three-outcome cases, the chairman's apparent voting power advantage under the plurality procedure does not translate into an advantage in securing the outcome he most prefers if voting is sophisticated.[1] Although limited to very simple situations under plurality voting, these results suggest that power over outcomes may be quite different from the greater "weight" accorded to one voter (the chairman). Indeed, in cases wherein there exists a paradox of voting, such an "advantage" may induce one's very worst outcome.

These results can be extended to more complicated situations. In general—as in the situation of cyclical majorities—the probability of occurrence of the aforementioned situations increases as the number of voters and outcomes—especially the latter—increases (see section 2.5).

Does a chairman or larger faction, with apparently greater voting power, have any recourse in such situations? Or do the strategic calculations of sophisticated voting inevitably nullify his edge over the other voters? We turn to a consideration of these questions in section 7.3.

---

1. There is a fourth distinct conflict situation, also comprising 12 cases, in which the first preferences of the three voters are all different but, under sophisticated (as well as sincere) voting, the chairman's first choice always wins. This situation is illustrated by the following preference scales: passers—(O, A, N); amenders—(A, O, N); defeaters—(N, O, A). In this situation, the chairman's (passers') first choice is the second choice of the other two voters. Since the sophisticated outcome (O) would be the same whichever of the three voters had the tie-breaking vote, however, even in this situation the chairman's tie-breaking vote offers no advantage; the passers would obtain their first-choice outcome anyway were one of the other voters the chairman and were voting sophisticated.

7.3. COUNTERSTRATEGIES OF A CHAIRMAN

Consider the first of the three conflict situations discussed in section 7.2 and illustrated by the following example: passers—(O, A, N); amenders—(A, O, N); defeaters—(N, A, O). The sophisticated outcome in this example is A, the second choice of the chairman (passers), whose straightforward (and sophisticated) strategy is to vote for O. If he voted for either other outcome, the social choice would remain A, so he has no counterstrategy to improve the social choice in his favor.

Consider the second conflict situation, illustrated by the following example: passers—(O, A, N); amenders—(A, N, O); defeaters—(N, A, O). In this situation, with the passers voting for outcome O, the outcome is indeterminate—O or A or N—depending on the sophisticated strategy choices ("vote for A" or "vote for N") of the other two voters (see section 1.8).

Can the passers, by departing from their sophisticated strategy ("vote for O"), ensure a better outcome for themselves? The answer is no: by voting for A (there is never any incentive for them to vote for their least-preferred outcome, N), they ensure that outcome O, their first choice, will never be chosen, but they cannot insure against the selection of outcome N (if the amenders and defeaters both vote for it). Hence, they have no counterstrategy to prevent their worst outcome from being chosen.

Consider the third conflict situation, illustrated by the following example: passers—(O, A, N); amenders—(A, N, O); defeaters—(N, O, A). In this situation, the sophisticated outcome is N, which is supported by the amenders and defeaters. Clearly, the passers have no voting strategy that will change this strategy choice of the other two voters.

We have shown that in all three conflict situations in which the sophisticated outcome is either indeterminate or the second or last choice of the chairman (passers), he has no voting counterstrategy by which to ensure himself of a better outcome, despite his extra voting power. To be sure, if communication among the voters were permitted and they could form coalitions, a coalition of the passers and amenders supporting outcome A would be invulnerable to challengers in the second situation (see section 1.9). This would at least ensure that the passers, by settling for their second choice, would not have to face the possibility that their last-choice outcome would be chosen.

Although a coalition of passers and amenders supporting outcome A could upset the sophisticated outcome N supported by the amenders and defeaters in the third conflict situation, this coalition is not stable. As in all cases where there exist cyclical majorities, no outcome is socially preferred to all others; hence, a coalition supporting any outcome is vulnerable to challenges. Even allowing for coalitions, therefore, the passers cannot ensure that the outcome least favorable to them, and supported by the other two voters, will not triumph in the end.

These results would appear to be pretty dismaying to a chairman: in 36 of the 48 cases in which the most-preferred outcomes of all three voters differ, sophisticated voting under the plurality procedure nullifies his apparent power advantage—specifically, his ability to obtain his most-preferred outcome if voting is sincere. Moreover, there appears to be no voting strategy, either individual or in concert with another voter, that can restore it. Is there any alternative for a chairman that remains once sincerity (innocence?) in voting is lost?

7.4. THE COUNTERSTRATEGY OF DECEPTION

A chairman is often in the unique position, after the other voters have already committed themselves, of being the last voter to have to make a strategy choice. Yet this position does not furnish a ready solution to his problem if voting is truly sophisticated, for sophisticated voting implies that voters act upon both their own preferences and a knowledge of the preferences of the other voters. If complete information about all voters' preference scales is available before voting—as it must be for voting to be sophisticated—then the order of voting is immaterial: all voters can predict sophisticated choices beforehand—and act accordingly. Moreover, as we showed in the section 7.3, even a chairman's (unexpected) deviation from a sophisticated strategy under the plurality procedure cannot generally effect for him a more favorable outcome.

Let us assume for purposes of the subsequent analysis that the chairman, by virtue of his unique position, can obtain information about the preference scales of the other two voters but they cannot obtain information about his preference scale. Assume further that each of the two regular members is informed of the other regular member's preference scale. Now, if voting is to be truly sophisticated, the chairman must inform the regular members of his preference scale; but, given our information assumptions, he is not compelled to tell the truth. The question is: can a chairman, by announcing a preference scale different from his true preference scale, induce a better (manipulated) sophisticated outcome for himself?

Given that voting is sophisticated, the chairman, because of his tie-breaking vote, will always have a straightforward strategy, as we showed in section 1.8: vote for his most-preferred outcome. Thus, the other voters need only know his (announced) first choice, and not his complete preference scale, to determine what his sophisticated (and sincere) strategy choice will be.

Define a *deceptive strategy* on the part of the chairman to be any *announced* most-preferred outcome that differs from his *honestly* most-preferred outcome. We call the use of a deceptive strategy by the chairman *tacit deception*, since the other members, not knowing his honest preference scale, are not able to determine whether or not his announcement is an honest representation of his most-preferred outcome. Tacit deception will be profitable for the chairman if it induces a more-preferred social choice for him than an honest representation of his preferences, given sophisticated voting by the other voters.

To illustrate this concept, consider the first conflict situation discussed earlier, represented by the following preference scales: passers—(O, A, N); amenders—(A, O, N); defeaters—(N, A, O). The chairman (passers), by announcing his first choice to be outcome A rather than outcome O, does not change the sophisticated outcome; it remains outcome A if he votes for outcome A rather than outcome O, which is his sophisticated (straightforward) choice.[2] Tacit deception is, therefore, not profitable for the chairman in this situation.

Assume now that the passers actually vote for outcome O after announcing their (dishonest) preference for outcome A. Then the (manipulated) sophisticated outcome will be O, their first preference. In other words, the passers can induce their best outcome by faking their (announced) preference scale and, contrary to their announcement, voting honestly in the end. We call this kind of deception, which involves not only announcing a deceptive strategy but taking *deceptive action* as well (i.e., voting differently from one's announced preference), *revealed deception*. It is deception that is revealed in the voting process and is clearly profitable for the passers in the first conflict situation.

Consider the second conflict situation discussed earlier, represented by the following preference scales: passers—(O, A, N); amenders—(A, N, O); defeaters—(N, A, O). The chairman (passers), by announcing his first choice to be outcome A rather than outcome N, can induce the sophisticated outcome A, which would seem better for him than the previous indeterminate sophisticated outcome that involves the risk that his worst outcome (N) will be chosen. Given that the passers prefer their second choice for sure to an indeterminate outcome whereby their last choice might be selected, tacit deception will be clearly profitable for them in this conflict situation.

The passers, however, can do even better in this conflict situation if, after announcing their first choice to be outcome A, they actually vote for their very best outcome, O, which wins if the voting of the other voters is sophisticated. As in the first conflict situation, then, revealed deception ensures selection of the best outcome for the passers.

Finally, consider the third conflict situation discussed earlier, represented by the following preference scales: passers—(O, A, N); amenders—

---

2. If the passers announced their first choice to be outcome N—their least-preferred outcome—they would thereby induce N as the sophisticated outcome (their last choice), which would obviously be a foolish tacit deception strategy on their part. However, if they then revealed their deception by voting for outcome O (see text), O would be the social choice of the voting body since the amenders and defeaters would split on outcomes A and N, respectively. Thus, there are situations in which a chairman's announcement for his least-preferred outcome may be profitable, though generally it seems that he can obtain at least as favorable an outcome through a less blatant deception strategy (e.g., announcement for his second most-preferred outcome). See Steven J. Brams and Frank C. Zagare, "Deception in Simple Voting Games," forthcoming.

TABLE 7.1 SOPHISTICATED OUTCOMES IN THREE CONFLICT SITUATIONS IN WHICH FIRST PREFERENCES OF THREE VOTERS DIFFER AND DECEPTION BY CHAIRMAN IS PROFITABLE

REPRESENTATIVE PREFERENCE SCALES		SOPHISTICATED OUTCOMES		
Chairman	Other members	No deception	Tacit deception	Revealed deception
1. (O, A, N)	(A, O, N); (N, A, O)	A	A	O
2. (O, A, N)	(A, N, O); (N, A, O)	O, A, N	A	O
3. (O, A, N)	(A, N, O); (N, O, A)	N	A	O

(A, N, O); defeaters—(N, O, A). The chairman (passers), by announcing his first choice to be outcome A rather than outcome O, can, as in the previous situation, induce the sophisticated outcome A. This outcome is preferred by the passers to the sophisticated outcome N, which they obtain when they honestly represent their preferences. They can do even better, however, if, after announcing their first choice to be outcome A, they vote for their most-preferred outcome, O, thereby ensuring its passage if the other voters vote sophisticatedly. As in the second conflict situation, therefore, the passers can obtain their second choice through tacit deception, their first choice through revealed deception.

In Table 7.1 we have summarized the sophisticated outcomes that result in the three conflict situations in which tacit or revealed deception by the chairman is profitable. Although simply a dishonest announcement may improve a chairman's position somewhat—as in the second and third situations, wherein a dishonest announcement ensures passage of the chairman's second most-preferred outcome—such an announcement, followed by a vote for one's most-preferred outcome (that flaunts this announcement) always ensures one's best outcome (O in our example).

Of course, revealed deception becomes apparent after the vote—unless it is secret—and probably cannot be used very frequently. If it were, one's announcements would quickly become unbelievable and lose their inducement value.

The deceptive strategy game we have sketched for the chairman can naturally be played by a regular member if he is privy to information that the chairman and the other regular member are not. (The results will not duplicate those for the chairman, however, because of the extra voting power he—the chairman—possesses.) We shall not carry this analysis further, though, because our main purpose has been to demonstrate that there is a resolution (of sorts) to the paradox of the chairman's position.[3] It requires, however, that we restrict the information available to some players in the game, which has the effect of endowing one player (the chairman) with still greater voting power.

This, it must be admitted, is itself a rather deceptive way out of a problem that seems genuine. If voting is sophisticated, or if coalitions can form, the chairman, despite his added "weight," will not necessarily exercise greater control over outcomes than the other members. In fact, the reverse might be the case, as in paradox-of-voting situations under the plurality procedure if voting is sophisticated. To derive greater insight into this and other anomalous aspects of voting power, we shall next explore related paradoxes of power in terms of two quantitative measures of voting power.

7.5. THE CONCEPT OF VOTING POWER

We have avoided up to now defining exactly what we mean by the "power" of an actor in voting situations. Intuitively, it seems clear that the chairman in our three-member voting body has more voting power than the other two members because of his ability to break ties as well as cast one vote like the other (regular) members. Yet, as shown in the previous sections, this fact does not help him to obtain his most-preferred outcome in certain situations. Unless we assume that the chairman's preferences are not known to the other members, but their preferences are known to him, he will not be in a position to deceive the other members into availing him of his best outcome and may, consequently, have to settle for his second or third most-preferred choice.

This paradox of the chairman's position suggests that a useful definition of voting power should incorporate the idea of *control over outcomes*.[4] As we shall show, such control is not in general perfectly correlated with the number of votes one casts or other factors (e.g., the ability to break ties) that weigh in the decision-making process. Rather, control over outcomes also depends on how frequently, on the average, one can pool one's votes with those of others to ensure an outcome favorable to oneself.

---

3. For a more systematic analysis of deceptive voting strategies, see Brams and Zagare, "Deception in Simple Voting Games," forthcoming; and Steven J. Brams, *Theory of Political Deception*, forthcoming.

4. The material that follows in this section is adapted from Steven J. Brams, *Game Theory and Politics* (New York: Free Press, 1975), pp. 157–158. As used here (and in subsequent definitions of voting power), the idea of "control over outcomes" excludes the preferences of actors, which were central in our implicit formulation of power in the previous sections of this chapter. Along with Nagel, I believe that a complete definition of power must include both preferences and outcomes (i.e., power is the causation of outcomes by preferences) and offer a formal synthesis in Brams, *Theory of Political Deception*, forthcoming. See Jack H. Nagel, *The Descriptive Analysis of Power* (New Haven, Conn.: Yale University Press, 1975), esp. chap. 3, who links preferences and outcomes descriptively (i.e., empirically), but not formally.

Although other definitions of influence and power stress the effects that actors can have on each other,[5] for the purpose of defining the power of players in voting games, an outcome-oriented measure is preferable to an actor-oriented measure. In large voting bodies or even the electorate, wherein the influence of each person on every other person is for all practical purposes negligible, an actor-oriented measure would suggest that no one has any power. In fact, if each person has one vote, each person has an equal chance to influence the outcome, which seems a more reasonable way to view power in voting situations.[6]

This view is not compatible with defining the voting power of an actor to be proportional to the number of votes he casts, because votes per se may have no bearing on outcomes. For example, in a 3-member voting body (a, b, c), in which a has 4 votes, b 2 votes, and c 1 vote, members b and c are powerless if the decision rule is simple majority (4 out of 7). Since the fact that members b and c together control $\frac{3}{7}$ of the votes is irrelevant to the selection of outcomes by this body, we call these members *dummies*. Member a is a *dictator*, on the other hand, since his votes by themselves are sufficient to determine the outcome, and only coalitions of which he is a member are winning. Note that there can be only one dictator in a voting body, whose existence renders all other members dummies, but there may be dummies without there being a dictator (an example of this will be given in section 7.8).

The votes cast by a member of a voting body are relevant in the selection of outcomes only in the context of the number of votes cast by other members and the decision rule of the voting body. Both measures of voting power that we shall develop in this chapter utilize this information, albeit in different ways.

7.6. TWO INDICES OF VOTING POWER

To illustrate these measures, consider a 3-member voting body with member weights (3, 2, 2), in which the decision rule is a simple majority of 4 out of 7 members. Following Banzhaf, we define the voting power of a member to be the *number of winning coalitions in which his defection from the coalition would render it losing*—which is a defection that we call *critical—divided by the total number of critical defections for all members.*[7]

---

5. For a good collection of readings on the concept of power, see *Political Power: A Reader in Theory and Research*, ed. Roderick Bell, David V. Edwards, and R. Harrison Wagner (New York: Free Press, 1969).

6. John F. Banzhaf III, "Weighted Voting Doesn't Work: A Mathematical Analysis," *Rutgers Law Review*, 19 (Winter 1965), pp. 329–330, n. 31.

7. John F. Banzhaf III, "Weighted Voting Doesn't Work: A Mathematical Analysis"; Banzhaf, "Multimember Electoral Districts—Do They Violate the 'One Man, One Vote' Principle?" *Yale Law Journal*, 75 (July 1966), pp. 1309–1388. Combined with a measure of citizen voting power in states, Banzhaf's index has been applied to the calculation of the power of states in the U.S. Electoral College in Banzhaf, "One Man, 3.312 Votes: A Mathe-

We call such winning coalitions, wherein the subtraction of one member would change its status from winning to losing, *minimal winning coalitions*.

We distinguish the two 2-vote members in our example by the subscripts 1 and 2 (2_1 and 2_2). There are three distinct minimal winning coalitions—($3, 2_1$), ($3, 2_2$), and ($2_1, 2_2$)—whose members overlap but are not all identical with those of any other such coalition. Clearly, the subtraction of the 3-vote member from ($3, 2_1$) and ($3, 2_2$), the 2_1-vote member from ($3, 2_1$) and ($2_1, 2_2$), and the 2_2-vote member from ($3, 2_2$) and ($2_1, 2_2$) would render each minimal winning coalition losing. Altogether, therefore, there are six critical defections for the three members of the voting body.

Since each member's defection is critical in two minimal winning coalitions, each member's proportion of voting power is $\frac{2}{6} = \frac{1}{3}$ by Banzhaf's definition. We may conveniently represent these fractional values for each member by the components of a "power vector," which we call the *Banzhaf index* of a voting body. For the voting body (3, 2, 2), its Banzhaf index is ($\frac{1}{3}, \frac{1}{3}, \frac{1}{3}$) under simple majority rule, which indicates that the voting power of the one 3-vote member is the same as that of each of the two 2-vote members.

As an alternative measure of voting power, Coleman considers a member's voting power to be linked to his ability to prevent the passage of a motion. Like Banzhaf, he relates this ability to a member's critical defections. Unlike Banzhaf, however, Coleman chooses the number of minimal winning coalitions—not the number of critical defections of all members—as his basis of comparison and defines a member's voting power to be the *proportion of minimal winning coalitions in which his defection is critical*.[8]

Since each member's defection in the voting body (3, 2, 2) is critical in two of the three minimal winning coalitions, each member's power to prevent action is $\frac{2}{3}$ by Coleman's measure of voting power.[9] We call the vector whose components give each member's preventive power the *Coleman index*, which for the voting body (3, 2, 2) under simple majority rule is ($\frac{2}{3}, \frac{2}{3}, \frac{2}{3}$). Unlike the components of the Banzhaf index, the components of the Coleman index do not necessarily sum to 1.

It is apparent in our example that the power values of members given by the Coleman index are simply double the values given by the Banzhaf

---

matical Analysis of the Electoral College," *Villanova Law Review*, 14 (Winter 1968), pp. 304–332. For related analyses of the Electoral College, see references in note 15, p. 20. For a variation on Banzhaf's index, see Peter C. Fishburn, *The Theory of Social Choice* (Princeton, N.J.: Princeton University Press, 1972), pp. 53–55.

8. James S. Coleman, "Control of Collectivities and the Power of a Collectivity to Act," in *Social Choice*, ed. Bernhardt Lieberman (New York: Gordon and Breach, 1971), pp. 277–287.

9. Coleman, in "Control of Collectivities and the Power of a Collectivity to Act," also defines another measure of individual voting power—the power of a member to initiate action—but this measure is essentially a mirror image of a member's power to prevent action. Since it exhibits the same paradoxical features (discussed in section 7.7) of the "preventive" measure defined in the text, we shall not consider it in the analysis that follows.

index. In general, since the numerators of the fractional values for each index are the same, the proportion (or percentage) of the total power held by each member will be the same. However, the Coleman power values for members of a voting body will not in general sum to 1 (or any other constant) but will depend on the composition and decision rule of the body.

To illustrate this point, consider the following example. At one extreme, assume that each member of a voting body of n members has a veto over the combined action of all the other members (as in most trial juries, where the decision rule is unanimity). In this case, the Coleman index attributes voting power equal to 1 to every member of the body since the defection of each member is critical in the single coalition (of all members) that is winning. On the other hand, the Banzhaf index attributes voting power equal to $1/n$ to every member because this is each member's proportion of the n critical defections (one for each member).

At the other extreme, assume that every member in an n-member voting body has one vote, and the decision rule is simple majority. By the Banzhaf index, each member has voting power equal to $1/n$ (as before), since the defection of every member is critical in the same number of minimal winning coalitions. By the Coleman index, however, each member's voting power will always be greater than $\frac{1}{2}$ because each is a member of more than one-half of all minimal winning coalitions and—by his defection—critical in this proportion, too.[10]

The sensitivity of the Coleman index to the decision rule is evident from our two previous examples, for which the Banzhaf index gives identical power values. (When members are not equally weighted, both indices are sensitive to the decision rule, as we shall show in section 7.7.) Although both indices are based on the same idea—the ability of members to cast critical votes and thereby block action through their defection from minimal winning coalitions—they summarize information about this ability in different ways. The Banzhaf index, whose component power values for all members of a voting body always sum to 1, highlights the *relative* amount of voting power possessed by members of different voting bodies. The Coleman index, by contrast, does not highlight a member's share of the total power but emphasizes his *absolute* ability to block or prevent action by his defection. In effect, the Banzhaf index assumes a constant-sum game—voting power can only be redistributed (by a change in the decision rule or member weights)—whereas the Coleman index assumes a variable-sum game in which everybody's power may go up or down simultaneously.

Despite the different conceptualizations of power embodied in each index, they both show up the same paradoxical feature of voting power.

---

10. The larger n is, the closer this proportion is to exactly one-half.

So, too, does still another index of voting power—the so-called Shapley-Shubik index[11]—which is a constant-sum index akin to the Banzhaf index.[12]

7.7. THE PARADOX OF NEW MEMBERS

In the previous section we showed that the power of members of the voting body $(3, 2, 2)$ is $(\frac{1}{3}, \frac{1}{3}, \frac{1}{3})$ according to the Banzhaf index and $(\frac{2}{3}, \frac{2}{3}, \frac{2}{3})$ according to the Coleman index, given a decision rule of simple majority (4 out of 7). If a new 1-vote member is added to this body so that it becomes $(3, 2, 2, 1)$, how does this increase in the size of the body affect the voting power of the original members, given a decision rule of simple majority (now 5 out of 8)?

In the enlarged voting body, there are six minimal winning coalitions: $(3, 2_1)$; $(3, 2_2)$; $(3, 2_1, 1)$; $(3, 2_2, 1)$; $(3, 2_1, 2_2)$; $(2_1, 2_2, 1)$. The defection of the 3-vote member is critical in five coalitions, each of the 2-vote members in two, and the 1-vote member in one, making for a total of twelve critical defections. The Banzhaf power values for the body $(3, 2, 2, 1)$ are, therefore, $(\frac{5}{12}, \frac{3}{12}, \frac{3}{12}, \frac{1}{12}) = (\frac{5}{12}, \frac{1}{4}, \frac{1}{4}, \frac{1}{12})$, and the Coleman power values are $(\frac{5}{6}, \frac{3}{6}, \frac{3}{6}, \frac{1}{6}) = (\frac{5}{6}, \frac{1}{2}, \frac{1}{2}, \frac{1}{6})$.

Note that a coalition of members [e.g., $(3, 2_1, 2_2)$] may be minimal winning with respect to the defection of one member (3) but not with respect to the defection of other members (2_1 and 2_2). For a coalition to be considered minimal winning, we require that it be so with respect to the defection of *at least one of*—but not necessarily all—its members.

While the power of the two 2-vote members decreases in the enlarged voting body, the 3-vote member surprisingly *increases* his power in this body. Specifically, his power increases from $\frac{1}{3} = 0.33$ to $\frac{5}{12} = 0.42$ by the Banzhaf index, and from $\frac{2}{3} = 0.67$ to $\frac{5}{6} = 0.83$ by the Coleman index, despite the fact that his proportion of votes decreases from $\frac{3}{7} = 0.43$ in

11. L. S. Shapley and Martin Shubik, "A Method of Evaluating the Distribution of Power in a Committee System," *American Political Science Review*, 48 (September 1954), pp. 787–792.

12. For a detailed comparison of the different power indices and the models on which they are based, see Steven J. Brams, *Game Theory and Politics* (New York: Free Press, 1975), chap. 5; descriptions and applications of the Banzhaf and Shapley-Shubik indices are also given in William F. Lucas, "Measuring Power in Weighted Voting Systems," Cornell University, Department of Operations Research Technical Report no. 227 (Ithaca, N.Y., September 1974). Axiomatizations of the Shapley-Shubik index are given in L. S. Shapley, "A Value for N-Person Games," in *Annals of Mathematics Studies* (*Contributions to the Theory of Games*, ed. H. W. Kuhn and A. W. Tucker), 28 (Princeton, N.J.: Princeton University Press, 1953), pp. 307–317; and Pradeep Dubey, "On the Uniqueness of the Shapley Value," Cornell University, Department of Operations Research Technical Report (Ithaca, N.Y., June 1974); an axiomatization of the Banzhaf index is given in Pradeep Dubey and Lloyd S. Shapley, "Some Properties of the Banzhaf Power Index" (unpublished paper, February 1975). Axioms that all the power indices satisfy are given in M. G. Allingham, "Economic Power and Values of Games," *Zeitschrift für Nationalökonomie*, forthcoming.

TABLE 7.2   VALUES OF VOTING POWER INDICES FOR MEMBERS OF ORIGINAL AND ENLARGED VOTING BODIES UNDER TWO DECISION RULES

DECISION RULE

WEIGHT OF MEMBER	SIMPLE MAJORITY				CONSTANT (5 VOTES)			
	Banzhaf index		Coleman index		Banzhaf index		Coleman index	
	Original	En-larged	Original	En-larged	Original	En-larged	Original	En-larged
3	0.33	0.43	0.67	0.83	0.60	0.42	1.00	0.83
2	0.33	0.25	0.67	0.50	0.20	0.25	0.33	0.50
2	0.33	0.25	0.67	0.50	0.20	0.25	0.33	0.50
1	—	0.08	—	0.17	—	0.08	—	0.17
Total	1.00	1.00	2.00	2.00	1.00	1.00	1.67	2.00

the original body to $\frac{3}{8} = 0.375$ in the enlarged body. On the basis of this redistribution of power caused by the addition of the 1-vote member to the original voting body, it seems reasonable to suppose that the 3-vote member would favor an *expansion* in the size of the voting body by one 1-vote member!

Lest one think that a member's greater power in the enlarged (versus the original) voting body is an artifact of a change in the decision rule [from 4 (out of 7) in our original body to 5 (out of 8) in our enlarged body], consider what the power of the three original members would be if they had operated under a decision rule of 5 (out of 7), the same as that assumed in the enlarged body. Then the defection of each of the two 2-vote members (2_1 and 2_2) would be critical in one coalition apiece [$(3, 2_1)$ and $(3, 2_2)$]; the defection of the 3-vote member would be critical in both these coalitions as well as in the coalition $(3, 2_1, 2_2)$. Hence, the Banzhaf power values of the voting body $(3, 2, 2)$ under a decision rule of 5 out of 7 are ($\frac{3}{5}, \frac{1}{5}, \frac{1}{5}$), and the Coleman power values are $(1, \frac{1}{3}, \frac{1}{3})$.

Comparing these values with the corresponding Banzhaf [$(\frac{5}{12}, \frac{1}{4}, \frac{1}{4}, \frac{1}{12})$] and Coleman [$(\frac{5}{6}, \frac{1}{2}, \frac{1}{2}, \frac{1}{6})$] power values in the enlarged voting body $(3, 2, 2, 1)$, we see that each of the two 2-vote members *increases* his voting power from $\frac{1}{5} = 0.20$ to $\frac{1}{4} = 0.25$ by the Banzhaf index, and from $\frac{1}{3} = 0.33$ to $\frac{1}{2} = 0.50$ by the Coleman index. Thus, when the decision rule is the same in the original and enlarged bodies (i.e., 5 votes), each of the two 2-vote members—rather than the 3-vote member—benefits from the addition of a 1-vote member to the original body. The changes in voting power for the two different decision rules are summarized in Table 7.2.

The simultaneous *decrease* in a member's proportion of votes in the enlarged voting body, and his *increase* in voting power, seems certainly paradoxical, especially since the new 1-vote member added to the voting body is not a dummy and—by his presence—deprives the other members together of some voting power. Under the decision rule of simple majority in the original and enlarged voting bodies, for example, he reduces the combined voting power of the three original members from a total of 1.00 to a total of 0.92 by the Banzhaf index, from a total of 2.00 to a total of 1.83 by the Coleman index. Despite this collective reduction in voting power of the three original members, however, the new member causes a redistribution in the share that remains so that the largest original member (3) benefits under simple majority rule.

When the decision rule is the same (5 votes) in both voting bodies, the two smaller original members (2_1 and 2_2) benefit, as we showed earlier. In the case of the Coleman index, however, their increase in voting power is not so startling because the total power of all members also increases from 1.67 in the original body to 2.00 in the enlarged body (see Table 7.2).

We say that there is a *paradox of new members* when one or more new members are added to a weighted voting body—with or without a change in the decision rule—and the voting power of one or more of the original members increases, rather than decreases. Although other paradoxes connected with the measurement of voting power have been identified[13]— one of which we shall describe in section 7.9—the paradox of new members is probably the one of greatest empirical interest. Before we discuss empirical examples of this paradox, however, it is useful to distinguish three patterns associated with its occurrence:[14]

1. One or more dummies are empowered.

2. One or more other members, excluding the largest (in terms of weight), are advantaged.

3. The largest member (in terms of weight) enhances his dominant position.

We have already illustrated the second and third patterns; in section 7.8 we shall give a real-life example of the first pattern.

In terms of practical politics, the third pattern is probably the most interesting. Conventional political wisdom suggests that a stratagem for diluting the power of the dominant member (or coalition) in a voting body is to increase the size of the body. There are numerous examples of this maneuver's being employed, ranging from Franklin Roosevelt's (unsuccessful) attempt to pack the Supreme Court in the 1930s to (successful)

---

13. See Brams, *Game Theory and Politics*, pp. 176–182.

14. The discussion that follows here and in sections 7.8 and 7.9 is based largely on Steven J. Brams and Paul J. Affuso, "Power and Size: A New Paradox," *Theory and Decision,* 7 (March 1976). Reprinted from *Theory and Decision* by permission of D. Reidel Publishing Company, Dordrecht, Netherlands.

TABLE 7.3   VALUES OF BANZHAF INDEX FOR FOUR CASES UNDER DECISION RULE OF SIMPLE MAJORITY

WEIGHT OF MEMBER	POWER VALUES OF BANZHAF INDEX			
	Case 1	*Case 2*	*Case 3*	*Case 4*
6	0.500	0.565	0.542	0.636
3	0.167	0.130	0.125	0.091
2	0.167	0.130	0.125	0.091
2	0.167	0.130	0.125	0.091
1	—	0.043	0.042	—
1	—	—	0.042	—
2	—	—	—	0.091

efforts by Democrats in the U.S. House of Representatives to enlarge the membership of the Rules Committee in the 1960s and 1970s. Granted, part of the rationale behind this sort of maneuver is usually the conviction that the new members will be positioned ideologically and behaviorally in opposition to the previously dominant faction—that is, they will join only *certain* coalitions, which violates the assumptions underlying the power indices. Nonetheless, it seems safe to assume that the advocates of increased size expect to benefit from changes in the formal structure of the voting body as well.

The third pattern of the paradox of new members, though, should cause us to think twice about the wisdom of this ploy. A striking example of this pattern, whereby the largest member does better when new members are added to a voting body, is shown in Table 7.3 using the Banzhaf index and assuming simple majority rule in all cases. The member with weight 6, and 46 percent of the total votes, has 50 percent of the voting power in the original body (case 1). Yet, when a new member of weight 1 is added to this body, decreasing the largest member's percentage of the total votes to 43 percent, the largest member's voting power increases from 50 to 57 percent (case 2). While the introduction of a second new member of weight 1 decreases everyone's power (case 3), his addition still gives an advantage to the largest member over and above that which he enjoyed in case 1 (54 percent versus 50 percent of the voting power). Incredibly, though, if instead of adding one or two members of weight 1 (cases 2 and 3), we add a single member of weight 2 (case 4), the largest member's power jumps from 50 percent to 64 percent. Evidently, one does not necessarily countervail the power of a previously dominant member by adding either several new members or a single member of greater weight.

Given the possibility of such dramatic shifts in unexpected directions, it is useful to explore both the conditions for the existence of the paradox and the probability of its occurrence. First, however, to establish that our explorations are not merely an academic exercise, we shall describe two different real instances of the paradox.

7.8. EMPIRICAL EXAMPLES OF THE PARADOX OF NEW MEMBERS

Article II, Section 1, of the United States Constitution provides for the election of a president by electors from each state equal to its number of senators and representatives; and, as modified by Article XII (ratified in 1804), for the election by the electors, on a separate ballot, of a vice president. Although there is no provision in the Constitution that the electors from each state must vote as a bloc, in fact since the beginning of the Republic the states, in an apparent effort to maximize their voting power, have almost invariably cast their votes as blocs.[15] This feature of voting in the Electoral College is known as "unit rule."

Given unit-rule voting, the Electoral College can, in effect, be considered a weighted voting body, with the states—casting different numbers of votes—as its members. This body grew from its 13 original members, when the Constitution was ratified in 1789, to 51 members in 1964, when the District of Columbia (casting three electoral votes) was admitted to membership. With the expansion of the Electoral College as new states were added to the Union, are there any instances in which the voting power of old members increased?

Eleven times in its history the Electoral College has increased in size while the original assigned weights of members remained intact.[16] Normally, this was the result of the admission of a state or a set of states to the Union during the interval between decennial apportionments. In two of these eleven cases, the computation of the Banzhaf index for the states showed up the occurrence of the paradox of new members: once with the expansion of the Electoral College from 17 to 18 members in 1812, and a second time with its expansion to 19 members in 1816.

We shall not offer details here except to note that the increases in voting power of some of the original members in each case were very small and probably have no empirical import.[17] A more significant, if less pure, case of the paradox of new members occurred with the recent

15. See Nelson W. Polsby and Aaron B. Wildavsky, *Presidential Elections: Strategies of American Electoral Politics*, 3rd ed. (New York: Charles Scribner's Sons, 1971), p. 108, n. 51.

16. See Svend Petersen, *A Statistical History of the American Presidential Elections* (New York: Frederick Ungar Publishing Co., 1963), Table 1, pp. 3–6.

17. For further information, see Brams and Affuso, "Power and Size: A New Paradox."

TABLE 7.4   VALUES OF BANZHAF INDEX FOR MEMBERS OF 1958 AND 1973 COUNCILS ON PROPOSALS FROM COMMISSION

MEMBER	1958		1973	
	Weight	*Banzhaf index*	*Weight*	*Banzhaf index*
France	4	0.238	10	0.167
Germany	4	0.238	10	0.167
Italy	4	0.238	10	0.167
Belgium	2	0.143	5	0.091
Netherlands	2	0.143	5	0.091
Luxembourg	1	0.000	2	0.016
Denmark	—	—	3	0.066
Ireland	—	—	3	0.066
United Kingdom	—	—	10	0.167

expansion of the European Community from six to nine members. Comprising the European Coal and Steel Community (ECSC), the European Economic Community (EEC), and the European Atomic Energy Commission (Euratom) since July 1, 1967, this international organization has had as its governing body a Council of Ministers, representing the national viewpoints of its members. The numbers of votes of each country in the original Council of the EEC, established by the Treaty of Rome in 1958, and the new Council, which replaced the old Council in 1973, are shown in Table 7.4.[18]

In Table 7.4 we have also indicated, according to the Banzhaf index, the voting power of each member of the old and new Councils when it considers policy proposals of the European Commission. (The Commission is a collegiate body of thirteen individual members, chosen by the member states, which serves as the administrative arm of the Council, the main decision-making body.) Action by the 1958 Council on proposals of the Commission required a qualified majority of 12 out of 17 votes; action by the 1973 Council requires a qualified majority of 41 out of 58 votes.

---

18. See *Traités Instituant les Communautés Européennes* (Communautés Européennes, 1971), Article 148, pp. 292–293, for voting weights of members of the original Council; and *Treaties Establishing the European Economic Communities* (Luxembourg: European Communities, 1973), Article 148, pp. 294–295, for voting weights of members of the new Council. I am grateful to Glenda Rosenthal for calling my attention to these changes in voting weights.

As is clear from Table 7.4, the admission of Denmark, Ireland, and the United Kingdom to membership in the European Community in 1973 diluted the voting power of all the members on the original Council except Luxembourg. Astounding as it may seem, Luxembourg exercised absolutely no influence on decisions of the original Council: the subtraction of its one vote could, under no circumstances, render a winning coalition losing, so its power according to the Banzhaf (as well as Coleman) index was necessarily zero. Unless its representative was able, in discussion, to influence the voting decision of representatives from other countries, he might as well have not attended Council meetings. Luxembourg's role as a dummy member on the 1958 Council seems not to have been previously recognized.[19]

When Luxembourg was given a second vote on the 1973 Council, its voting power increased to 0.02 by the Banzhaf index, which would seem to confirm the existence of a paradox of new members. (Its existence is also indicated by the Coleman index.) Strictly speaking, however, this increase in Luxembourg's voting power on the new Council does not meet the conditions of the paradox illustrated earlier. In our previous examples of the paradox, the weights of the original members did not change when new members were added to a voting body, though we did allow the decision rule to change. Yet, in the case of the Council, the weights of the old members did change when new members were added.

This fact, though, would not appear to violate the spirit of the paradox. For while Luxembourg's votes were doubled on the new Council, the votes of all the other original members were increased by a factor of two and one-half. The fact that Luxembourg still managed to increase its voting power, despite its having proportionally fewer votes on the new Council—relative to the other original members—than on the old Council, would seem to be an even more striking manifestation of the inverse relationship between power and size than is illustrated by the examples discussed earlier.

Although this fact is not related to the paradox, it is interesting to note in passing that the next smallest countries on the new Council—Denmark and Ireland, which were each given three votes, one more vote than Luxembourg—have more than four times the voting power of Luxembourg according to the Banzhaf index. Clearly, weight and voting power

19. Ronald Rogowski's calculation of Luxembourg's "probability of unique determination" on the original Council is not zero, but the substantive meaning of this concept—at least in the context of measuring voting power—is not at all clear. See Ronald Rogowski, *Rational Legitimacy: A Theory of Political Support* (Princeton, N.J.: Princeton University Press, 1975), p. 135, Table 3.4. For another example of a voting body with dummy members that ultimately led to the reassignment of weights to members when this fact was uncovered and challenged in the courts, see Banzhaf's discussion of the voting power of members of the Nassau County Board of Supervisors in Banzhaf, "Weighted Voting Doesn't Work: A Mathematical Analysis," pp. 338–340. For a report on the continuing litigation concerning representation on the Nassau County Board, see *New York Times,* November 17, 1974, p. 43; and *New York Times,* June 15, 1975, section 4, p. 6.

may diverge significantly. Given that "the weighting of votes takes some account of the differences in population of the various Member States . . . ,"[20] this divergence will obviously affect the correlation between voting power and population.

When the Council does not act on proposals that it receives from the European Commission but instead develops its own proposals, the decision rule for the 1958 Council required not only a qualified majority of 12 votes but also the assent of at least four of the six members. For the 1973 Council, the assent of at least six of the nine members is required, in addition to a qualified majority of 41 votes.[21] This latter provision has ensured that "the four large countries, voting en bloc, cannot dominate the smaller nations on any issue."[22] Nonetheless, though these slightly more stringent decision rules afforded Luxembourg some nonzero voting power on both the 1958 and 1973 Councils, Luxembourg still gained power on the 1973 Council, according to the Banzhaf index, raising its proportion from 0.024 in 1958 to 0.026 in 1973.

7.9. EXPECTED FREQUENCY OF THE PARADOX OF NEW MEMBERS

The mathematical conditions that give rise to the paradox of new members are rather complex and appear to have no simple interpretation.[23] These conditions are of less practical interest, anyway, than the expected frequency of the paradox. To gain some insight into the probability of occurrence of the paradox, one can, with the aid of the computer, generate a large number of voting bodies and determine how frequently the paradox occurs, on the average, when new members are added to voting bodies.

---

20. *Encyclopedia of European Community Law: European Community Treaties* (New York: Matthew Bender, 1974), vol. BII, pt. B10, p. B10118.

21. There are, in addition, some decisions on which the Council may take action by simple majority (at least five out of nine members since 1973) and some which require unanimity (all nine members). In a comment on the Treaty article on voting procedures, it is noted that "in practice unanimity is still generally sought by the Council and voting occurs rarely." *Encyclopedia of European Community Law: European Community Treaties*, p. B10118. For further details on the Council of Ministers, see Gerhard Mally, *The European Community in Perspective: The New Europe, the United States, and the World* (Lexington, Mass.: D. C. Heath and Co., 1973), pp. 105–107; and *European Community: The Facts* (Washington, D.C.: European Community Information Service, 1974), p. 4. Both of the latter publications contain erroneous information on voting weights and decision rules in the Council. Conversation with staff members of the European Community Information Service, New York City, February 25, 1975. Correct information on weights and rules can be found in Keesing's research report, *The European Communities* (New York: Charles Scribner's Sons, 1975), pp. 22–24; and Uwe Kitzinger, *Diplomacy and Persuasion* (London: Thames and Hudson, 1973), p. 95.

22. *European Community: The Facts*, p. 4.

23. See Brams and Affuso, "Power and Size: A New Paradox," for a specification of these conditions in terms of generating functions.

As a basis for their probabilistic calculations, Brams and Affuso[24] generated all partitions of the integers 2 through 18 and used these partitions to define a sample space of weighted voting bodies with between 2 and 18 members.[25] The partitions of the integer 5, for example, define six weighted voting bodies with between 2 and 5 members: (4, 1); (3, 2); (3, 1, 1); (2, 2, 1); (2, 1, 1, 1); (1, 1, 1, 1, 1).

Adhering to the restriction that the combined weight of all members is never greater than 18 in the enlarged voting body, Brams and Affuso tested whether the addition of one or more members to all 2-member, 3-member, . . . , 17-member voting bodies in the sample produced the paradox of new members. They assumed that a decision rule of simple majority was operative in both the original and enlarged voting bodies in computing the power indices.

An abbreviated table of results of this computation using the Banzhaf index is shown in Table 7.5. (The Coleman index produces similar results.) For bodies whose number of original members varies between 2 and 7, Table 7.5 shows the probabilities of occurrence of the paradox when between 1 and 6 members are added that increase the bodies' sizes to between 3 and 13 members. (Given in parentheses below these probabilities are the numbers of cases sampled for relevant partitions of the integers 2 through 18.) The results reveal that the probability of the paradox *tends* to decrease—with qualifications, to be spelled out subsequently—as more new members are added (reading across the rows) and as the size of the body increases (reading down the columns).

Although these trends confirm our expectations that the paradox is less likely to occur in large bodies, or when several new members are added, it is surprising that the probability values are as high as they are. All the probabilities, for example, exceed 0.45 when one new member is added to each of the original bodies (with between 2 and 7 members). Even when as many as 5 members are added to a 5-member body— thereby doubling its size—the probability of the paradox is still a relatively high 0.25 (see Table 7.5).

Very small bodies with between 2 and 4 original members that are enlarged by 1 to 5 additional members contribute some nonuniformity to the trends mentioned earlier. The reason is that for bodies containing very few members, their enlargement does not generate many additional power distributions. For example, in a 2-member body, there are by the Banzhaf index only two distinct power distributions—(0.50, 0.50) or (1, 0); that is, either the members have equal voting power or there is a dictator. The

---

24. Brams and Affuso, "Power and Size: A New Paradox."

25. The partitions of a positive integer are the ways of writing that integer as a sum of one or more positive integers. Thus,

$$3 = 2 + 1 = 1 + 1 + 1$$

give the three partitions of the integer 3.

TABLE 7.5 PROBABILITIES OF THE PARADOX OF NEW MEMBERS[a]

NUMBER OF ORIGINAL MEMBERS	NUMBER OF NEW MEMBERS ADDED					
	1	2	3	4	5	6
2	0.459 (444)	0.620 (960)	0.666 (1245)	0.669 (1197)	0.661 (959)	0.646 (690)
3	0.492 (711)	0.483 (1245)	0.446 (1387)	0.405 (1187)	0.371 (871)	0.344 (581)
4	0.578 (797)	0.548 (1197)	0.475 (1187)	0.416 (932)	0.374 (636)	0.332 (400)
5	0.561 (719)	0.442 (959)	0.357 (871)	0.290 (636)	0.248 (410)	0.204 (244)
6	0.529 (567)	0.389 (690)	0.302 (581)	0.237 (400)	0.184 (244)	0.143 (139)
7	0.463 (412)	0.290 (462)	0.194 (365)	0.126 (237)	0.086 (138)	0.054 (74)

[a] Based on the application of the Banzhaf index to all partitions of the integers 2 through 18. Simple majority rule is assumed in the calculation of the Banzhaf index; the numbers in parentheses indicate the numbers of cases examined. From Brams and Affuso, "Power and Size: A New Paradox."

addition to this body of one member may result in three different power distributions—(1, 0, 0), (0.33, 0.33, 0.33), or (0.60, 0.20, 0.20).

While two of these three distributions for a 3-member body will always produce a paradox if there is a dictator in the original 2-member body, when this original body is progressively enlarged by the addition of 2, 3, and 4 new members, proportionally more power distributions generate the paradox. As can be seen in the progression of probability values in the first row of Table 7.4, they first increase before the more general trend of decreasing probabilities with increasing numbers of additional members takes hold.

It would appear that the probability of the paradox approaches zero as the number of original members approaches infinity (and the number of new members remains finite). Brams and Affuso conjecture that the probability of the paradox is *never* zero, however, for any finite weighted voting body (trivial exceptions excluded, such as bodies in which all members have equal weight). That is, they hypothesize that it is *always* possible to add one or more new members to any (nontrivial) finite weighted voting body and create a paradox of new members.

Whether there exists a voting body invulnerable to the paradox is of less practical import than the probability of occurrence of the paradox.

At least in small and moderate-size bodies, this probability is reasonably high. (Of the 24,744 changes in voting body size included in Table 7.4, 11,352, or 45.8 percent, result in the paradox.) Since most weighted voting bodies tend to be relatively small, it would seem that the paradox cannot be dismissed as an unlikely aberration. Certainly the real instances of its occurrence described in section 7.8 demonstrate that its existence is not strictly hypothetical.

7.10. THE PARADOX OF QUARRELING MEMBERS

In this section we shall describe a second paradox associated with the indices of voting power about which relatively little is known. Its expected frequency of occurrence has not been computed, nor has it been studied empirically, but it seems no less strange than (and probably as real as) the paradox of new members.

This paradox involves placing restrictions on winning coalitions that are allowed to form in voting bodies. We may suppose, for example, that two members are involved in a quarrel and refuse to join together to help form a winning coalition.[26] Although one might suspect that they could succeed only in hurting each other, it is a curious fact that the quarrel between two members may actually redound to *their* benefit by increasing both their individual and combined voting power. We call this phenomenon the *paradox of quarreling members*.

As an example, consider again the weighted voting body consisting of members (3, 2, 2), for which we showed in section 7.7 that for the decision rule of 5 out of 7 the Banzhaf power values are $(\frac{3}{5}, \frac{1}{5}, \frac{1}{5})$ and the Coleman power values are $(1, \frac{1}{3}, \frac{1}{3})$. Assume that the quarreling members of this voting body are the two 2-vote members. Then there will (as before) be one minimal winning coalition in which the defection of one of these members is critical—$(3, 2_1)$—and one in which the defection of the other member is critical—$(3, 2_2)$. The 3-vote member is also critical in each of these coalitions, but he is not critical in the coalition $(3, 2_1, 2_2)$, for this coalition is precluded by the quarreling restriction that prevents coalitions containing *both* 2-vote members (as well as the 3-vote member) from forming. Thus, by both the Banzhaf and Coleman indices, the power of the 3-vote member will be twice as great as the power of each 2-vote member, yielding for members (3, 2, 2) Banzhaf power values of $(\frac{1}{2}, \frac{1}{4}, \frac{1}{4})$ and Coleman power values of $(1, \frac{1}{2}, \frac{1}{2})$.

Since the power values for each of the two 2-vote members (0.25 by the Banzhaf index, 0.50 by the Coleman index) are greater than their respective

---

26. For a formalization of this idea, based on the Shapley value, which suggested the name for this paradox, see D. Marc Kilgour, "A Shapley Value for Cooperative Games with Quarrelling," in *Game Theory as a Theory of Conflict Resolution*, ed. Anatol Rapoport (Dordrecht, Netherlands: D. Reidel Publishing Co., 1974), pp. 193–206. Kilgour establishes the conditions under which the paradox described in the text occurs for the Shapley-Shubik index but not for the Banzhaf index or the Coleman index.

power values (0.20 and 0.33) if they do not quarrel and coalition formation is unrestricted, there is an incentive for them to quarrel to increase their shares of the voting power. It would appear, therefore, that power considerations—independently of ideological considerations—may inspire conflicts among members of a voting body simply because such conflicts enhance the quarreling members' relative (Banzhaf) and absolute (Coleman) voting power.

7.11. SUMMARY AND CONCLUSION

We began our analysis by showing that in several conflict situations in a three-member voting body whose members choose among three alternatives under the plurality procedure, the tie-breaking vote of a chairman may not enable him to obtain his most-preferred outcome if voting is sophisticated. His illusory extra voting power in such situations we referred to as the paradox of the chairman's position. We showed how a chairman can improve his position through a strategy involving either tacit or revealed deception, but the use of such a strategy depends on his having information about the preference scales of other members that they do not have about his preference scale. We concluded that the paradox of the chairman's position in conflict situations in which his tie-breaking vote works to his disadvantage is quite real; this conclusion suggested the need for looking at the relationship between votes and voting power in quantitative and more systematic terms.

Toward this end, we defined two indices of voting power, due to Banzhaf and Coleman, both of which measure an actor's ability to control the selection of outcomes in a weighted voting body. We showed that whereas both indices tap an actor's ability, by changing his vote, to change the outcome in a voting body, the Banzhaf index—as a relative measure—assumes a constant-sum game and the Coleman index—as an absolute measure—assumes a variable-sum game.

Both power indices were shown to be vulnerable to the paradox of new members, which occurs when new members are added to a voting body and the voting power of at least one of the original members increases, rather than decreases, as a result of the body's enlargement. This phenomenon seems paradoxical, we argued, because we commonly think that the smaller the proportion of votes that an actor controls, the less will be his voting power.

We showed that the paradox of new members can occur whether the decision rule changes or stays the same when the original body is enlarged. Moreover, it is not necessarily the case that adding more or weightier new members mitigates the effects of the paradox, as one of our hypothetical examples demonstrated.

We described two real instances of this paradox in the Electoral College when new states were added to the Union and the voting power of some of the original states increased. Because these power changes were practically negligible, however, we questioned whether they could have had any noticeable empirical consequences (even if they were perceived by the participants, which seems highly unlikely). On the other hand, although Luxembourg also increased its voting power only marginally on the European Community Council of Ministers when the Council's membership was enlarged from six to nine members, the fact that it started out as a dummy—according to one of the decision rules used by the Council—makes this case much more significant. For Luxembourg did benefit from a qualitative change in its power position; that this change seems to have gone undetected underscores the capricious nature of constitution writing—done mostly by lawyers uninformed as to the significance of the weights and decision rules they set down—even today.

Using the Banzhaf index, we next gave expected frequencies for the occurrence of the paradox of new members based on partitions of the integers 2 through 18. Although the probabilities of the paradox's occurrence tend to decrease as the size of the original voting body, and the number of members added, increase, they are surprisingly high in relatively small weighted voting bodies.

We then briefly described the paradox of quarreling members whereby members of a weighted voting body who refuse to join the same winning coalition may, by their refusal, increase their voting power. The expected frequency of occurrence of this paradox, and empirical manifestations of conflicts it may have engendered, have not been studied.

Although we cannot say much about the paradox of quarreling members, our analysis of the paradox of new members indicates that it is neither contrived nor improbable—and this seems probably also true of the paradox of quarreling members. Of course, one might still argue that these paradoxes are a creation of indices that only imperfectly reflect power realities in actual voting bodies. But to make this argument cogent, one must specify what the "realities" are.

Although political, historical, ideological, and other constraints have an evident effect on one's ability to control outcomes in an actual weighted voting body, the power indices nonetheless seem to provide very useful measures of a priori voting power based on members' weights and the decision rule of the body. The fact that they are founded on more or less plausible coalition models, and have been widely applied to the analysis of numerous real weighted voting bodies, would seem to indicate their general appeal as intellectual constructs.[27] At a more practical level, the Banzhaf index has been accepted by the New York State Court of Appeals

---

27. See Brams, *Game Theory and Politics*, chap. 5. For an attempt to validate the Banzhaf and Shapley-Shubik indices as applied to the analysis of congressional-presidential power in the United States, see Steven J. Brams and Lee Papayanopoulos, "Legislative Rules and Legislative Power" (Paper delivered at the Seminar on Mathematical Models of Congress, Aspen, Colo., June 16–23, 1974.)

as a basis for assigning weights to representatives on that state's County Boards of Supervisors.[28]

Given the widespread use and acceptance of the power indices, it would seem that aberrations that they show up must be taken seriously. Instead of thinking of the paradoxes of new members and quarreling members as "aberrant," however, it seems preferable to view them as reflecting aspects of voting power whose existence would have been difficult to ascertain in the absence of precise quantitative concepts. These concepts, by throwing into bold relief subtle relationships between the power of members and the size of, and conflict within, a voting body, enable us to comprehend more fully different dimensions of that power.

It is a limitation in our thinking and models, not an aberration in the phenomenon, that has heretofore led us to equate power with size and the lack of conflict. (Indeed, it is the nature of the conflict itself between the chairman and the other members, based on their different preference scales, that put the chairman at a disadvantage, and gave an advantage to the other members, in the voting situations discussed at the beginning of this chapter.) Taken together, the paradoxes of the chairman's position, new members, and quarreling members suggest that there may be instabilities in power relationships and structures that have heretofore not been evident. Given our general lack of understanding of the nature and exercise of power in voting situations, the conditions that lead to these instabilities would certainly seem to merit further study.

---

28. Ronald E. Johnson, "An Analysis of Weighted Voting as Used in Reapportionment of County Governments in New York State," *Albany Law Review*, 34 (Fall 1969), pp. 317–343; Robert W. Imrie, "The Impact of Weighted Voting on Representation in Municipal Governing Bodies of New York State," *Annals of the New York Academy of Sciences* (*Democratic Representation and Apportionment: Quantitative Methods, Measures, and Criteria*, ed. L. Papayanopoulos), 219 (New York: New York Academy of Sciences, 1973), pp. 192–199.

8

A PARADOX OF PREDICTION

8.1. INTRODUCTION

In a book on paradoxes, it is perhaps both instructive and appropriate to conclude with a recently invented paradox that is not, strictly speaking, a paradox of politics. It is a problem formulated by a physicist, William A. Newcomb, in 1960, elucidated by a philosopher, Robert Nozick, in 1969,[1] popularized by a mathematician in 1973,[2] and—despite the fact that it generated a huge response from many different people—remains, in the opinion of Nozick, a more open problem than ever.[3]

This fact seems testimony to some of the deep questions the paradox raises—particularly related to the existence of free will—which I shall only touch upon in this chapter. What I do hope to do is indicate the relevance of Newcomb's problem to some very interesting questions in politics and show—through the illustration to be developed presently—how philosophical issues almost inevitably intrude on what, in the beginning, may appear to be only hard-headed practical questions. I also hope that the subsequent discussion and analysis will demonstrate that if many profound questions have already been raised by great political thinkers of the past, there yet remain many questions to ask, as well as to answer. Not only are there new ways of looking at some of these questions, as I have tried to show in earlier chapters, but there also remain significant new problems

With the exception of section 8.3, this chapter is based on Steven J. Brams, "Newcomb's Problem and Prisoners' Dilemma," *Journal of Conflict Resolution*, 19 (December 1975). The permission of the Publisher, Sage Publications, Inc., to adapt material from this article is gratefully acknowledged.

1. Robert Nozick, "Newcomb's Problem and Two Principles of Choice," in *Essays in Honor of Carl G. Hempel*, ed. Nicholas Rescher (Dordrecht, Netherlands: D. Reidel Publishing Co., 1969), pp. 114–146. For further discussion of the paradox, see M. Bar-Hillel and A. Margalit, "Newcomb's Paradox Revisted," *British Journal for the Philosophy of Science*, 23 (November 1972), pp. 295–304; G. Schlesinger, "The Unpredictability of Free Choices," *British Journal for the Philosophy of Science*, 25 (September 1974), pp. 209–221; and Isaac Levi, "Newcomb's Many Problems," *Theory and Decision*, 6 (May 1975), pp. 161–175.

2. Martin Gardner, "Mathematical Games," *Scientific American*, July 1973, pp. 102–108.

3. See Nozick's reply to those who responded to Gardner's *Scientific American* article (see note 2 above) in Martin Gardner, "Mathematical Games," *Scientific American*, March 1974, pp. 102–108.

which contemporary political philosophers will undoubtedly raise, if not always satisfactorily resolve.

A persuasive resolution to Newcomb's problem, due to John A. Ferejohn, will be offered in section 8.4. However, our main analysis in this chapter will be devoted to showing the relationship between Newcomb's problem and Prisoners' Dilemma, the latter game being a "symmetricized" version of the former in its payoff structure. Moreover, the assumption made about one player in Newcomb's problem, when applied to both players in Prisoners' Dilemma—one considered as a leader and the other as a follower—offers a resolution to this dilemma that is generally consistent with the resolution offered by metagame theory. Unlike metagame theory, however, the solution proposed is not based on the *assumption* that players can successively predict each other's strategy choices before the game is played but rather is derived as a *consequence* of calculations that maximize the players' expected utility.

8.2. NEWCOMB'S PROBLEM

Imagine the following situation. There are two boxes, B1 and B2. B1 contains $1,000; B2 contains either $1,000,000 or nothing, but you do not know which. You have a choice between two possible actions:

1. Take what is in both boxes.
2. Take only what is in B2.

Now what is in B2 depends on what action some superior Being predicted you would take beforehand. If he predicted you would (1) take what is in both boxes—or would randomize your choice between the two actions —he put $0 in B2; if he predicted you would (2) take only what is in B2, he put $1,000,000 in B2. Hence, you are rewarded for taking only what is in B2—provided the Being predicted this choice—though you have some chance of getting even more ($1,001,000) if you take what is in both boxes and the Being incorrectly predicted that you would take only what is in B2. On the other hand, you do much less well ($1,000) if you take what is in both boxes—and the Being predicted this action—and worst ($0) if you take what is in B2 and the Being incorrectly predicted that you would take what is in both boxes.

These payoffs are summarized in the payoff matrix of Figure 8.1. Clearly, the very best ($1,001,000) and very worst ($0) outcomes occur when the Being's predictions are incorrect, the intermediate outcomes ($1,000,000 and $1,000), when the Being's predictions are correct.

Note that the Being's strategies given in Figure 8.1 are predictions, not what he puts in B2. We could as well define his two strategies to be "Put $1,000,000 in B2" and "Put $0 in B2," but since these actions are in one-to-one correspondence with his predictions about what you take, it

FIGURE 8.1 PAYOFF MATRIX FOR NEWCOMB'S PROBLEM

		BEING	
		Predicts you take only what is in B2	*Predicts you take what is in both boxes*
YOU	*Take only what is in B2*	$1,000,000	$0
	Take what is in both boxes	$1,001,000	$1,000

does not matter whether we consider the Being's strategies to be predictions or actions. (Since the Being's predictions precede his actions, they are perhaps the more basic indicator of his behavior.)

From the perspective of the game theorist, what does matter is that the Being's strategies are not the "free" choices usually assumed of players in the normal-form representation of a game (i.e., its representation by a payoff matrix). But this is not a game in the usual sense, which renders its Figure 8.1 representation vulnerable to attack (as will be shown in section 8.4). Moreover, the solution that will be proposed in section 8.6 to a symmetrical version of this game rests on a different model of player choices.

On first blush, it would appear, Newcomb's problem does not present you with a problem of choice. Your second row strategy—take what is in both boxes—dominates your first row strategy—take only what is in B2— since whatever the Being predicts, your payoffs are greater than those in your first row. Thus, you should always take what is in both boxes, which assures you of at least $1,000, as contrasted with a minimum of $0 for your first row strategy.

This choice is complicated, however, by your knowledge of the past performance of the Being, who is (or seems) "superior" precisely because his predictions have always been correct. (The Being may be thought of as God, but the paradox described subsequently retains its full force if he is regarded as a superior intelligence from another planet, or a super-computer capable of discerning your thoughts and using this knowledge to make highly accurate predictions.) Although you do not know what his prediction is in the present choice situation, it will, you believe, "almost surely" be correct. Thus, if you choose your dominant strategy of taking what is in both boxes, the Being will almost certainly have anticipated this action and left B2 empty. Hence, you will get only $1,000 from B1.

On the other hand, if you choose your first row strategy and take only what is in B2, the Being, expecting this, will almost surely have put $1,000,000 in B2, which would seem a strong argument for your choosing this strategy, despite the dominance of your second row strategy. This argument is based on the principle of maximizing *expected utility*—associated with money in this case—which is the sum of the payoffs associated with each of the outcomes in each row times the probability that each will occur. (Recall that we made a similar calculation in section 5.3, but the payoff units were undefined.)

Assume, for purposes of illustration, that though you have near perfect confidence in the predictions of the Being, you conservatively estimate that the probability of his being correct is only 0.9. Then, the expected utility of your first row strategy (take only what is in B2) is

$$(\$1,000,000)(0.9) + (\$0)(0.1) = \$900,000,$$

whereas the expected utility of your second row strategy (take what is in both boxes) is

$$(\$1,001,000)(0.1) + (\$1,000)(0.9) = \$101,000.$$

Evidently, to maximize your expected utility you should take only what is in B2. (In fact, the probability that the Being is correct need only be greater than 0.5005 in this example to make the expected utility that you derive from your first row strategy exceed that which you derive from your second row strategy.)

This conflict between the dominance principle, which prescribes taking what is in both boxes, and the expected-utility principle, which prescribes taking only what is in B2, is the heart of the paradox. Although each principle can be supported by very plausible arguments, the choices that each prescribes will in general be in conflict, given the excellent powers of prediction assumed on the part of the Being.

This paradox, it should be pointed out, is not the product of any hidden or suppressed assumptions. You are assumed fully to understand the choice situation, the Being knows that you understand, and so on. Furthermore, no kind of "backwards causality" is assumed to be at work, whereby your present actions are influenced by the Being's past predictions. The Being is assumed to have made a prediction—say, a week before you make your choice—and put either $1,000,000 in B2 or nothing. The money is there or it is not there, and nothing that you think or do can subsequently change this fact.

What is your choice? Nozick reports:

. . . I have put this problem to a large number of people, both friends and students in class. To almost everyone it is perfectly clear and obvious what should be done. The difficulty is that these people seem to divide almost evenly on the problem, with large numbers thinking that the opposing half is just being silly.[4]

---

4. Nozick, "Newcomb's Problem and Two Principles of Choice," p. 117.

Although respondents to Gardner's first *Scientific American* article favored the expected-utility principle by better than two to one, Nozick concludes in his reply to the respondents that "the [148] letters do not, in my opinion, lay the problem to rest."[5]

8.3. AN INTERPRETATION IN POLITICS

Restating a problem in a different context sometimes clarifies some of its ambiguities and makes perspicuous the difficulties implicit in its original formulation. Although the interpretation of Newcomb's problem offered in this section does not disarm either the arguments supporting the dominance principle or the arguments supporting the expected-utility principle, it does add to the original statement of the problem some less ethereal qualities. Insofar as our "political" interpretation faithfully reflects the anomalous aspects of this problem, it would seem that these aspects cannot be dismissed as a "mere" curiosity of no practical significance. Almost all dilemmas of human choice—including those, like Newcomb's problem, with nonhuman or theological overtones—come to be mirrored in political life, though not all such dilemmas are easy to identify, much less resolve.

To exorcise the mystical element from Newcomb's near omnicient Being, we first consider political situations in which the ability to make predictions is highly valued. There are, of course, many such situations in politics, but the definition of Newcomb's problem also demands that the actor making the predictions be able to reward, in some manner, the actor about whose choices he is making predictions.

It is not easy to think of political situations in which persons who make predictions *reward others*, rather than *are rewarded themselves*, for the correctness of their predictions. If we extend the notion of reward, however, from that of compensating others *by direct payments* to compensating others *by taking or not taking a particular course of action oneself*, then rewards to others frequently attend the predictions politicians make.

Consider the following situation. Three persons, A, B, and C, consider entering the race for their party's nomination for the presidency. Person A announces his candidacy first, saying that he will enter all the primaries. Person B, though an acknowledged candidate, announces that he will defer his decision on whether or not to enter the primaries, presumably to assess his chances should person C also decide to enter the primaries. Person B—the Being in Newcomb's problem—reasons as follows:

> Person C will undoubtedly not make a decision on whether or not to enter the primaries until the last minute—too late for me to organize an effective primary compaign should I decide to enter the primaries. Therefore, in order

---

5. Nozick's reply in Gardner, "Mathematical Games," *Scientific American*, March 1974, p. 108.

FIGURE 8.2 PAYOFF MATRIX FOR PERSON C IN NOMINATION RACE

| | | PERSON B (KENNEDY) | |
		Predicts C will enter	*Predicts C will not enter*
PERSON C (HUMPHREY)	*Will enter*	1. 50-50 chance	3. Loses
	Will not enter	2. Better than 50-50 chance	4. Less than 50-50 chance

to determine my own best course of action, I must make a prediction before-hand about whether he will enter the primaries.

1. If I (correctly) predict that C will enter, I should not enter myself but instead let A and C fight it out in the primaries; C will almost certainly win in most of the primaries, but I would have a 50-50 chance of beating him in the convention (and he would have a 50-50 chance of beating me).

2. If I (incorrectly) predict that C will enter, I should not enter myself and A will run unopposed in the primaries. A's victories under these circumstances will not be very impressive, though; because C has better credentials as a compromise candidate than I do, however, he would have a better than 50-50 chance of beating both A and me in the convention, where his middle-of-the-road position will be most advantageous.

3. If I (incorrectly) predict that C will not enter the primaries, and I therefore decide to enter, C as the compromise candidate will almost certainly lose in a three-way primary race, where his middle-of-the-road position will be least advantageous.

4. If I (correctly) predict that C will not enter the primaries, and I therefore decide to enter, I can almost certainly beat A in the primaries. With the strong primary support that I receive, C, even as a compromise candidate, would have less than a 50-50 chance of beating me in the convention.

The payoffs for these four outcomes are summarized in Figure 8.2.

An implausible scenario? I would suggest that the 1968 race for the Democratic presidential nomination among Eugene McCarthy (A), Robert Kennedy (B), and Hubert Humphrey (C) quite closely approximated this scenario. McCarthy announced first, fought Kennedy in the primaries, to whom he lost in the final and crucial California primary before Kennedy was assassinated. If Kennedy had lived, he probably would have stood a good chance of beating Humphrey in the convention, as suggested by outcome 4 (outcome descriptions apply to person C, Humphrey).

Outcome 2 supposes that if McCarthy had run unopposed in the primaries, Humphrey could probably have captured the nomination in the convention. This seems plausible because, even with considerable support from Kennedy delegates in the convention, McCarthy did in fact lose the nomination to Humphrey in 1968.

Outcome 3 says that Humphrey would have lost to Kennedy or McCarthy if he had entered the primaries. This seems highly likely, given the success McCarthy had in discrediting the Johnson administration—and by implication, Humphrey—in the New Hampshire and Wisconsin primaries. In Indiana and the later primaries that both Kennedy and McCarthy entered, stand-ins for the Johnson administration fared badly.

Outcome 1 is the most difficult to relate to the 1968 Democratic race. It says that if Humphrey had entered the primaries against McCarthy only, he would have triumphed, but Kennedy would have had an even chance of defeating him in the convention. Although it is conceivable that if Humphrey had successfully divorced himself from the Vietnam policy of the Johnson administration, he could have met the McCarthy challenge on the left in the primary battles, it is less conceivable that Kennedy would have posed a serious threat to Humphrey's candidacy in the convention if Kennedy had not entered the primaries. This latter proposition does become more plausible, however, if we assume that the primaries could have exposed weaknesses in Humphrey's position that, the convention delegates believed, would compromise his chances in the general election. Yet, though there are precedents for primary winners' losing their party's nomination in the convention (in the 1952 Democratic convention, Estes Kefauver lost to Adlai Stevenson, who did not enter the primaries; but Stevenson, unlike Kennedy, was not running against an officeholder from the previous administration), it seems fair to admit that the scenario for outcome 1 does not match very well events as they might have unfolded in 1968.

If our scenario does not fit perfectly the events in any actual presidential nomination race, it seems certainly possible to imagine two candidates in a three-candidate race thinking in the terms we have described. Indeed, Robert Kennedy—the Being in our example—agonized for several weeks over whether or not to enter the primaries in 1968. Not only did he face the question of whether Humphrey would enter the primaries after Johnson took himself out of the race just prior to the Wisconsin primary, but he also had to assess how he would do against McCarthy and possible stand-ins (e.g., favorite sons) for the Johnson administration if Humphrey did not run in the primaries. In this sense, Kennedy was forced to make predictions not only about Humphrey's actions but also about those of his surrogates who might run; given these predictions, Humphrey (and possible stand-ins) themselves faced choices, based in part on the intelligence (or clairvoyance) they attributed to Kennedy in being able to predict their own behavior. Thus, it would seem that the payoff matrix in Figure 8.2 summarizes a hypothetical, but not unrealistic, situation that two candidates might face in their mutual attempts to divine each other's probable choices.

8.4. WHICH PRINCIPLE, AND IS THERE A CONFLICT?

In Newcomb's problem, an asymmetry is assumed in both the rules and actions of the two players in the prediction-choice game. The Being (person B in Figure 8.2) is assumed to be a phenomenally good guesser, but no such superior intelligence is attributed to person C. Furthermore, player B is assumed to make the first move, but in fact this gives him neither an advantage nor a disadvantage because his choice (based on his prediction) is not communicated to person C. Thus, we could just as well assume that the two players make simultaneous choices; the essential nature of the game remains unchanged.

What we have added to Newcomb's formulation is that person B not only makes a prediction about C's behavior but chooses an action—to enter or not to enter the primaries—that is consistent with this prediction (i.e., is his best course of action if his prediction is correct). We assume that this action is not known to person C before he makes his own choice of whether or not to enter the primaries, but we do assume that it has an effect on C's payoff (as well as B's). This assumption is necessary to motivate the rewards (or penalties) that would be bestowed on person C, for political science—unlike philosophy—does not readily admit a Being who disburses payments solely on the basis of the (in)correctness of his predictions and another player's subsequent choices.

The most reasonable source for such payments would seem to be the *consequent actions* that person B (the Being in Newcomb's problem) takes after making his prediction. He, as well as person C, wants to be a maximizer, but he is capable only, in the representation of Figure 8.2, of making (good) predictions, not independently choosing one of the two columns in the payoff matrix.

Person B's predictions, however, structure the payoffs for person C—through B's consequent actions (on whether or not to enter the primaries himself) based on these predictions—in a manner consistent with Newcomb's problem. Since person C's second row strategy (will not enter) dominates his first row strategy (will enter) in Figure 8.2—as does the row player's second strategy dominate his first in Figure 8.1—he should, according to the dominance principle, not enter the primaries, which happens to be the decision Humphrey made in 1968.

As we have indicated, person B, though he does not choose columns in the payoff matrix—his predictions presumably are based on information he has about person C—does use his predictions to determine his own best course of action. These predictions *indirectly* influence person C's choices because they determine person B's own best course of action, which defines in part the payoffs in Figure 8.2.

By the conditions of Newcomb's problem, person B's predictions may, in addition, *directly* influence person C's choices. If, in the extreme case, C's confidence in B's ability to predict his behavior is absolute, C's choice is clear. Since he cannot possibly outsmart C—because B would know this and act accordingly in making his prediction—C should enter the primaries. Correctly predicting this, B would not enter, but would wait until the convention to contest the nomination, which—as described by outcome 1—would give C a 50-50 chance of winning the nomination. This is better than the "less than 50-50 chance" he would have if he did not enter and C correctly predicted this choice. Thus, at least in the extreme case wherein C's confidence in B's predictive powers is absolute, C should ignore the dominance principle and enter the primaries. Apparently, Humphrey did not rate Kennedy's predictive powers that highly in 1968.

If we could attach numerical values to the payoffs in Figure 8.2, we could calculate exactly what confidence (i.e., probability of being correct) person C would have to have in person B in order for the expected-utility principle not to conflict with the dominance principle. As we indicated in section 8.2, for the monetary values given in Figure 8.1, the dominance principle and the expected-utility principle both prescribe the same strategy (C's second) when the probability that the Being's prediction is correct is less than 0.5005. Such a low probability value obviously conflicts with the presumed predictive powers of the Being, however, which is precisely why there is a paradox of prediction.

Is there any solution to this paradox that resolves the apparent inconsistency between the dominance principle and the expected-utility principle? John A. Ferejohn has shown that if Newcomb's problem is reformulated as a *decision-theoretic* rather than a *game-theoretic* problem, the apparent inconsistency between the two principles disappears.[6]

Recall from section 3.2 that in a model of decision making under risk, we assume that the action an actor takes does not lead to a particular outcome with certainty but to a set of possible outcomes with certain probabilities of occurring. When we conceptualize the problem in these terms, then, the person making the choice of either B2 or both boxes in Newcomb's problem does not view the Being as making predictions *about what he will choose* but rather making predictions *that are correct or incorrect* (see Figure 8.3).

Observe that your two best outcomes in the payoff matrix of Figure 8.1 ($1,000,000 and $1,001,000) are both associated with the Being's

---

6. Personal communication, May 27, 1975. Nigel Howard has also shown these two principles to be consistent in a metagame representation of Newcomb's problem. Personal communications, March 27, 1975 and June 25, 1975. Whereas Howard's metagame resolution of the paradox retains the assumption that Newcomb's problem is a game, Ferejohn criticizes precisely this assumption, as we shall show.

FIGURE 8.3   NEWCOMB'S PROBLEM AS A DECISION-THEORETIC PROBLEM

| | STATE OF NATURE | |
	Being correct	Being incorrect
Take only what is in B2	$1,000,000	$0
Take what is in both boxes	$1,000	$1,001,000

YOU

predicting that you will take only what is in B2 (first column of Figure 8.1). In the decision-theoretic payoff matrix of Figure 8.3, by contrast, these outcomes are the diagonal elements, each being associated with a different "state of nature," which is assumed to be either a correct or an incorrect prediction on the part of the Being. Because your best choice depends on what state of nature obtains in the decision-theoretic representation (if the Being is correct, take only what is in B2; if the Being is incorrect, take what is in both boxes), neither of your two actions dominates the other.

Since you do not have a dominant strategy in the decision-theoretic representation of Figure 8.3, there no longer exists a conflict between the expected-utility principle and the dominance principle. Now the sole determinant of whether you should take only what is in B2, or you should take what is in both boxes, to maximize your expected utility are the probabilities that you associate with each state of nature. If the probability that the Being is correct is greater than 0.5005, then you should take only what is in B2; if this probability is less than 0.5005, then you should take what is in both boxes; and if this probability is exactly 0.5005, then you would be indifferent between (equally inclined toward) your two actions.

How persuasive is this resolution of Newcomb's problem? If you believe that the Being has no control over which state of nature obtains in Figure 8.3, then the Being is not properly a player in a two-person game of the kind assumed in Figure 8.1; hence, the appropriate representation of Newcomb's problem is decision-theoretic. To be sure, the probabilities of being in each state are not specified by Newcomb's problem, so the decision-theoretic representation does not answer the question of whether you should take only what is in B2 or you should take what is in both boxes. However, this representation does demonstrate that there is no conflict between the dominance principle and the expected-utility principle.

On the other hand, if you believe that the Being has some control over which state of nature obtains—which is a question quite different from whether he can predict your choice (which he almost surely can)—then he is not an entirely passive "state of nature," at least with respect to being correct; hence, the game-theoretic representation of Figure 8.1 is the appropriate one. However, it must be said that there is nothing in the original statement of Newcomb's problem to indicate that the Being's choices are anything but mechanistic—that is, the correctness of his prediction about your action is *not* assumed to depend in any way on your choice. Or, to put it another way, though you are assumed to exercise free will with respect to the action you take, the Being exercises no free will with respect to what he puts in B2; his "choice" is dictated solely by his prediction.

The fact that the Being's prediction is assumed to be almost surely correct would seem to imply that you are indeed playing a game against nature whose two states—Being correct or Being incorrect—occur with the same relative frequency whatever you do. Given that this is the proper interpretation of Newcomb's problem, then Ferejohn's ingenious decision-theoretic reformulation of the problem convincingly resolves the presumed conflict between the dominance and expected-utility principles.

If we can dispose of Newcomb's problem in this manner, it is still intriguing to ask what consequences the predictive ability assumed on the part of the Being would have if *both* actors in Newcomb's problem could make genuine choices as players in a game. For in practically any interpretation of Newcomb's problem in politics, such as that given in section 8.3, there is an obvious arbitrariness in attributing superior predictive powers to one actor but not the other. Despite the vaunted intelligence and strategic skills of the Kennedy organization, it seems a bit absurd to designate him—or, for that matter, Humphrey—as the Being in Newcomb's problem. There is, probably, more symmetry than asymmetry in the roles that candidates assume in a political campaign, and it is useful to try to build this symmetry into Newcomb's problem. This we shall do in section 8.5 and show that it leads us back to an already familiar game.

8.5. NEWCOMB'S PROBLEM "SYMMETRICIZED": BACK TO PRISONERS' DILEMMA

We may generalize the payoff matrix of Newcomb's problem in Figure 8.1 to that shown in Figure 8.4, where the payoffs in the matrix represent *utilities* of the outcomes to the row player (A), A_1 representing his best payoff, A_2 next, and so on. The dominance principle says that player A should choose strategy a_2, the expected-utility principle says that player A should choose strategy a_1, given that A considers B's ability to predict his (A's) choices to be "sufficiently good." More precisely, if p is the subjective probability that A believes B's prediction about his strategy choice will be correct, then the expected-utility principle would prescribe that A should choose strategy a_1 if

$$A_2p + A_4(1 - p) > A_1(1 - p) + A_3p.$$

To convert Newcomb's problem into a symmetrical prediction-choice game, assume not only that player B can make predictions about player

FIGURE 8.4 GENERALIZED PAYOFF MATRIX FOR PLAYER A IN NEWCOMB'S PROBLEM

		PLAYER B	
		Predicts a_1	*Predicts a_2*
PLAYER A	a_1	A_2	A_4
	a_2	A_1	A_3

FIGURE 8.5 PAYOFF MATRIX FOR PLAYER B

		PLAYER B	
		b_1	b_2
PLAYER A	*Predicts b_1*	B_2	B_1
	Predicts b_2	B_4	B_3

A's choices but A can make predictions about B's choices as well. If player B's ranking of the outcomes duplicates player A's in Figure 8.4— but now, with the rows and columns interchanged, A is assumed to be the predictor and B the chooser—the payoff matrix for player B will appear as in Figure 8.5, with B_1 representing his best payoff, B_2 next, and so on. As was true for player A in the Figure 8.4 game, here the dominance principle and the expected-utility principle prescribe different strategy choices for player B if he (B) considers player A's ability to predict his choices to be sufficiently good.

If we combine the payoffs in the two asymmetrical prediction-choice games into a single payoff matrix, we get the game shown in Figure 8.6 (in which only the player's strategies, but not their predictions about the other player's strategy choices, are shown). The payoff matrix for this game gives the outcomes for both players, where, for each cell entry (A_i, B_j), A_i represents the payoff to the row player, and B_j the payoff to the column player. Lo and behold, the ranking of outcomes by both players in this game generated by the symmetric play of Newcomb's prediction-choice game defines the classic 2 × 2 Prisoners' Dilemma game (see section 3.2)!

Recall that the dilemma for the players in this game lies in the fact that whereas they both prefer outcome (A_2, B_2) to outcome (A_3, B_3), the former outcome is not in equilibrium: each player has an incentive to shift to his second (dominant) strategy, given that the other player sticks

---

**FIGURE 8.6 COMBINED PAYOFF MATRIX
FOR PLAYERS A AND B**

	PLAYER B b_1	b_2
PLAYER A a_1	(A_2, B_2)	(A_4, B_1)
a_2	(A_1, B_4)	(A_3, B_3)

---

to his first (dominated) strategy. Both players are therefore motivated to "play it safe" and choose their dominant second strategies (a_2 and b_2), which—unfortunately for them—yields the "noncooperative" outcome (A_3, B_3) that both find inferior to the "cooperative" outcome, (A_2, B_2).

8.6. A SOLUTION TO PRISONERS' DILEMMA

The fact that the problems of choice in Newcomb's problem and Prisoners' Dilemma are related should not obscure the fact that the latter is a two-person game—in which both players can make free and independent choices—whereas the former seems best conceptualized as a (one-person) game against nature, or a situation of decision making under risk. However, the condition in the symmetric version of Newcomb's problem that each player knows that the other player can predict—with a high degree of accuracy—which strategy he will choose does have a surprising consequence for the play of Prisoners' Dilemma: it provides an incentive for each player *not* to choose his second dominant strategy (a_2 or b_2).

True, if one player knows that the other player will almost surely choose his second strategy, then he should also choose his second strategy to insure against receiving his worst payoff (A_4 or B_4). As a consequence of these choices, the noncooperative outcome (A_3, B_3) will be chosen.

But now assume that one player knows that the other player plans—at least initially—to select his first strategy. Then one would ordinarily say that he should exploit this information and select his second strategy, thereby realizing his best payoff (A_1 or B_1). But this tactic will not work, given the mutual predictability of choices we have assumed on the part of both players in this symmetric version of Newcomb's problem. For any thoughts by one player of "defecting" from his strategy associated with the cooperative but unstable outcome, (A_2, B_2), would almost surely be detected by the other player. The other player then could exact retribution —and at the same time prevent his worst outcome from being chosen— by switching to his own noncooperative strategy. Thus, the mutual predictability of strategy choices that we have assumed in the symmetric version of Newcomb's problem helps to insure against noncooperative choices by *both* players and stabilize the cooperative solution to Prisoners' Dilemma.

More formally, assume player A contemplates choosing either strategy a_1 or a_2 and knows that player B can correctly predict his choice with probability p and incorrectly predict his choice with probability $1 - p$. Similarly, assume that player B, facing the choice between strategy b_1 and b_2, knows that player A can correctly predict his choice with probability q and incorrectly predict his choice with probability $1 - q$. Given these probabilities, we shall show that there exists a "choice rule" that *either* player can adopt that will induce the other player to choose his cooperative strategy—based on the expected-utility criterion—given that the probabilities of correct prediction are "sufficiently high."[7]

A *choice rule* is a conditional strategy based on one's prediction about the strategy choice of the other player. In the calculation to be given shortly, we assume that one player adopts a choice rule of *conditional cooperation*: he will cooperate (i.e., choose his first strategy) if he predicts that the other player will also cooperate by choosing his first strategy; otherwise, he will choose his second (noncooperative) strategy.

Assume player B adopts a choice rule of conditional cooperation. Then if player A chooses strategy a_1, B will correctly predict this choice with probability p and hence will choose strategy b_1 with probability p and strategy b_2 with probability $1 - p$. Thus, given conditional cooperation on the part of B, A's expected utility from choosing strategy a_1 will be

$$E(a_1) = A_2 p + A_4(1 - p).$$

Similarly, his expected utility from choosing strategy a_2 will be

$$E(a_2) = A_1(1 - p) + A_3 p.$$

Comparing $E(a_1)$ and $E(a_2)$,

$$A_2 p + A_4(1 - p) \overset{?}{>} A_1(1 - p) + A_3 p,$$

$$(A_2 - A_3)p \overset{?}{>} (A_1 - A_4)(1 - p),$$

$$\frac{p}{1 - p} \overset{?}{>} \frac{A_1 - A_4}{A_2 - A_3},$$

we see that this inequality is satisfied, and $E(a_1) > E(a_2)$, whenever p (in comparison to $1 - p$) is "sufficiently large." If, for example, the utilities associated with player A's payoffs are $A_1 = 4$, $A_2 = 3$, $A_3 = 2$, and

---

7. Recall that inducement takes a noncooperative—rather than cooperative—form in the sequential-primary game described in Chapter 5. For a different concept of inducement, based on players' misrepresentation of their preferences in 2 × 2 games, see Steven J. Brams, "Deception in 2 × 2 Games," forthcoming; and Brams, *Theory of Political Deception*, forthcoming.

$A_4 = 1$, then the expected utility of player A's first strategy will be greater than that of his second strategy if

$$\frac{p}{1-p} > \frac{4-1}{3-2},$$

$$p > 3(1-p),$$

$$4p > 3,$$

$$p > \frac{3}{4}.$$

That is, by the expected-utility criterion, player A should choose his first (cooperative) strategy if he believes that player B can correctly predict his strategy choice with a probability greater than $\frac{3}{4}$, given that player B responds in a conditionally cooperative manner to his predictions about A's choices. Note that whatever the utilities consistent with player A's ranking of the four outcomes are, p *must* exceed $\frac{1}{2}$.

What happens if player B adopts a less benevolent choice rule? Assume, for example, that he always chooses strategy b_2, whatever he predicts about the strategy choice of player A. In this case, if A now adopts a conditionally cooperative choice rule, he will choose strategy a_1 with probability $1 - q$ and strategy a_2 with probability q. Thus, given conditional cooperation on the part of A, B's expected utility from always choosing strategy b_2 will be

$$E(b_2) = B_1(1-q) + B_3 q.$$

Similarly, his expected utility from always choosing strategy b_1 will be

$$E(b_1) = B_2 q + B_4(1-q).$$

Comparing $E(b_1)$ and $E(b_2)$, we can show, in a manner analogous to the comparison of the expected utilities of strategies given previously for player A, that $E(b_1) > E(b_2)$ if

$$\frac{q}{1-q} > \frac{B_1 - B_4}{B_2 - B_3},$$

i.e., whenever q (in comparison to $1 - q$) is "sufficiently large." Subject to this condition, therefore, player B would *not* be well advised always to choose strategy b_2 if player A adopts a conditionally cooperative choice rule. Clearly, a choice rule of noncooperation on the part of one player is inconsistent with a choice rule of conditional cooperation on the part of the other player.

8.7. COOPERATION OR NONCOOPERATION?

We have now shown that if one player—call him the *leader*—(1) adopts a conditionally cooperative choice rule and (2) can predict the other player's strategy choice with a sufficiently high probability, the other player—call him the *follower*—maximizes his own expected utility by also cooperating, given that he can detect lies on the part of the leader with a sufficiently high probability. Thereby both players "lock into" the cooperative solution, which—it will be recalled—is unstable in Prisoners' Dilemma when the players do not have the ability to predict each other's strategy choices.

There is one question that remains, however. Given that the follower maximizes his expected utility by cooperating when the leader adopts a choice rule of conditional cooperation, how does the follower know when the leader adopts such a choice rule in the first place? The answer is that he does not, unless the leader announces his intention to adopt this choice rule.

To escape the dilemma, therefore, we must assume that there is some communication between the players. Moreover, we must assume that one player (the leader) announces a choice rule to which the other player (the follower) responds. If neither player takes the initiative, nothing can happen; if both players take the initiative simultaneously and announce the choice rule of conditional cooperation, each presumably will await a commitment from the other before committing himself, and nothing again will happen. Should the players simultaneously announce different choice rules, the resulting inconsistencies may lead to confusion, or possibly an attempt to align the rules or distinguish the roles of leader and follower.[8]

The only clean escape from the dilemma, therefore, occurs when the two players can communicate and take on the distinct roles of leader and follower. Although, strictly speaking, permitting communication turns Prisoners' Dilemma into a game that is no longer noncooperative, communication alone is not sufficient to resolve the dilemma without mutual predictability. For what is to prevent the leader from lying about his announced intention to cooperate conditionally? And what is to prevent the follower from lying about his announced response to select his cooperative strategy?

The insurance against lies that players have with mutual predictability is that the lies can be detected with probabilities p and q. If these probabilities satisfy the previous inequalities, then it pays for the follower to cooperate in the face of a choice rule of conditional cooperation, and the leader to cooperate by then choosing his cooperative strategy, too. Otherwise, the insurance both players have against lying will not be sufficient to make cooperation worth their while, and they should, instead, choose their noncooperative dominant strategies. We conclude, therefore,

---

8. The so-called Stackelberg solution in duopoly theory in economics also distinguishes between a "leader" and a "follower." See John M. Henderson and Richard E. Quandt, *Microeconomic Theory: A Mathematical Approach*, 2d ed. (New York: McGraw-Hill, 1971), pp. 229–231.

that a mutual ability to predict strategy choices on the part of both players offers them a mutual incentive to choose their cooperative strategies.

8.8. RELATIONSHIP TO METAGAME SOLUTION

The solution to Prisoners' Dilemma proposed here has some similarities to the solution of this game prescribed by metagame theory, but there are also some significant differences. In this theory, it will be recalled, the successive iteration of conditional strategies by the players yields some in the end at whose intersection the cooperative outcome is in equilibrium.

The choice rule of conditional cooperation we have posited assumes, in effect, the existence of a first-level (or "leader") metagame, which gives the follower a motive to cooperate against the leader's tit-for-tat conditional strategy (see section 4.3). But unlike Howard, we do not carry the analysis to a second-level (or "follower-leader") metagame in which the leader is given a motive to play tit-for-tat against the follower's own tit-for-tat policy, once removed.

The reason we eschew this stepwise backward reasoning is that it seems unnecessary if—as assumed of the Being in Newcomb's problem earlier—players' predictions (in the *preplay* leader-follower negotiation phase of the game) precede their choices (in the *play* of the game). Clearly, the proposal of conditional cooperation by the leader in the preplay phase is sufficient to initiate the process of cooperation. Then, however the players become aware of each other's powers of prediction, prediction probabilities that satisfy the previous inequalities are sufficient to protect the players against either's reneging on an agreement that is reached. For given that each player knows that the other player's probability of predicting his own strategy choice is sufficiently high, he knows that he probably cannot "get away with" a sudden switch in his strategy choice in the play of the game, because this move will already have been anticipated with a high probability in the preplay phase. Hence, the assumption that (preplay) predictions precede (play-of-the-game) choices —and both players know this—deters "last-minute" intrigue that would render the cooperative outcome unstable.

The advantage offered by a leader-follower model that distinguishes unambiguously between the preplay and play phases of a game lies not only in its ability to truncate the iterative calculations of metagame theory. It also offers an advantage in highlighting the circumstances under which players would come to harbor tit-for-tat expectations in the first place. If they come to realize, in the preplay phase of the game, that their later choices in the play of the game are, to a sufficiently high degree, predictable, they will be robbed of their incentive to violate an agreement, given that they are expected-utility maximizers.

In this manner, the leader-follower model suggests circumstances under which an *absolutely* enforceable contract will be unnecessary. When the prediction probabilities of the players are sufficiently high (which depends on the utilities assigned by the players to the outcomes), an agreement to cooperate—reached in leader-follower negotiations in the preplay phase of the game—can be rendered "enforceable enough" so as to create a probabilistic kind of equilibrium that stabilizes the cooperative outcome.

By introducing probabilities of correct prediction *as parameters* in the preplay phase of a game, one is able to place the metagame solution to Prisoners' Dilemma within a rational-choice framework. What emerges as a solution is, in essence, a consequence of the rationality assumption (i.e., that players maximize expected utility) rather than the assumption that there exists some kind of consciousness of predictability among players. This is not to denigrate the metagame solution but rather to show that there is a compelling rationale for its existence within a rational-choice framework.[9]

To what extent do players in real-world political games think in the terms we have described? This is a difficult question to answer generally, but one specific illustration of this kind of thinking may persuade the reader that it is certainly not unknown, at least in the field of foreign policy decision making. In describing a highly classified mission, code-named Holystone, that allegedly involved reconnaissance by United States submarines inside Soviet waters, one U.S. government official was quoted as saying:

> One of the reasons we can have a SALT [Strategic Arms Limitation Talks] agreement is because we know of what the Soviets are doing, and Holystone is an important part of what we know about the Soviet submarine force.[10]

Some implications of this remark will be touched upon in section 8.9.

8.9. REAL-WORLD IMPLICATIONS OF THE ANALYSIS

We have shown that the basic assumption about the predictability of choices in Newcomb's problem, when applied to not one but both players in Newcomb's prediction-choice game, defines a Prisoners' Dilemma in which the cooperative solution has considerable appeal. This appeal, it must be acknowledged, requires that one player (the leader) take the initiative and propose to the other player (the follower) a choice rule of conditional cooperation. It does not, however, require a binding and

---

9. In fairness to Howard, he argues that metagame equilibrium choices are rational, but in a "stability" rather than an "expected-utility" sense. See Nigel Howard, *Paradoxes of Rationality: Theory of Metagames and Political Behavior* (Cambridge, Mass.: MIT Press, 1971), pp. 61–63. The introduction of cardinal utilities (and probabilities) would seem to strengthen his rationality argument, though at the admitted cost of complicating his rather spare ordinal game model.

10. *New York Times*, May 25, 1975, p. 42.

enforceable contract between the two players, which some analysts have argued is the only way to ensure cooperation. Nor does it require that the players rely solely on good will and mutual trust to bring about the cooperative outcome. Rather, our analysis suggests that there is a third (middle?) road to cooperation—mutual predictability of choices—that renders the cooperative strategies less risky for both players.

If such predictability obtains, then a contract is unnecessary, for violations will be predictable with a high probability in the preplay phase of the game, and appropriate sanctions can be applied to the violator in the play of the game. But because such retribution works to the disadvantage of both players, the ability by both players to predict each other's choices serves also to reinforce trustworthy behavior, which is exactly what is not encouraged in Prisoners' Dilemma without mutual predictability.

We showed that this resolution of Prisoners' Dilemma bears some resemblance to the metagame solution to this game but offers, in addition, a model that rationalizes its existence in terms of the expected-utility calculations of players. This has the advantage of placing the metagame solution within a probabilistic, rational-choice framework.

The kind of mutual predictability assumed in our leader-follower model, it seems, has given impetus to negotiations between the superpowers in SALT and laid the groundwork for certain arms-limitation agreements recently. With each superpower's reconnaissance satellites (and submarines, à la Holystone!) able to detect substantial violations quickly, the abrogation of an agreement by one party will be known before its consequences prove disastrous to the other party and prevent it from taking appropriate countermeasures. With little to be gained from such a violation and perhaps much to be lost, it is less likely to occur. In this manner, space age technology has fostered arms-control agreements that—because of the ease with which violations could previously be kept secret—have been so difficult to obtain in the past.

Arms races are not the only situations that have the characteristics of a Prisoners' Dilemma game, as we showed in Chapter 4. Situations like vote trading, in which individuals can gain from cooperation but also have an incentive not to cooperate to improve their payoffs still more, seem nearly universal.

Perhaps the most poignant statement of the problem inherent in such situations is the now famous article by Garrett Hardin, "The Tragedy of the Commons."[11] Although Hardin focuses on the population problem—contending that the social costs of overpopulation do not offer individual incentives for people to have fewer children—he treats this as one of a class of tragedy-of-commons problems "without a technical solution." It

---

11. Garrett Hardin, "The Tragedy of the Commons," *Science*, 162 (13 December 1968), pp. 1243–1248; see also Beryle L. Crowe, "The Tragedy of the Commons Revisited," *Science*, 166 (28 November 1969), pp. 1103–1107.

would seem that our mutual predictability model does offer a "technical" solution, though for many-person games (like the population problem) it seems less meaningful and applicable. The reason is that "leaders" in such games are not so able as in two-person games to punish, by their own noncooperative actions, noncompliance by "followers."[12] Rather, it seems, followers as well as leaders would have to agree to the imposition of sanctions against noncompliance, enforceable by some higher authority (e.g., the state), that make it more rewarding to cooperate than not to cooperate—whatever the choices of the other players—which, of course, transforms Prisoners' Dilemma into another (more benign) game.

8.10. SUMMARY AND CONCLUSION

We began this chapter by describing a hypothetical problem of prediction, invented by William A. Newcomb, that previous philosophical analysis had suggested involved a fundamental conflict between two principles both supportable by plausible arguments. The problem involves two actors, one a superior Being capable of predicting with great accuracy the choice of another actor. The problem for the actor making the choice is that, on the one hand, he is motivated to select the action that dominates his other action. On the other, knowing the predictive capabilities of the Being, the other action may well provide a greater reward, based on its expected utility for any reasonable supposition about the Being's probability of making a correct prediction. This conflict between the dominance principle and the expected-utility principle constitutes what we called a paradox of prediction.[13]

To illustrate such a conflict, we developed an extended political example involving two candidates in a three-way race for their party's presidential nomination. Instead of postulating a superior Being, however, we made the consequent actions that one candidate takes, based on his predictions, the basis for payoffs to the other candidate. We pointed out that there was some arbitrariness in assuming one candidate to be the actor who makes predictions and the other candidate the actor who does (or does not) respond to his knowledge that these predictions are very probably correct. This hypothetical example, nevertheless, seemed to provide a reasonably close analogue to the situation faced by candidates Kennedy and Humphrey in the 1968 race for the Democratic presidential nomination.

Following Ferejohn, we next showed that the conflict between the dominance and the expected-utility principles could be persuasively

---

12. Relationships between two-person and n-person Prisoners' Dilemmas are discussed in Henry Hamburger, "N-Person Prisoner's Dilemma," *Journal of Mathematical Sociology*, 3 (1973), pp. 27–48; and Russell Hardin, "Collective Action as an Agreeable N-Person Prisoner's Dilemma, *Behavioral Science*, 16 (September 1971), pp. 472–481.

13. It is not the only such paradox. See, for example, Martin Gardner, "Mathematical Games," *Scientific American*, March 1963, pp. 144–154.

resolved if Newcomb's problem were reformulated as a decision-theoretic problem rather than a game. In the decision-theoretic representation, which seemed accurately to reflect the original statement of the problem, neither action is dominant for the person making the choice of which box(es) to choose (or campaign strategy to follow). In the absence of a dominant strategy, therefore, the expected-utility principle cannot run amok of the dominance principle.

To divest Newcomb's problem of the asymmetry in predictive capabilities and choices of the two actors, we next assumed that both actors know that the other actor can predict their choices with a high degree of accuracy. Combining into a single game the two games generated by both sets of choices, we showed that choices in the resulting game defined a two-person Prisoners' Dilemma game. However, the additional condition that each player know that his strategy choices are almost surely predictable by the other player gave each an incentive to choose his cooperative—rather than noncooperative but dominant—strategy, given that one player (the leader) adopts a choice rule of conditional cooperation to which the other player (the follower) responds.

This mutual predictability condition, applied to Prisoners' Dilemma, offered a rationale within a probabilitic, rational-choice framework to explain circumstances under which conditional strategies in the theory of metagames that yield a cooperative and stable outcome might come to be adopted in this game. As an empirical example, we suggested that mutual predictability may well be the basis for the limited agreements so far achieved in SALT. Even in elections, which have an unmistakably more zero-sum character than arms races, such information may enable two candidates to avoid a Prisoners' Dilemma-type situation whereby they eliminate each other in a race only to see a third—and less desirable candidate, from their point of view—win. On the other hand, many-person Prisoners' Dilemma games with large numbers of players—such as that exemplified by the population problem—seem much more difficult to solve without intervention by a higher authority like the state.

One may, of course, regard the mutual predictability solution to Prisoners' Dilemma to be a paradox itself because—as in Newcomb's problem treated as a game—it shows up a conflict between the dominance principle and the expected-utility principle. It seems more constructive, however, to stress the fact that one can calculate, from players' payoffs, probabilities that indicate thresholds at which the cooperative solution in Prisoners' Dilemma can be rendered stable and the paradox of cooperation thereby circumvented. The serendipitous value that the analysis of one (apparent) paradox has offered to another seems a nice note on which to end this book.

INDEX

A

The purpose of this paper is to propose a theory of diplomatic change and to test it against post-war ~~data on~~ ambassadors changes in Washington D.C. This analysis has implications for understanding the role of diplomats in foreign relations as well as a ~~more~~ general goal-maximizing theory of political recruitment